# FLORENTINE CODEX

# Florentine Codex

## General History of the Things of New Spain

FRAY BERNARDINO DE SAHAGUN

# Introductions and Indices

Introductions, Sahagún's Prologues
and Interpolations, General Bibliography,
General Indices

By

ARTHUR J. O. ANDERSON
SCHOOL OF AMERICAN RESEARCH

CHARLES E. DIBBLE
UNIVERSITY OF UTAH

Prefacio

By

MIGUEL LEÓN–PORTILLA

IN THIRTEEN PARTS

PART I

Published by
The School of American Research and The University of Utah

Monographs of the School of American Research

Number 14, Part I        Santa Fe, New Mexico        1982

DEDICATED TO THE MEMORY OF
EDGAR L. HEWETT
AND
SYLVANUS G. MORLEY

# CONTENTS

List of Illustrations . . . . . . . . . . . . . . . . . . . . . . . . . . . . . . . . . . . . . . . . . . .   ix

Prefacio by Miguel León–Portilla . . . . . . . . . . . . . . . . . . . . . . . . . . .   xiii

INTRODUCTIONS by Arthur J. O. Anderson and Charles E. Dibble
Variations of a Sahaguntine Theme by Arthur J. O. Anderson . . . . . . . .   3

Sahagún's *Historia* by Charles E. Dibble . . . . . . . . . . . . . . . . . . . . . . .   9

The Watermarks in the *Florentine Codex* by Charles E. Dibble . . . . . . . .   25

Sahagún: Career and Character by Arthur J. O. Anderson . . . . . . . . . . .   29

SAHAGUN'S PROLOGUES AND INTERPOLATIONS translated
   from the Spanish by Charles E. Dibble

Book I: The Gods
   Prologue . . . . . . . . . . . . . . . . . . . . . . . . . . . . . . . . . . . . . . . . .   45
   To the Sincere Reader . . . . . . . . . . . . . . . . . . . . . . . . . . . . . . .   50

Book II: The Ceremonies
   Prologue . . . . . . . . . . . . . . . . . . . . . . . . . . . . . . . . . . . . . . . . .   53
   To the Sincere Reader . . . . . . . . . . . . . . . . . . . . . . . . . . . . . . .   57
   Exclamation of the Author . . . . . . . . . . . . . . . . . . . . . . . . . . .   57
   Comment on the Sacred Songs . . . . . . . . . . . . . . . . . . . . . . . . .   58

Book III: The Origin of the Gods
   Prologue . . . . . . . . . . . . . . . . . . . . . . . . . . . . . . . . . . . . . . . . .   59

Book IV: The Soothsayers
   Prologue . . . . . . . . . . . . . . . . . . . . . . . . . . . . . . . . . . . . . . . . .   61
   To the Sincere Reader . . . . . . . . . . . . . . . . . . . . . . . . . . . . . . .   62

Book V: The Omens
   Prologue . . . . . . . . . . . . . . . . . . . . . . . . . . . . . . . . . . . . . . . . .   63
   Appendix Prologue . . . . . . . . . . . . . . . . . . . . . . . . . . . . . . . . .   63

Book VI: Rhetoric and Moral Philosophy
   Prologue . . . . . . . . . . . . . . . . . . . . . . . . . . . . . . . . . . . . . . . . .   65

Book VII: The Sun, Moon and Stars, and the Binding of the Years
   Prologue . . . . . . . . . . . . . . . . . . . . . . . . . . . . . . . . . . . . . . . . .   67
   To the Reader . . . . . . . . . . . . . . . . . . . . . . . . . . . . . . . . . . . . .   67

Book VIII: Kings and Lords
   Prologue . . . . . . . . . . . . . . . . . . . . . . . . . . . . . . . . . . . . . . . . .   69

Book IX: The Merchants
   Prologue . . . . . . . . . . . . . . . . . . . . . . . . . . . . . . . . . . . . . . . . .   71

Book X: The People

Prologue .................................................... 73

Author's Account Worthy of Being Noted .................... 74

Book XI: Earthly Things

Prologue .................................................... 87

To the Sincere Reader ....................................... 88

Note ........................................................ 89

Note Also ................................................... 91

Eighth Paragraph ............................................ 93

Maize ....................................................... 96

Book XII: The Conquest

To the Reader ............................................... 101

INDICES compiled by Arthur J. O. Anderson

Subject Matter .............................................. 105

Persons and Deities ......................................... 117

Places ...................................................... 123

BIBILOGRAPHY .............................................. 131

# LIST OF ILLUSTRATIONS

Cover of the Florentine Codex—x

Fr. Bernardino de Sahagún—xi

Fig. 1. Sahagún's signature—18

Fig. 2. Sahagún's handwriting—18

Fig. 3. Sahagún's handwriting—18

Fig. 4.   Watermark A—26

Fig. 5.   Watermark B—26

Fig. 6.   Watermark C—26

Fig. 7.   Watermark D—26

Fig. 8.   Watermark E—26

Fig. 9.   Watermark F—26

Fig. 10.  Watermark G—27

Fig. 11.  Watermark H—27

Fig. 12.  Watermark I—27

Fig. 13.  Watermark J—27

Fig. 14.  Watermark K—27

Fig. 15.  Watermark L—27

The embossed leather cover that presently binds the Florentine Codex. Photograph by Dr. G. B. Pineider; permission to use this illustration was granted by the Biblioteca Medicea-Laurenziana.

El V.ᵉ P.ᵉ Fr Bernardino Sahagun, varon estatico y Doctissimo, uno de los primeros que leyeron Theologia en este Colegio, donde vivìo mas de 40 a.ˢ ocupado en enseñar, trabajàr, y escrivìr las doctissimas, y utilissimas obras de que hace Catalog la Bibliothèca Mexicana T 1º nº 608 Murio año de 1590. Photograph by Constantino Reyes–Valerio. Dr. Guillermo Bonfil, director of the Instituto Nacional de Antropología e Historia, Mexico City, kindly granted permission to reproduce this painting. This portrait of Fray Bernardino de Sahagún is in the Museo Nacional de História, Mexico City.

# PREFACIO

*by* Miguel León–Portilla

Con este volumen—a la vez último y primero—culmina el prolongado y admirable esfuerzo de sacar a luz el *Códice Florentino*, su texto en náhuatl con traducción al inglés, notas, amplios estudios introductorios e índices analíticos. Con esmero, celo y aun cariño, a semejanza de fray Bernardino de Sahagún, los modernos nahuatlatos Arthur J. O. Anderson y Charles E. Dibble han rescatado así de nueva forma este gran tesoro de testimonios según la tradición indígena sobre la historia y la cultura de los antiguos mexicanos. Puesto que aquí mismo, en el capítulo intitulado "Variations on a Sahaguntine Theme," Anderson hace una recolección sobre el origen del proyecto que ahora contemplamos plenamente realizado, me fijaré en este Prefacio en otros dos puntos que tengo como de principal interés.

En primer lugar quiero poner de relieve lo que significa este rescate del *Códice Florentino*. En seguida intentaré un esbozo de las personalidades de quienes han cumplido esta tarea, mis colegas y amigos, Charles E. Dibble y Arthur J. O. Anderson.

Volvamos la mirada hacia un pasado de hace poco más de cuatro siglos, el año de 1580. Fue entonces cuando fray Rodrigo de Sequera, Comisario General en la orden franciscana, cumplida su visita en México, emprendió viaje de regreso a España. Consigo llevaba cuatro volúmenes de texto bilingüe, en idiomas mexicano y castellano. Fray Bernardino de Sahagún le había entregado esa obra manuscrita, con muchas y hermosas ilustraciones en color. Sequera, conociendo los libros que por largo tiempo venía preparando Sahagún con auxilio de sus informantes indígenas, "se contentó mucho de ellos y mandó al autor que los tradujese en romance, y proveyó de todo lo necesario para que se escribiese de nuevo, en la lengua mexicana en una columna, y el romance en la otra, para los enviar a España. . . ."

Cinco años más tarde, en 1585, el mismo fray Bernardino, recordando que fray Rodrigo se había llevado esos volúmenes, añadió que "nunca me ha escripto en qué pararon aquellos libros . . . y no sé en cuyo poder estén agora. . . ." En realidad mucho tiempo transcurrió antes de que los interesados en la historia del México indígena tuvieran noticia de la suerte de tales libros y pudieran aprovechar su contenido. Otros manuscritos de Sahagún habían pasado antes a España en cumplimiento de la requisición ordenada por Felipe II en 1577. Por fortuna sabemos hoy que no se perdieron, ni los libros que viajaron con Sequera ni los que fueron enviados en cumplimiento de la real orden. Estos últimos, con los *Memoriales* y la primera versión en náhuatl de la *Historia*, fueron a parar, unos a la Biblioteca del Palacio Real, y otros a la de la Real

Academia de la Historia, en Madrid. Son los que ahora se conocen como *Códices Matritenses.* Los cuatro volúmenes entregados a fray Rodrigo de Sequera, dañada tal vez su encuadernación original, fueron reempastados, distribuido su contendio en tres volúmenes. Por hallarse en la Biblioteca Medicea Laurenziana de Florencia (Manuscrito 218–220 de la Colección Palatina), se les conoce como *Códice Florentino, Historia general de las cosas de Nueva España,* de fray Bernardino de Sahagún.

No me compete referir aquí cómo se inició el redescubrimiento de la amplia obra de Sahagún y cuáles han sido las publicaciones de la misma, bien sea de la *Historia* en castellano o de los textos en náhuatl. De ello trata ampliamente Dibble en otro capítulo de este mismo volumen. Las aportaciones, a partir de las iniciadas por Carlos María de Bustamante en 1829–1830 y lord Edward Kingsborough en 1830, han sido en distintos grados valiosas. La lista de los estudiosos de la obra Sahagún es ya bastante larga e incluye a Eduard Seler, Francisco del Paso y Troncoso, Ignacio Alcocer, Angel María Garibay K., Leonhard Schultze Jena, Wigberto Jiménez Moreno, Howard F. Cline y otros varios de tiempos más recientes, entre los que deseo incluirme. Meritorios como son los trabajos de estos investigadores, ninguno de ellos había logrado el rescate completo de los materiales recogidos por Sahagún e incluidos o en los *Códices Matritenses* o en el *Florentino.* Han sido Dibble y Anderson quienes, con celo y paciencia que, como en el caso de fray Bernardino, calificaré de franciscanos, emprendieron y llevaron a buen término la magna empresa de estudiar, paleografiar, traducir al inglés y anotar el texto completo en náhuatl de los doce libros del *Códice Florentino.* Curiosamente su interés por realizar esta tarea se despertó a cuatro siglos de distancia del momento en que Sahagún, en 1547, concluía la transcripción de lo que sería más tarde el libro VI de su *Historia,* el de los *huehuetlatolli,* que él intituló "De la Rethorica y Filosofía Moral y Teología de la Gente Mexicana. . . ."

Nuestros colegas son oriundos del Suroeste de los Estados Unidos, lo que equivale a decir que la cultura mexicana nunca les fue extraña. Arthur nació en Phoenix, Arizona, en 1907 y Charles en Layton, Utah, en 1909. Trasladada la familia del primero a tierras mexicanas, su niñez y primera juventud transcurrieron en Guadalajara. Por lo que toca a Charles sus contactos con México se produjeron también desde época relativamente temprana, hacia 1936, cuando contaba 27 años de edad. Entonces se trasladó a la capital de la República para obtener la maestría y el doctorado en la Universidad Nacional Autónoma de México.

Charles y Arthur—Carlos y Arturo, como con afecto los llamamos en México—son personas que muy pronto se ganan la confianza y el aprecio. Su bondad y su carácter sincero se reflejan en sus rostros. Carlos sonríe siempre con los ojos, en tanto que Arturo un poco más serio, deja luego entrever su actitud comprensiva y condescendiente. En el *tonalli* o destino de Carlos y Arturo estuvo interesarse por la cultura de los nahuas, y a partir de un encuentro en Santa Fe de Nuevo México, trabajar juntos por mucho tiempo en su empresa acerca del *Codice Florentino.* Allí se hallaba también Sylvannus Morley quien animó a ambos a realizar dicho trabajo.

Dibble, con su doctorado obtenido en México, laboraba en el Departamento de Antropología de la Universidad de Utah. Anderson, doctorado a su vez en la University of Southern California, tenía entonces a su cargo los departamentos

de historia, así como de publicaciones, de la School of American Research y del Museo de Nuevo México en Santa Fe. Ambos poseían conocimientos suficientes del idioma náhuatl. Asociados en el proyecto del *Códice Florentino*, adoptaron el siguiente procedimiento: cada uno preparaba su propia versión de las distintas partes del códice, la que luego enviaba al otro para su revisión crítica. De ambos esfuerzos procedería a la postre la versión adoptada. Uno y otro elaboraban asimismo las notas. En ocasiones se reunían en Santa Fe o en Salt Lake City y también en la ciudad de México. Allí consultaban con Angel Maria Garibay K., Byron McAfee y otros pocos nahuatlatos. En tal contexto fue cuando conocí y empecé a estimar grandemente a Carlos y Arturo.

Este último preparó casi siempe la transcripción final del trabajo correspondiente a cada libro. Carlos se ocupaba de otros aspectos, como los relacionados con las ilustraciones. Uno y otro, para ampliar sus conocimientos sobre Sahagún y su obra, realizaron varios viajes no ya sólo a México sino también a España e Italia.

Además, a medida que avanzaban en su proyecto, iban publicando otros trabajos, todos en estrecha relación con la obra Sahaguntina y el mundo de la cultura náhuatl. Por desgracia no me es posible transcribir aquí la lista de sus publicaciones, entre ellas "El Inventario Anatómico Sahaguntino" y las *Rules of the Aztec Language* ( A Translation with Modifications of Clavijero's *Reglas*...), debidas a Anderson o las ediciones del *Códice Xólotl* y del *Códice en Cruz*, preparadas por Dibble.

Trabajadores sinceros en el mundo de la cultura, humildes y sencillos, precisamente por su condición de sabios verdaderos, Carlos y Arturo han tendido nuevo puente de amistad entre su país y México. Con razón este último ha reconocido públicamente sus méritos al otorgarles en 1981 las insignias de la Orden Mexicana del Aguila Azteca. Gracias a estos colegas, siempre sonrientes y dispuestos a ayudar, tenemos ahora la mejor de las posibles respuestas a las inquietudes que en 1585 expresó Sahagún: ya sabemos "en qué pararon aquellos libros . . ." Paleografiado su texto náhuatl, traducido y anotado, es ya asequible testimonio del México antiguo que ha pasado a enriquecer la cultura universal. Por otra parte los mismos libros en preciosa reproducción facsimilar, hecha recientemente por el Gobierno de México, pueden ser también fácilmente consultados.

La tarea realizada por Charles E. Dibble y Arthur J. O. Anderson es ejemplo digno de emularse. Textos sahaguntinos, como los que integran los *Primeros Memoriales* y otros más, merecen también concienzudo estudio. Tiempo es de proseguir por el camino abierto por ellos, para conocer mejor los logros del extraordinario mundo de cultura que floreció en Mesoamérica.

Miguel León–Portilla
Instituto de Investigaciones Históricas
Universidad Nacional de México
Septiembre de 1981

# INTRODUCTIONS

by Arthur J. O. Anderson and Charles E. Dibble

# Variations on a Sahaguntine Theme

*by* Arthur J. O. Anderson

The name *Florentine Codex* was adopted as the standard appellation for this edition of Sahagún's text of the *General History of the Things of New Spain* on which Charles E. Dibble and I have worked because the late Edgar L. Hewett[1] so designated it, though he was not the first to use that name. More formally Hewett referred to it as "the Great Florentine Codex." It has other labels—quite often *Manuscrito florentino* in Mexico; or Laurentian or Laurenziano, following the style of Eduard Seler. Officially it is the manuscript of the Biblioteca Medicea–Lorenziana Palat. 218–220, and, as Dibble explains elsewhere in this volume, it has been known to be in that library since the 1790s. A century later it was attracting scholars, through whom it became increasingly prominent. Seler's brilliant pioneering research with Sahagún's manuscripts from the turn of the century on, and Francisco del Paso y Troncoso's studies and production of a facsimile edition of the Madrid Codices and the illustrations of the Florentine manuscript kept bringing the texts to the attention of other scholars.

It had long been Hewett's hope, he once told me, to persuade Adolph Bandelier to translate Sahagún's Nahuatl text into English (Hewett presumably referred specifically to the *Florentine Codex*), for Bandelier was a good linguist and had some mastery of Nahuatl. I never knew the full extent of Bandelier's knowledge, but there are passages in his journals and in his publications that leave no doubt about his familiarity with Nahuatl terminology. How-ever, since Bandelier died in 1914 no such project was possible.

For events connected with the celebration of New Mexico's Coronado Quartocentennial (1940), Hewett had interested the late Lansing Bloom, then associate professor of history at the University of New Mexico and editor of the *New Mexico Historical Review*, in devoting part of a sabbatical leave in Europe (1938–1939) to microfilming a number of archival sources. Included among the items Professor Bloom delivered to the School of American Research in 1939 was a complete microfilm of the *Florentine Codex*, along with authorization to publish. This must have been the first microfilm to be made of that document. Today microfilms are more easily obtainable, and with the Mexican government's publication in 1980 of a magnificent color facsimile, the *Florentine Codex* is now perfectly reproduced and more easily available to researchers.[2]

In the months that followed, Miss (later Dr.) Bertha P. Dutton[3] and Miss Hulda Hobbs (now Mrs. Finis Heidel), then associates of the School of American Research and curators of the Museum of New Mexico, made eight-by-ten-inch enlargements of each of the approximately 2,500 negatives of Bloom's microfilm, a huge task for which they have never received adequate recognition. The results of their darkroom work were excellent. Using these enlargements, Charles Dibble and I have produced our translation of the *Florentine Codex*; from them, too, copies were later photostated for presentation to the Museo Na-

---

1. Hewett was founder and first director of the School of American Archaeology (of the Archaeological Institute of America), which was later reorganized and renamed School of American Research. Through Hewett's initiative, the School secured its photocopy of the *Florentine Codex*. See his *Fray Bernardino de Sahagún and the Great Florentine Codex*.

2. An edition of 2,000 was published by the Secretaría de Gobernación (Prof. Enrique Olivares Santana, secretary), and publication was supervised by the Archivo General de la Nación (Dra. Alejandra Moreno Toscano, director).

3. She later became director of the Museum of Navaho Ceremonial Art, Santa Fe, New Mexico, and is now retired.

cional, Mexico City, and to a few interested American libraries.

My involvement with the Nahuatl of Sahagún's *General History* began soon after 1940, when, having heard the late Sylvanus G. Morley speak enthusiastically about the existence of the microfilm, I was kindly allowed to use School–Museum library sources freely and to study a number of defective microfilm enlargements that had been discarded. In due course, Hewett, knowing of my interest in the Codex, placed me on a Sahagún committee to further the translation and publication of Sahagún's texts and in 1945 asked me to join the staff of the School of American Research and Museum of New Mexico. There matters stood until Hewett's death on the last day of 1946.

Sylvanus G. Morley, who succeeded Hewett as director of the School of American Research and of the Museum of New Mexico, provided the strong new impetus that actually launched the translating of the Codex. Most importantly, Morley simultaneously added Charles E. Dibble's knowledge of Mexican codices and laid the foundations for successfully funding publication of the Codex. This came about through negotiations with A. Ray Olpin, then president of the University of Utah, that brought in Utah anthropology professor Charles E. Dibble as co-translator and co-editor. In short, an agreement with the University of Utah to share equally the costs and benefits of publication was to guarantee permanence and support to the venture. The work was to appear as Monograph Number 14 of the School of American Research in thirteen parts: an introductory volume, followed by the twelve Books of the Codex proper (hence some apparent anomalies in the numbering of the Books of the Codex and the parts of the Monograph). Morley, with Dibble and me, sketched the course we were expected to follow. We estimated that in five years, with Dibble and me on schedules that would permit us each half time for the translating–editing–publishing project, we could complete the work, bringing it out as a bilingual account like the original, with a Nahuatl column matched by one in English on each page. The English version was to follow the Nahuatl as closely as it conveniently could, and since both the original Spanish and Nahuatl were written in the sixteenth century, the English was to be modified by appropriate, not too obtrusive archaisms. Morley recommended specifically the English of the King James version of the Holy Bible. Each of the twelve Books was to be completed separately, in an order convenient for the translator-editors, and published as soon as completed. Illustrations were to be taken from the Paso y Troncoso facsimile edition because those in the photographic reproduction of the Codex that we were using, while in many ways more characteristically "Aztec," occasionally lacked clarity and were often marred by ink that had soaked through from the other side of the page. This was the general course laid out not long before Morley died in 1948. We have followed it as closely as we could, with the support of the subsequent directors of the School of American Research—Boaz Long, Wayne Mauzy, Edward Weyer, and now Douglas Schwartz—and many officials of the University of Utah including presidents, deans, and department chairmen, among whom we may especially mention those who were pioneers in promoting it there—President A. Ray Olpin, Dean O. Meredith Wilson, and the late Harold W. Bentley, then director of the University of Utah Press.

Developments when the Honorable Boaz Long became director of the School of American Research and of the Museum of New Mexico resulted in few modifications of the course outlined in 1948 by Morley, Dibble, and me. In the main, the project was continued as originally sketched, though the collapse of the five-year plan represented an unavoidable casualty. The University of Utah did, however, maintain Dibble on a half-time schedule for the agreed term of five years. If Morley had lived, the *Florentine Codex* undoubtedly would have been better for it and completed more quickly. His broad and deep knowledge of Mesoamerican prehistory, of the type of technical writing and publication involved, and of sources of financial support would have contributed enormously. Without Morley, Dibble and I continued as best we could, and in fact, for the next few years, were able to bring out a volume a year.

The order in which we have translated the Books of the Codex has been governed by two factors. For one, when we started, Eduard Seler's were the only translations of considerable sections available.[4]

---

4. I estimate that, in all, he had translated what amounts to less than one-third of the content of the *Florentine Codex*; he used, however, sometimes the Florentine and sometimes the Madrid manuscripts.

In terms of the Codex, these represented Books I, II, III, and XII, and brief selections from others. It was logical, considering the reverence we felt for his work, to start with those Books of the Codex for which we could use Seler's translations as a control, though we maintained constant comparisons with the works of others then available—mostly Garibay's, since other Mexican experts were not yet active in this field. As to the other factor, we took the Books easiest to translate first, and tried to gauge which of the succeeding, more difficult ones would be the least troublesome to tackle. We also soon learned that Books XI and VI, which we earlier had decided to leave until the last, were always useful to refer to (XI for various technical information and VI for figures of speech) and that the standard Spanish versions of those books were sometimes as helpful, or almost as helpful, as the Nahuatl. We have always made as much use as we could of Sahagún's Spanish; even though it is far from a literal rendition, Sahagún is, after all, the ultimate authority. We knew that Book VI, because of its difficult, florid, formal language, would have to come at the very end of the translated series. The preliminary volume—the first of the Monograph's thirteen parts—would have to follow even later because it would contain indices, bibliography, various kinds of introductory sections or chapters, the prologues, and the occasional interpolations we had customarily omitted because they were written in Spanish.

Considering the contents planned for Part 1 and our original five-year deadline, some omissions and peculiarities in each translation of the Books of the Codex are understandable. None of the twelve Books contains its own bibliography. Hence footnote citation had to be full in order to make up, even if awkwardly, for the lack of a formal list of works consulted. None of the Books contains an index (except for the partial one in Book XI); all this indexing is in Part 1. Each published Book does, however, contain a complete table of contents and list of illustrations, as well as a central section with the illustrations themselves. For lack of a formal introduction, we have twice appended temporary forewords.

Some of these difficulties in the general approach and organization were at least partially foreseen when our procedures and goals were sketched and agreed upon in 1948. If we had known, however, that the five-year limit would prove to be impossible, we would no doubt have provided each Book with an index and bibliography, simplified our footnote citations, and made other adjustments.

As to our intellectual approach, I have already noted perhaps the most basic factor: our frequent turning, for interpretation of parts of the Nahuatl text obscure to us, to Sahagún's Spanish text. Of course we have added as many other reliable ancient and modern sources as we could find. We have been most fortunate in having many expert colleagues to whom we turned for advice. Names that occur to me at once are, in Mexico, the late Angel María Garibay K., the late Byron McAfee, the late Rafael García Granados, Miguel León-Portilla, the late José Gurría Lacroix, and Alfredo López Austin; in the United States, Elizabeth and the late Dudley T. Easby, Jr.; in England, the late Herbert Maryon, O. B. E.; in Spain, the late José Tudela de la Orden, Manuel Ballesteros Gaibrois, and José Alcina Franch. . . . We have always received the greatest encouragement and help from the University of Utah Press and all who are connected with it. Most particularly we are grateful to its director, Norma B. Mikkelsen, and her copy editor, Peggy Lee, both of whom have labored mightily with us in the revision of the Books representing our earliest work and in the preparation of the present volume with its indices, bibliography, and other such materials. It is due to them, too, that now for the first time all the Books of the *Florentine Codex* are in print and available. To these we no doubt owe more than we realize; they have never hesitated to advise and help us. For assistance along more concrete lines, I have been beholden for a fellowship and two grants awarded by the John Simon Guggenheim Memorial Foundation, and Dibble for three grants to him from the National Science Foundation.

Another general principle, applied as strictly as we could, was to avoid inserting interpretations or opinions of what our translation was bringing to light. Most of our notes should, we thought, attempt to clarify meanings of Nahuatl terms, suggest permissible alternatives, or draw attention to conflicting or contradictory possibilities. Thus the translation, if accurate enough, could be used by other scholars as material to support or question theory or hypothesis.

Since the inclusion of an interlinear translation (or its equivalent) had been judged impractical, it was

necessary to attempt a satisfactory compromise by making the English follow the Nahuatl sequence of ideas as closely as possible while at the same time producing a version in readable English. It had also been suggested that it might be possible to take advantage of some features in normal Nahuatl syntax that approximate English syntax. I think it is possible to refer continually from our version to the native one without too much inconvenience. The method perfected by Seler, and used rewardingly by a number of others, of matching Nahuatl phrase against non-Nahuatl phrase is no doubt more efficient, but it is not suitable for producing what we hoped would be a satisfactory compromise between a literal and a literary text.

We are aware of the fluctuations between the more literal and the more literary translation as we have moved from one Book to another. The circumstance has not concerned us unduly since we feel that we have adequately conveyed the meaning. In some instances we have been moved by the context, in some by the terminology in Sahagún's Spanish text, in others by the various authorities we have consulted.

Doing as we did involved considerable fundamental give-and-take. Perhaps the detail most troublesome and, at times, disconcerting to us has been the differences in verb concepts. Simple tense, aspect, or mood equivalents presented little trouble on the whole, but how to preserve what one hoped might be graceful English in the face of the demands made upon meanings by directional auxiliary suffixes, direction-pointing prefixes, verbs compounded with verbs indicating movement or direction or position—verbs like "come" or "go" or "be" compounded with one another or with themselves—has been a tax upon our imagination or ingenuity and, quite likely, the patience of the casual reader.

Though one could take advantage of English–Nahuatl syntactical correspondences to the degree that they may exist, tense sequences are irreconcilable. Hence, we have usually reduced the passage to the past tense with the tense sequences as in English. Otherwise a disordered effect might disconcert the reader. The essential meanings are there, however, and anyone who knows Nahuatl can sort out the tenses and attendant refinements.

Our favoring past tense over present is connected with our need to use the Aztec form of second person singular when called for. English "you" is ambiguous; the Aztec use of the second person singular is absolutely unambiguous. In using the English equivalent, we have kept in mind Morley's suggestion that we sometimes use the language of the King James Bible; resorting to a fairly consistent past tense has avoided some exaggeratedly archaic effects.

Other areas where we have taken liberties are in paragraphing and sentence forming. Since divisions are rarely indicated on the manuscript except for sections or chapters, the paragraphing in the *Florentine Codex* as published is mostly our doing. Even the division into sentences has often been our responsibility. Fortunately, mistakes in judgment are likely to have been relatively few, though it is not always possible to be certain which of a series of statements are independent and which are subordinate. With the spoken language there might be less doubt. In the unstandardized written Nahuatl of the sixteenth century, punctuation marks and initial capital letters are of no help in determining the structure of a sentence. Although punctuation marks are plentifully if not invariably used, we could not and did not ignore them, nor could we be bound or guided by them.

Though complicated, the orthography of the various Sahagún Nahuatl manuscripts presented fewer problems even though we may sometimes have been influenced by our assumptions as to the general context. Reproduced here is a summary of orthographical correspondences (not all from Sahagún's amanuenses) that illustrates the situation. Though most terms presented no problems, a study of Molina's *Vocabulario de la lengua Mexicana*, a work well standardized for its time, will show other possible booby traps that may catch the unwary.

*Summary of Orthographical Correspondences*

*h* sometimes indicates a glottal stop; cf. *hicac, tlahtoani, teteuh*

*i* for *y*: *tlaquaquaia* for *tlaquaquaya*; *iacattiuitze* for *yacattiuitze*

*j* for *i*: *jmjtzcuinoan* for *imitzcuinuan*; *njmā* for *niman*

*n* for *m*: *ipanpa* for *ipampa*; *quenman* for *quemman*

*n* (final) is sometimes omitted: *mictla* for *mictlan*

*o* for *u*: *jmjtzcuinoan* for *imitzcuinuan*; *cioatl* for *ciuatl* (or *cihuatl*)

*u* and *hu* may be used indiscriminately: *yuan, yhuan* (as well as *yoan, ihuan*, etc.); *ciuatl, cihuatl*

*u* for *o*: *uncan* for *oncan*; *teteu* for *teteo*; *chicunavi* for *chiconaui* (or *-nahui*)

*v* for *o*: *vtlica* for *otlica*; *vncan* for *oncan*

*v* for *u*: *iacattivitze* for *yacattiuitze*; *vevetque* for *ueuetque* (or *huehuetque*)

*y* for *i*: *yn* for *in*; *yoanj* for *iuani*

' indicates omission: *q'nnaoatia* for *quinnauatia*; *aq'n* for *aquin*

~ indicates omission: *y* or *i* for *in*; *çã* for *çan*; *njmã* for *niman*; *teamã* for *teaman*; *oticallaq* for *oticallaque*; *tlaciuhq* for *tlaciuhque*; *yqc* for *iquac*; *q'nqque* for *quinquaque*; *motetepexiqtz* for *motetepexiquetz*; *tlaõcaiotitivi* for *tlaoncayotitiui*; *tlauãqui* *tlauanqui*; *õcã* for *oncan*, etc., etc.

^ sometimes indicates a glottal stop: *tê, yê, tlâtlachichina* (but its use is also often problematical)

—after Arthur J. O. Anderson,
*Rules of the Aztec Language*
(Salt Lake City: University
of Utah Press, 1973).

*Note*: The standard against which comparisons are made, when they apply, is Rémi Siméon's *Dictionnaire de la langue nahuatl ou mexicaine*. On a threefold distinction in apostrophe-like and tilde-like marks, see "Types and Conventions of Colonial Nahuatl Documentation," *in* Arthur J. O. Anderson, Frances Berdan, and James Lockhart, *Beyond the Codices*. In transcribing, we have adopted the standard apostrophe and tilde to indicate omissions.

Our practice has been to reproduce the Nahuatl text as accurately as possible from the manuscript (except for the paragraphing), standardize the spelling of Nahuatl terms in our English text in conformity with Siméon's *Dictionnaire de la langue nahuatl ou mexicaine*, and editorialize as little as possible in our translation and the explanatory notes.

Occasionally there has been trouble with the handwriting of Sahagún's amanuenses, but on the whole it is easy to read, and our impression is that they made remarkably few errors. A few corrected passages have proved to be quite hard to decipher, notably in Book VI where in several short passages we were able to decipher not only the corrections but what had been corrected, and where in a series of pages ink had soaked through to the Nahuatl column from the Spanish column on the reverse of the page. Dibble definitively settled the reading of a number of difficult passages by personal examination and hand-copying them in Florence in 1960. Glosses or corrections in Sahagún's own hand are very rare, fortunately, since the *Florentine Codex* was compiled

over a span of time when his hand trembled virtually uncontrollably and his writing is exceedingly hard to read.[5]

So much for some of the mechanical problems in dealing with the Codex.

We completed our translation in 1969, four hundred years after Sahagún had finished the Nahuatl version (1559–1569), which, as the late J. Eric S. Thompson then reminded us, is a figure that fits nicely in the Mexican vigesimal system of counting. The *Florentine Codex* is now published as twelve books in eleven volumes constituting Parts 2 to 13 of the School of American Research's Monograph Number 14. This volume is Part 1, and as the volume that contains general introductory material (as well as the indices, bibliography, etc.), it precedes the translations of Sahagún's Nahuatl text.

As for the future, there still remain parts of the Madrid Codices that could be translated into English without duplicating what is in the *Florentine Codex*. We have already used such materials in Books I (revised edition), VII, and VIII. A supplementary volume or series of volumes would be well justified and might indeed incite others to bring out English translations of other classics of the same period now available only in Spanish, German, or French.

Those who have seen the original manuscript in Florence will agree that for all its having been rather hurriedly copied, as Sahagún complains in one of his prefaces and as is here and there quite evident, it is beautiful to behold. Until the Mexican government's recently published color facsimile, few reproductions have done justice to the vividness and spirit of the illustrations, including the uncompleted ones in black and white. The Paso y Troncoso facsimiles, though good, are, after all, just European draftsmen's copies. Ornamental space fillers and some capital letters are nicely worked out in color; the arrangement, balance, and spacing of the pages are pleasing; the handwriting is usually attractive and mature looking. Mesoamericanists still lack either a complete critical edition of the Spanish text or a complete English version of any of the standard Sahagún Spanish versions of the *General History*, even though a century and a half has elapsed since the Bustamante and Kingsborough editions. Because the Spanish ver-

5. On problems of decipherment, cf. also "Types and Conventions of Nahuatl Documentation," *in* Arthur J. O. Anderson, Frances Berdan, and James Lockhart, *Beyond the Codices*.

sions are available, it would be better to have no English version than only a poor one, but considering how quickly after its publication Clavijero's *Historia antigua de México* found an English translator and a publisher, it is unbelievable that we still have only Fanny Bandelier's work on Books I–IV (Bernardino de Sahagún, *A History of Ancient Mexico*).

To the future also belongs significant expansion of information on Sahagún's life and work. I mention this with some feeling, having spent a good deal of time in 1955, 1958, 1960, and 1968–1969 in Spain looking for additional archival materials on Sahagún and questioning experts. Dibble has similarly persistently sought and inquired. I suspect that as a Franciscan of the strict observance, Sahagún was somewhat indifferent to personal recognition, and for various reasons few official documents other than those we know of are available. But it may be possible to add new data from time to time to what we have.

It is obvious that the Codex is important as a body of linguistic information. It was to serve, as Sahagún said, as a net to trap all the elements of the Nahuatl language spoken by the ancient Mexicans. From what Sahagún wrote in his asides in the *General History*, we know that he was consciously educating his less well-informed colleagues; much of his teaching was of the structure and meaning of the language. Hence it should be possible to compile from it and other translated Nahuatl documents and existing dictionaries and vocabularies a more complete dictionary than any now extant. What Sahagún's compilations can contribute to clarifying and adding to our knowledge of classical Nahuatl grammar has already been demonstrated. Garibay did so in his *Llave del náhuatl*, and in this respect J. Richard Andrews and the late Thelma D. Sullivan have followed his example with their important though quite different grammars.[6]

Studies of the use of both Spanish and Nahuatl by literate natives throughout the colonial period, as a part of the acculturation of Indians and *mestizos*, as well as of the Spanish language as it was being modified, can be added to the works of such authorities as Robelo and Davila Garibí in the way that Frances Karttunen and James Lockhart are successfully demonstrating.[7]

\*      \*      \*

Hewett used to speculate whether the Nahuatl text hid information or actualities sharply different from what we might call the official point of view—that is, the Spanish text. Of this there is no sign. Even if Sahagún and his colleagues quarreled among themselves or were often at odds with much of Spanish officialdom, they show no anti-establishment sentiments, and the amanuenses and informants were as good Christians and supporters of the Spanish régime as possible, given their origin, time, and place. On the other hand, sometimes statements in one part of the Codex vary from or contradict statements in another part. Informants supplied data at different times and under different situations and represented different places and social stations. These are some of the features worth studying and making allowances for, along with other circumstances that make the coverage of the Florentine and Madrid Codices occasionally uneven or incomplete. But they remain the best sources of their kind. The documents are valuable because their compilers had so much to tell us. Even though, as Hewett used to maintain, it is impossible for the western European to understand fully the Indian mind,[8] if, with works like Sahagún's, we can in time penetrate more deeply into ancient Mexican ways of thinking, the Codex may yet have much more to divulge. For there now is available a complete Nahuatl text from which scholars of the present and future, with their increasingly greater knowledge of the ancient Aztecs and their language, can continue to draw more accurate and refined conclusions.

6. Angel M. Garibay K., *Llave del náhuatl*; J. Richard Andrews, *Introduction to Classical Nahuatl*; Thelma D. Sullivan, *Compendio de la gramática náhuatl*.

7. Cf. their *Nahuatl in the Middle Years*; "Textos en náhuatl del siglo xvii"; also James Lockhart, "Y la Ana lloró."

8. Cf. Hewett, *Fray Bernardino de Sahagún*, p. 1.

# Sahagún's Historia

*by* Charles E. Dibble

The inception of and preparation for Sahagún's *Historia* dates from his arrival in New Spain in 1529. It was during his first years, the decade of the thirties, that we find him actively cooperating in the selecting and training of the young natives who were to become his constant collaborators.

Through the early efforts of Fr. Pedro de Gante, Fr. Andrés de Olmos, Motolinía (Fr. Toribio de Benavente), and others, spoken Nahuatl had been converted into written form utilizing Spanish letters.[1] Building on this pioneer endeavor, the Franciscan Order arrived at two decisions with respect to the policy of conversion and education. First, the focus of missionary effort was to be directed toward the children who in due time would become the teachers of the parent generation; secondly, instruction was to be in Latin and Nahuatl in preference to Spanish.[2]

Sahagún was a participant in founding and directing the early primary schools and was engaged in the instruction of the youth. References in Mendieta[3] and Torquemada[4] record his residence in the monastery at Tlalmanalco during the years Fr. Martín de Valencia was custodian, 1530–1533. The evidence suggests his presence rather than his residence there. A statement by Mendieta, "during his early years he was guardian of important monasteries,"[5] would indicate that, if not constantly at Tlalmanalco, he was nonetheless active in one or more of the many Franciscan monasteries that had been founded by 1531.[6]

The sons of native rulers and native nobility were assembled near the monasteries where, besides Christian doctrine, they were taught to read, write, preach, and sing. Basic Christian doctrine was taught in Latin and Nahuatl.[7] These early schools must have been well attended since Gante mentions the daily instruction of five to six hundred boys.[8]

An outgrowth of the successful functioning of the elementary schools was the founding of the Royal College of Santa Cruz on January 6, 1536, in the monastery at Santiago, located in Tlatelolco. It was known as the Colegio de Santa Cruz de Tlatelolco. Instructors in Latin were Fr. Arnaldo de Bassacio, Fr. Bernardino de Sahagún, and Fr. Andrés de Olmos. Rhetoric, logic, and philosophy were taught by Fr. Juan de Gaona. All four instructors were acknowledged masters of the Nahuatl language.[9]

Sahagún informs us that some seventy of the most capable boys, those best able to read and write, were selected from the elementary schools to be housed and instructed at the College.[10] These select students, instructed by the acknowledged scholars of the Order, produced immediate and favorable results. Mastering Latin and the writing of their native Nahuatl, they became effective aides in proselyting and in translating Christian sermons and texts into Nahuatl.[11]

Sahagún remained at the College during its first four years, 1536–1540, and it was during these years

1. Angel María Garibay K., *Historia de la literatura náhuatl*, Vol. I, p. 15.

2. Robert Ricard, *La conquista espiritual de México*, pp. 129–40.

3. Gerónimo de Mendieta, *Historia eclesiástica indiana*, Vol. IV, p. 37.

4. Juan de Torquemada, *Tercera parte de los veinte i un libros rituales i monarchia indiana*, Tomo III, p. 411.

5. Mendieta, *Historia eclesiástica indiana*, Vol. IV, p. 115.

6. Ricard, *La conquista espiritual de México*, pp. 157–59.

7. *Códice Franciscano*, pp. 55–61. See also "Carta de Fray Martín de Valencia, Custodio, y de otros religiosos de la orden de San Francisco, al Emperador Don Carlos, 1532," in *Cartas de Indias. Publicadas por primera vez por el Ministerio de Fomento*, pp. 54–61.

8. See "Carta de Fray Pedro de Gante al Emperador D. Carlos, 1532," in *Cartas de Indias*, pp. 51–53.

9. Mendieta, *Historia eclesiástica indiana*, Vol. III, p. 67.

10. See Sahagún's interpolation, Book X, this volume.

11. Mendieta, *Historia eclesiástica indiana*, Vol. III, p. 68.

that the pattern of religious and scholastic collaboration which made the *Historia* possible was forged. While the personnel of the student collaborators changed over the years, the nature of the teacher-student team persisted. Sahagún, perhaps to a greater degree than his colleagues, acknowledged his dependence on those he had instructed. He wrote:

> And they, being knowledgeable in the Latin language, inform us of the properties of the words, the properties of their manner of speech. And they correct for us the incongruities we express in the sermons or write in the catechisms. And whatever is to be rendered in their language, if it is not written congruently in the Latin language, in Spanish, and in their language, cannot be free of defect. With regard to orthography, to good handwriting, there are none who write it other than those reared here.[12]

An early, if not the earliest, example of Sahagún's efforts is a *Sermonario* in Nahuatl presently in the Edward E. Ayer collection of the Newberry Library in Chicago, Illinois.[13] While the date is given as 1540, it is safe to assume that the lengthy sermons and *Santoral* are the products of the 1536–1540 years in the College, where the motivation of the school was the production of such works. Thus by 1540 the collaborators were identified and the pattern of collaboration was established. The organization, the editing, and the planning were under the direction of Sahagún, while the mechanics of writing and the proper phrasing depended on those trained in the Royal College of Santa Cruz. It remained only to change the focus of interest from Christianity in the Bible to native culture in the codices and the memories of the old men.

The first evidence of work that relates to and forms part of the *Historia* appears in 1547. This is the material that eventually became Book VI. At the end of Book VI is the statement: "This was translated into the Spanish language by the said Father, Fray Bernardino de Sahagún, in this year of 1577, thirty years after it had been written in the Mexican language."[14]

Book VI is mainly a collection of sermons, prayers, and orations by the elders designed to instruct the people in proper conduct. A similar work, collected by Fr. Andrés de Olmos and called *Huehuetlatolli, The Discourses of the Elders*, is assigned also to the year 1547.[15] Scholars differ in assigning the responsibility for these two collections. They are both attributed to Sahagún or to Olmos, or Book VI is attributed to Sahagún and the *Huehuetlatolli* to Olmos.[16] Both Franciscans were acknowledged masters of the Nahuatl language, both were instructing in the College, there was undoubtedly considerable sharing of information, and there was, as phrased by the late Howard F. Cline in personal correspondence, the "Franciscan doctrine of anonymity and borrowing." Nevertheless, the evidence favors crediting Sahagún with Book VI. We have Sahagún's statement plus the fact that the discourses of Book VI are in the language of the ruling class, whereas those of the *Huehuetlatolli* are in the language of the common folk, suggesting two different sources for the material.

The place where the discourses of Book VI were gathered is not known. Garibay suggests Tepepulco or Tenochtitlan–Tlatelolco but favors Tenochtitlan–Tlatelolco.[17] However, two factors favor considering Tepepulco as the locale. Tezcatlipoca was especially venerated in the Texcocan region and the six prayers to Tezcatlipoca in Book VI would point to Texcoco or neighboring Tepepulco. Also, ten years later, when Sahagún formally initiated the compilation of his *Historia*, he moved to Tepepulco, which suggests an earlier working relationship with native leaders such as don Diego de Mendoza.[18]

In 1555 Sahagún was in Tlatelolco and at this time he prepared a native account of the Conquest, which subsequently became Book XII of his *Historia*. This information is contained in his revised version of the Conquest published in 1585. Therein he states that the Tlatelolcan version was written more than thirty years earlier.[19]

12. See Sahagún's interpolation, Book X, this volume.

13. Ayer MS No. 1485, Newberry Library, Chicago.

14. Bernardino de Sahagún, *Florentine Codex, Book VI, Rhetoric and Moral Philosophy*, translated by Charles E. Dibble and Arthur J. O. Anderson, p. 260.

15. Fr. Juan Bautista, *Huehuetlatolli, o, pláticas de los viejos.*

16. See Joaquín García Icazbalceta, *Bibliografía mexicana del siglo XVI*, pp. 342, 472. Also see Federico Gómez de Orozco, "Huehuetlatolli," *Revista Mexicana de Estudios Antropológicos*, Vol. III, No. 2, pp. 157–66; Garibay, *Historia de la literatura náhuatl*, Vol. I, p. 426.

17. Garibay, *Historia de la literatura náhuatl*, Vol. I, p. 439.

18. See Prologue to Book II, this volume.

19. Carlos María de Bustamante, ed., *La aparición de Ntra. Señora de Guadalupe de Mexico . . .*, p. 1: "*Cuando escribí en este pueblo del Tlatilulco los doce libros de la historia de esta Nueva-España (por los cuales envió nuestro señor el rey D. Filipe, que los tiene allá), el nono libro fué de la conquista desta tierra. Cuando esta escritura se escribió, (que ha ya mas de treinta años) todo se escribió en lengua mexicana.*"

In 1558 Fray Francisco de Toral became Provincial of the Franciscans in Mexico. Sahagún's nearly twenty years of missionary and literary efforts were of such quality as to motivate Toral's ordering him: "to write in the Mexican language that which seemed to me useful for the indoctrination, the propagation and perpetuation of the Christianization of these natives of this New Spain and as a help to the workers and the ministers who indoctrinate them."[20]

The charge given to Sahagún by Toral, Sahagún's motivations in accepting the charge, and his method of gathering the data were anticipated by earlier work within the Order.[21] In his Prologue to Book II, Mendieta comments:

> It is known that in the year 1533 D. Sebastián Ramírez de Fuenleal (at the time he was Bishop of Hispaniola) being president of the Real Audiencia of Mexico and the saintly man Fr. Martín de Valencia being custodian of the Order of our Father St. Francis in this New Spain, the Father Fr. Andrés de Olmos of said Order (because he was the best interpreter of the Mexican language at that time in this land, and a wise, judicious man) was charged by both to put the ancient customs of these native Indians, especially those of Mexico, Texcoco, and Tlaxcalla, in a book, that there be some memory thereof, that the evil and imponderable might be better refuted and, if there were something good, that it might be recorded even as many things of other gentiles are recorded and remembered. And the said Father did so. Having seen all the paintings of ancient customs which the chiefs and leaders of these provinces possessed, and the oldest men having given answers to all he wanted to inquire of them, he made a very extensive book of all this.[22]

Toral's request of Sahagún and Mendieta's account of the labors of Olmos make it clear that Sahagún, in the inception of his *Historia*, followed the procedures practiced by Olmos and that the purpose of the enterprise was essentially religious. While Olmos, Motolinía, and Sahagún are acknowledged as the New World's first ethnographers and linguists, a term used by Garibay, "ethnographic missionaries," seems to accurately assess their activities.[23]

Sahagún's plan and organization varied as the work progressed. However, from the beginning he formed a general listing of the topics to be discussed as well as the order of their presentation. Schooled in the tradition of Medieval European scholars at the University of Salamanca, he took their works as his model. In a detailed study Garibay concludes the model for the *Historia* was Pliny's *Historia Naturalis*.[24] Robertson sees parallels with *De Proprietatibus Rerum* by Bartholomaeus Anglicus.[25]

Our knowledge of the developmental stages of Sahagún's *Historia* derives from two principal sources. In his Prologues to the separate Books, especially Books I and II, he chronicles the successive stages of compilation and revision. Also we have access to many of his early drafts and subsequent revisions, known collectively as the Madrid Codices, "Codices Matritenses"; one is in the library of the Royal Palace and is usually known as the Palace Manuscript, a second is in the library of the Royal Academy of History and is usually known as the Academy Manuscript. Annotations, corrections, translations, and revisions in Sahagún's unmistakable handwriting are frequent in both manuscripts.

In addition to the originals of the Madrid Codices, there exist the photographic facsimiles of the two manuscripts reproduced by Francisco del Paso y Troncoso, a Mexican scholar who, during the years 1892–1916, while residing in Europe had the illustrations from the *Florentine Codex* and Madrid Codices copied and the text of the Madrid Codices photographed. This material, although bearing the

---

20. See Prologue to Book II, this volume.

21. Garibay, *Historia de la literatura náhuatl*, Vol. II, p. 29. See also Georges Baudot, *Utopie et histoire au mexique: les premiers chroniqueurs de la civilisation mexicaine (1520–1569)*, pp. 119–157.

22. Mendieta, *Historia eclesiástica indiana*, Vol. I, pp. 81–82: "*Pues es de saber, que en el año de mil y quinientos y treinta y tres, siendo presidente de la Real Audiencia de México D. Sebastián Ramírez de Fuenleal (obispo que a la sazón era de la isla Española), y siendo custodio de la órden de nuestro Padre S. Francisco en esta Nueva España el santo varón Fr. Martín de Valencia, por ambos a dos fué encargado el padre Fr. Andrés de Olmos de la dicha órden (por ser la mejor lengua mexicana que entonces había en esta tierra, y hombre docto y discreto), que sacase en un libro las antigüedades de estos naturales indios, en especial de México, y Tezcuco, y Tlaxcala, para que de ello hubiese alguna memoria, y lo malo y fuera de tino se pudiese mejor refutar, y si algo bueno se hallase, se pudiese notar, como se notan y tienen en memoria muchas cosas de otros gentiles. Y el dicho padre lo hizo así, que habiendo visto todas las pinturas que los caciques y principales de estas provincias tenían de sus antiguallas, y habiéndole dado los más ancianos respuesta a todo lo que les quiso preguntar, hizo de todo ello un libro muy copioso.*"

23. Garibay, *Historia de la literatura náhuatl*, Vol. II, p. 21.

24. *Ibid.*, pp. 69–71.

25. Donald Robertson, *Mexican Manuscript Painting of the Early Colonial Period*, p. 170. Glass, however, observes that the Medieval model is characteristic of the early stages but does not apply to all stages of the reorganization. See John B. Glass, *Sahagún: Reorganization of the Manuscrito de Tlatelolco, 1566–1569*, pp. 21–22.

11

dates 1905–1907, saw limited distribution prior to 1927.[26]

In 1558, responding to the commission, Sahagún prepared an outline (*minuta o memoria*) of the topics to be developed. In 1558 or 1559, equipped with his outline, he moved to Tepepulco, in the vicinity of Texcoco. Gathering the leaders of the village, including don Diego de Mendoza, an elderly native, he requested and was provided with ten or twelve elderly informants conversant in the aboriginal practices and beliefs. Following his outline, he requested information on specific topics. Responding to his requests the native informants provided the information in the form of paintings (codices) which they subsequently explained verbally. Four Latin scholars, native students he had previously trained at the College, wrote the verbalized explanation in Nahuatl to the side or at the foot of the corresponding painting.[27]

The native aides were referred to as *colegiales*, students of the College; *grammaticos*, those skilled in grammar; or *latinos*, those skilled in Latin. There were also *escribanos*, scribes, who prepared the finished manuscript. This would seem to indicate his judicious utilization of the individual skills of his various students.[28]

The first organization of the work,[29] called the plan of Tepepulco, is contained in the *Primeros Memoriales* (fols. 250r–303v of the Palace MS, and fols. 51r–85v of the Academy MS). Therein he organized his work into chapters and subdivided the chapters into paragraphs. They appear in the following order:

Chapter 1, [The Gods (Teteo; Dioses)], 14 paragraphs.

Chapter 2, Matters relating to the Heavens and to the Region of the Dead (Ilhuicayotl iuan Mictlancayotl; Cielo e Infierno), 7 paragraphs.

Chapter 3, The Rulership (Tlatocayotl; Señorio), 17 paragraphs.

Chapter 4, Human Things (Tlacayotl; Cosas Humanas), 11 paragraphs.

There is evidence of a fifth chapter in this first plan. This is based on the now lost Sanz Manuscript[30] and the occurrence of a fifth chapter in the subsequent plan.

As explained by Sahagún, and as the *Primeros Memoriales* reveal, he drew his information from the paintings and the verbalized explanations. Garibay notes that the texts and paintings dealing with the ceremonies and the array of gods follow an aboriginal pattern developed in the native priests' school (calmecac): The informants provided Sahagún with a double version, the visual and the accompanying oral explanation memorized by the novices in the school.[31] If the topics required by his outline were not forthcoming by way of the codices, Sahagún resorted to the compilation of a vocabulary to complete the outline. For specific rituals, such as the offering of copal, sweeping, the piercing of the tongue, etc., the vocabulary was secured first, after which the corresponding illustration was added by the native artist. Subsequently, the Nahuatl text explaining the term and the illustration was added. On topics such as food, drink, tools, games, ailments, he compiled a vocabulary of characteristic terms which were supplemented and explained later. As López Austin has documented in a recent study, Sahagún's outline varied as his work progressed and likewise varied according to the subject matter under consideration. At times Sahagún followed his outline faithfully, yet at other times the informant's answer prompted him to ask additional questions; on occasions he encour-

26. Bernardino de Sahagún, *Historia general de las cosas de Nueva España*, ed. Francisco del Paso y Troncoso. For a description of the content of each volume (Vols. V, VI, VII, and VIII), see Silvio Zavala, *Francisco del Paso y Troncoso: su misión en Europa, 1892–1916*, pp. 335–36.

27. See Prologue to Book II, this volume.

28. See Miguel León-Portilla, *Ritos, sacerdotes y atavíos de los dioses*, pp. 9–19.

29. The stages of Sahagún's work and the manuscripts relating to the *Historia* are presented in summary. For greater detail see: García Icazbalceta, *Bibliografía mexicana*, pp. 344–87; Wigberto Jiménez Moreno, *Fray Bernardino de Sahagún y su obra*; Luis Nicolau D'Olwer, *Fray Bernardino de Sahagún (1499–1590)*; Manuel Ballesteros Gaibrois, *Códices matritenses de la Historia general de las cosas de la Nueva España de Fr. Bernardino de Sahagún*; H. B. Nicholson, "Sahagún's 'Primeros Memoriales,' Tepepolco, 1559–1561," in *Handbook of Middle American Indians*, pp. 207–18; Luis Nicolau D'Olwer and Howard F. Cline, "Sahagún and His Works," in *Handbook of Middle American Indians*, pp. 186–207; Charles Gibson and John B. Glass, "A Census of Middle American Prose Manuscripts in the Native Historical Tradition," in *Handbook of Middle American Indians*, pp. 360–70.

30. José Fernando Ramírez, "Códices mejicanos de Fr. Bernardino de Sahagún," *Boletín de la Real Academia de la Historia*, Vol. VI, p. 90; Nicholson, "Sahagún's 'Primeros Memoriales,'" p. 208.

31. Bernardino de Sahagún, *Historia general de las cosas de Nueva España*, ed. Angel María Garibay K. (hereafter referred to as Sahagún, Garibay ed.), Vol. I, pp. 35, 36.

aged his informant to digress or pursue his own order of presentation.[32] As a result, the overall organization of the *Historia* is clearly the handiwork of Sahagún, yet the degree to which the finished Nahuatl text can be traced to Sahagún's promptings and editing or to the order and mode of presentation of his informants and grammarians varies measurably.[33]

In 1561 Sahagún moved to Tlatelolco. Of this period he wrote:

> Taking all my writings I went to dwell in Santiago del Tlatelolco, where, gathering the leaders, I presented the matter of my writings to them, and requested that they assign me some capable leaders with whom to examine and discuss the writings which I brought recorded from Tepepulco. The governor with his councilmen assigned me as many as eight or ten leaders, selected from among all, very capable in their language and in their ancient customs. Cloistered in the College with them and with four or five students of the College, all trilingual, for a year or more, all I brought written from Tepepulco was amended, explained and expanded. And all was re-written in a poor hand, because it was written in great haste.[34]

The above quotation gives us the important procedures of the Tlatelolco period. The drafts of this period are known collectively as the *Manuscrito de Tlatelolco* and this MS consists of three parts:

1. The *Primer manuscrito de Tlatelolco* (ca. 1561–1562) consists of two fragments wherein the Nahuatl text fills the full width of the page: (a) The *Memoriales complementarios* gives a description of the Goddess Tlazolteotl that eventually became chapter 12 of Book I in the *Historia*, and adages regarding the sun and moon that were subsequently left out of the *Historia*; (b) The text of the *Segundos memoriales* that eventually became chapter 1 of Book VIII in the *Historia*.

2. The *Memoriales en tres columnas* (ca. 1563–1565) is a draft of Sahagún's envisaged three-column text. Only short sections contain the three columns with the Nahuatl text in the center column, a Span-

ish paraphrase in the left column, and a glossary (*scholia*) of Nahuatl terms in the right column. The remainder of the MS contains only the central Nahuatl column. This MS retained the earlier chapter organization.

3. The *Memoriales con escolios* (ca. 1565) is a finished copy in a clear hand; the beginning of a three-column manuscript that Sahagún never completed. The Nahuatl column occupies the center of the page, the Spanish paraphrase is in the left column, and the glossary (*scholia*) in the right column. It is a slightly revised copy of the sections in *Memoriales en tres columnas* that contain three columns. After Sahagún's reorganization, this text became Chapters 1–5 of Book VII and Chapters 1, 2, and part of 3 in Book X.

In 1565 Sahagún moved to the convent of San Francisco de Mexico. In the Prologue to Book II he wrote: "Having acted as mentioned in Tlatelolco, I came to dwell with all my writings in San Francisco de Mexico, where for three years, alone, I examined and re-examined all my writings. And I again amended them and divided them into Books, into twelve Books, and each Book by chapters, and some Books by chapters and paragraphs."[35]

In contrast to the work at Tlatelolco, which was due principally to the labors of the informants and the students, Sahagún continued to work alone. He writes in the first person singular. We are thus able to reconstruct his successive organizations by reviewing his notations and deletions as they occur throughout the text, but specially at the beginning and end of each Book. The work was in five separately bound units corresponding to a five chapter organization. Glass has observed that the location of Sahagún's notations on the left margin of the folios would require their removal from the two-hole binding.[36] As indicated by the glosses in Sahagún's hand, he reorganized the *Manuscrito de Tlatelolco* and included the earlier material on rhetoric and the Conquest that eventually became Books VI and XII respectively. The earlier chapters were divided into books, chapters, and some chapters were divided into paragraphs. Jiménez Moreno's study gives three successive organizations—the first of nine Books, the second of twelve Books, and the third being a fin-

---

32. Alfredo López Austin, "The Research Method of Fray Bernardino de Sahagún: The Questionnaires," in *Sixteenth Century Mexico: The Work of Sahagún*, pp. 111–49.

33. See Donald Robertson, "The Sixteenth Century Mexican Encyclopedia of Fray Bernardino de Sahagún," *Cuadernos de Historia Mundial*, Vol. IX, No. 3 (1966), pp. 617–28; Miguel León-Portilla, "Problematics of Sahagún," in *Sixteenth-Century Mexico: The Work of Sahagún*, pp. 235–55; Nicholson, "Sahagún's 'Primeros Memoriales,'" pp. 207–18.

34. See Prologue to Book II, this volume.

35. See Prologue to Book II, this volume.

36. Glass, *Sahagún*, pp. 3–4.

ished copy of the twelve Books that is known as the *Manuscrito de 1569*.[37]

In a meticulous study of Sahagún's glosses, Glass modifies Jiménez Moreno's earlier study. Glass documents four stages or organizations (stages A–D) as "three years of editing, review and reorganization (ca. 1566–68). The main activity of this period was the addition of Spanish book and chapter titles, none of which disturbed the physical order of the original Nahuatl texts," and a fifth stage or organization (stage E), which entailed the "editorial preparation for the copy known as the *Manuscrito de 1569* (ca. 1568–69)." He further characterizes the stages of reorganization: "In this reinterpretation of the reorganization of the Manuscrito de Tlatelolco during 1566–69, the revisions in the book and chapter numbers are envisioned as a continuous evolutionary process during which the five capitulos of the Tlatelolco manuscript of 1565 were transformed into the finely divided chapters of the 12 books of the Florentine Codex."[38]

The *Manuscrito de 1569* was, apparently, Sahagún's finished copy of the twelve Books divided into chapters and paragraphs, "put in final form in a clear hand." His native students "amended and added many things to the twelve Books when they made a clear copy."[39] Arranged as a three column copy, only the Nahuatl text of the twelve Books was completed; the Spanish column and the glosses were yet to be added.[40] The whereabouts of this *Manuscrito de 1569* is not known.

By the 1570s a new generation of missionaries had emerged. The spiritual climate had changed. The inquisition had been formally installed in New Spain.[41] In 1570, at the Chapter meeting, some members of the governing assembly looked upon Sahagún's work with disfavor, resulting in the withdrawal of financial support for scribes. The Provincial, Fr. Alonso de Escalona, impounded Sahagún's writings and scattered the individual Books throughout the province. Thus the writings remained relatively untouched for a period of five years, 1570–1575.[42]

The retrieval of the Books and the subsequent task of providing a Spanish text began with the arrival of Fr. Miguel Navarro as Commissary General. With his authorization, Sahagún spent about a year gathering his scattered writings.[43]

The Father Commissary General Fray Rodrigo de Sequera arrived in New Spain in 1575. Sahagún wrote in the Prologue to Book II that Sequera saw the writings, was pleased with them, ordered the author to translate them into Spanish, and provided the encouragement and means therefor. Sequera intended to send them to Señor Juan de Ovando, who had seen an earlier summary of the Books.[44] A letter from Archbishop Pedro Moya de Contreras to the king, dated March 28, 1576, states that he, Moya, urged Sequera to have the *Historia* written in Spanish and Mexican in order that it could be forwarded to the king. Moya further suggested a royal order be issued to this effect. Baudot publishes the Moya letter in a detailed study of Sequera, wherein he favors attributing the initiative for the translation of the *Historia* to Sequera rather than to Moya.[45]

In Sahagún's own words, there was no one to encourage the completion of the translation into Spanish until the arrival of Fr. Sequera, an indication that some translation into Spanish had been undertaken prior to 1575.[46]

In the Prologue to Book II, Sahagún recorded that he had prepared a summary (in Spanish) of all the Books and all the chapters of each Book in addition to the Prologues. He sent this MS to Spain with Fr. Miguel Navarro and Fr. Gerónimo de Mendieta.[47] This *sumario* dates from 1570. Its whereabouts is not known.

The Spanish text of the earlier *Memoriales con Escolios* (ca. 1565) appears virtually unaltered as the first six chapters of Book VII and Chapters 1, 2, and part of 3 of Book I.

Fols. 1–24 of the Palace MS contain a Spanish text known as *Memoriales en Español*. It contains the 22 chapters of Book I, without the appendix, and the

37. Jiménez Moreno, *Fray Bernardino de Sahagún*, p. 32.
38. Glass, *Sahagún*, pp. 33–34.
39. See Prologue to Book II, this volume.
40. See Prologue to Book I, this volume.
41. See Ricard, *La conquista espiritual de México*, pp. 148–50.
42. See Prologue to Book II, this volume.

43. See Prologue to Book II, this volume.
44. See Prologue to Book II, this volume.
45. Georges Baudot, "Fray Rodrigo de Sequera, avocat du diable pour une histoire interdite," *Cahiers du Monde Hispanique et Luso-Brésilien*, Caravelle 12 (1969), p. 62.
46. See Prologue to Book II, this volume.
47. See Prologue to Book II, this volume.

13 chapters of Book V, without the appendix. Since Book V is included and the text refers to chapters in Books II, IV, and VI of the *Historia*, the MS dates after Sahagún's final ordering of his Books in 1569.

On December 25, 1570, at a time when his work was being critically assessed, Sahagún sent a summary in Spanish to Pope Pius V entitled *Breve compendio de los ritos idolatricos de Nueva España*.[48] The *Compendio* contained a digest of parts of Book I and the Prologue, Chapters 1–19, and Chapter 24 of Book II. With minor variations the materials of Book II were included in the Florentine text. However, only Chapter 24 (Toxcatl) represented a translation from Nahuatl; the Prologue and Chapters 1–19 were composed in Spanish.

Building on these sections of the *Historia* which had been translated into Spanish by 1570, Sahagún continued the translation during 1576 and 1577. The frequent references to current events of 1576 and 1577 in the Spanish text make clear the translation was completed during these years.[49]

Sahagún prepared two bilingual versions of his *Historia*.[50] One was the Enriquez manuscript prepared during the years 1576–1577 and transmitted to Spain in 1578 as attested in his letter to Philip II dated March 26, 1578.[51] The fate of this version is not known. A second bilingual version prepared during the years 1578–1579, known as the Sequera manuscript, was given to Sequera to transmit to the king.[52] Sequera returned to Spain in 1580.[53] It is generally affirmed that the Sequera manuscript of 1578–1579 is the Florentine Codex.[54]

## THE FLORENTINE CODEX

In selecting *Florentine Codex* as the title of our translation of the Sahagún manuscript, we have followed the lead of two scholars, Paso y Troncoso[55] and García Icazbalceta.[56] We also, thereby, do homage to its fortunate and vigilant preservation in the Biblioteca Medicea–Laurenziana in Florence, Italy.

Sahagún's *Historia* is without title in the Florentine MS. However, as Paso y Troncoso noted in 1896, evidence of the title page and traces of the title still remain. The title page was removed at the second binding leaving a thin strip of the left margin which contains traces of the title.[57]

Fol. 1 of the Palace MS, which is also the first folio of *Memoriales en Español*, contains the title: *historia vnjuersal, de las cosas de la nueua españa: repartida en doze libros, en lengua mexicana, y española. fecha por el muy reuerendo padre, fray bernardino de sahagun: frayle de sanct francisco, de obseruancia.*

The original title page of the Tolosa MS is defective, reading: *. . . sal, de las cosas de la nueua s . . . libros y quatro volumines en lengua española. Compuesta y copillada Por el muy R.do P.e fr. bernaᵒ de saagun de la orden de los Frayles menores de obseruancia.*

Preceding the original title page is one of a later date which reads: *Historia universal de las cosas de la Nueva España, en doce libros y quatro volumenes en lengua Española. Compuesta y copilada por el M. R.do P.e Fr. Bernardino de Sahagun, de la orden de los Frayles menores de observancia.*

The final folio of the Tolosa MS contains the following note in the handwriting of the scribe: *"Fin de*

---

48. The MS is in the Vatican archives: Cod. Archivi vaticani AA Arm. 1-XVIII, 1816. Oliger published the text of the MS and compared the text with the Historia. See Livarius Oliger, *Breve compendio de los ritos idolátricos de Nueva España*. See also W. Schmidt, "Fray Bernardino de Sahagún O. Fr. M. 'Un breve compendio de los ritos ydolátricos que los yndios desta nueva España usauan en el tiempo de su infidelidad,'" *Anthropos*, 1:302–17.

49. Three manuscripts attributed to Sahagún, but postdating the Florentine Codex, are not discussed. They are: *Calendario de las fiestas y meses de estos naturales*. (Codex Ixtlilxochitl part 3); *Kalendario mexicano latino y castellano; Arte adivinatoria*. See Gibson and Glass, "A Census of Middle American Prose Manuscripts," pp. 366, 369–70; Walter Lehmann, "Der sogenannte Kalender Ixtlilxochitls. Ein Beitrag zur Kenntnis der achtzehn Jahresfeste der Mexikaner." *Anthropos*, 3:988–1004; Roberto Moreno, "Guia de las obras en lenguas indígenas existentes en la Biblioteca Nacional," pp. 38–43; Georges Baudot, "The Last Years of Fray Bernardino de Sahagún (1585–90)," pp. 180–84.

50. Cf. Bustamante, ed., *La aparición*, p. 334: *"los cuales libros que fueron doce, envió por ellos nuestro señor el rey D. Filipe, y se los envié yo por mano del Sr. D. Martin Henriquez, Visorey que fué desta tierra, y no sé que se hizo dellos, ni en cuyo poder están agora. Llevólos despues desto el P. Fr. Rodrigo de Sequera, desque hizo su oficio de comisario en esta tierra, y nunca me ha escripto en que pararon aquellos libros que llevó en lengua mexicana y castellana, y muy historiados."*

51. The Sahagún letter is published in Baudot, "Fray Rodrigo de Sequera," p. 65.

52. See note 50.

53. Nicolau D'Olwer, *Fray Bernardino de Sahagún*, p. 179.

54. *Ibid.* Nicolau D'Olwer and Cline, "Sahagún and His Works," p. 196; Jiménez Moreno, *Fray Bernardino de Sahagún*, p. 40.

55. Zavala, *Francisco del Paso y Troncoso*, p. 6.

56. García Icazbalceta, *Bibliografía mexicana*, p. 353.

57. Cf. Francisco del Paso y Troncoso, "Estudios sobre el códice mexicano del P. Sahagún conservado en la Biblioteca Mediceo-Laurenziana de Florencia," *Anales del Museo Nacional de Arqueología, Historia y Entología*, 4ª Epoca, Vol. 4 (1926), pp. 316–20; see esp. p. 317.

*la Historia general compuesta Por el Muy R.ᵈᵒ P.ᵉ fray ber.ⁿᵒ de sahagun."*

The *Historia* has been variously designated by scholars: *Historiam Universalem Nova Hispania* by Fr. Juan de San Antonio in 1732,[58] *Historia Mexicana* by Bandini in 1793;[59] *Historia general de las cosas de Nueva España* by Bustamante in 1829;[60] and *Historia de las cosas de la Nueva España* by Paso y Troncoso in 1896.[61] We have selected the title in current usage: *General History of the Things of New Spain.*[62]

The existence of the Florentine MS in the Medicea–Laurenziana Library was brought to the attention of scholars by the bibliographer Angelo Maria Bandini in 1793.[63] His Latin description of the MS contains selections of the Spanish text from the Prologues, the Book titles, and the Chapter headings. The MS appears to have remained relatively unstudied until its continuing existence in the Medicea–Laurenziana Library was mentioned by P. Fr. Marcelino de Civezza in 1879.[64]

The date of acquisition by the Laurentian Library and its provenance remain conjectural. Nuttall reasoned that its earlier history was shared with the Codex Magliabecchi; that both manuscripts were sent to Florence for the approval of Medici Pope Leo XI prior to 1605; that it came into the possession of the bibliophile Magliabecchi, librarian for Cosimo I de' Medici, grand Duke of Tuscany.[65] Detlef Heikamp suggests that the illustrations from the *Florentine Codex*[66] served artist Lodovico Buti as a model for the frescoed ceilings of the Armoury of the Uffizi

Gallery.[67] The frescoes were painted in 1588 by Buti. Heikamp also suggests that the *Florentine Codex* was purchased by Ferdinand I de' Medici.[68] This would place the MS in Florence prior to 1588.[69]

Spanish scholars were aware of the Florentine MS by 1882 when Cayetano Rosell informed members of the Royal Academy of History of its existence.[70] In 1883 Antonio María Fabié, a member of the Academy, informed the 5th International Congress of Americanists, held in Copenhagen, that he had studied the Sahagún MS in Florence.[71]

In his article on Sahagún for his *Bibliografía mexicana del siglo XVI*, first published in 1886, García Icazbalceta published the Bandini description of the Florentine.[72] He had collaborated with Francisco del Paso y Troncoso in writing the Sahagún article, and, at that time, according to Paso y Troncoso, their only knowledge of the Florentine MS was by way of the Bandini description.[73]

At the first session of the 7th International Congress of Americanists, held in Berlin October 2–5, 1888, Eduard Seler reported that he had examined the Florentine MS and described many of its illustrations.[74] At the same Congress Seler presented a paper entitled *Das Tonalamatl der Aubin'schen Sammlung und die verwandten Kalenderbücher,* wherein he made frequent reference to the "Sahagun–Manuskrit dèr Biblioteca Laurentiana zu Florenz."[75] In the spring of 1892 Seler sent his wife, Cæcilie Seler-Sachs, to Florence to personally copy parts of the Florentine text.[76] This copy enabled Seler to prepare the Nahuatl text and a German translation of parts of Books III, IV, V, VI, X, and all of Book XII for publication.[77]

Daniel G. Brinton examined the MS in the Laurentian Library in April 1889. He copied the Nahuatl

58. Juan de San Antonio, *Bibliotheca universa franciscana,* Vol. I, p. 214.

59. García Icazbalceta, *Bibliografía mexicana,* p. 358.

60. Carlos María de Bustamante, *Historia general de las cosas de Nueva España.*

61. Paso y Troncoso, "Estudios sobre el códice mexicano," p. 316.

62. Cf. Bernardino de Sahagún, *Historia general de las cosas de Nueva España,* Editorial Pedro Robredo. See also *Historia general de las cosas de Nueva España,* ed. Miguel Acosta Saignes, and Sahagún, Garibay ed.

63. Angelo Maria Bandini, *Bibliotheca Leopoldina Laurentiana, seu Catalogus Manuscriptorum qui nuper in Laurentiana translati sunt.*

64. Marcelino de Civezza, *Saggio di Bibliografia Geografica Storica Etnografica Sanfrancescana,* p. 525.

65. Zelia Nuttall, "Francisco Cervantes de Salazar," *Anales del Museo Nacional de Arqueología. Historia y Etnología,* 4ª Epoca, Vol. 4 (1926), p. 302.

66. Detlef Heikamp, *Mexico and the Medici,* pp. 19–20, plates 37–38, 40–42.

67. *Ibid.,* p. 21, plates 30–31.

68. *Ibid.,* pp. 20, 41.

69. Donald Robertson, "Mexican Indian Art and the Atlantic Filter: Sixteenth to Eighteenth Centuries," in *First Images of America,* p. 489.

70. *Boletín de la Real Academia de la Historia,* Vol. II, p. 184.

71. *Ibid.,* Vol. III, p. 209.

72. García Icazbalceta, *Bibliografía mexicana,* pp. 358–59.

73. Cf. Paso y Troncoso, "Estudios sobre el códice méxicano," p. 316.

74. *Congrès International des Américanistes, Compte–Rendu de la Septième session, Berlin,* 1888, p. 90.

75. *Ibid.,* pp. 521–735.

76. Eduard Seler, *Einige Kapitel,* p. viii.

77. *Ibid.,* pp. xiii–xvi.

text of the hymns to the gods and five illustrations from Book II, which he utilized the following year, 1890, in his English translation of the hymns.[78] Furthermore, in his publication he added: "When in Florence, in 1889, I had an accurate copy made of the Nahuatl text and all the figures of the first book of Sahagún's History."[79]

Don Francisco del Paso y Troncoso's mission to Europe covered the years 1892–1916. In 1893, through the offices of D. Gonzalo A. Esteva, Mexico's minister in Italy, Paso y Troncoso received the permission of the Italian government to reproduce the illustrations and copy the Florentine text.[80] The artist Genaro López was employed to prepare the illustrations, the work being completed in 1894.[81] Proceeding from Madrid to Florence in 1894, Paso y Troncoso utilized the next two years to make a loyal copy of the Florentine text, a labor that was done at his own expense.[82] After completing his personal copy of the Florentine, Paso y Troncoso published a short study of the Codex in which he related it to the Tolosa MS, identified it as one of the two originals sent to Spain by Sahagún, and cited evidence that the three-volume MS was earlier bound in four volumes. At this time he planned to publish the Florentine in its original four-volume organization.[83]

In 1898, familiar with the Madrid manuscripts and the Florentine MS, Paso y Troncoso projected a definitive edition of Sahagún's writings. It was to be organized as follows:

Vols. I–IV. The Nahuatl text of the Florentine matched with the Spanish text of the Códice Castellano de Madrid (Tolosa MS).

Vol. V. Illustrations from the *Florentine Codex*.

Vol. VI. Nahuatl text of the Palace MS.

Vol. VII. Nahuatl text of the Academy MS.

Vol. VIII. A literal translation of the Nahuatl texts of the Palace, Academy, and Florentine manuscripts.

Vols. IX–XII. A Sahagún dictionary (Vocabulario Sahaguntino).

Vols. XIII–XV. Commentary on the texts and a general index.[84]

In his plans for publication, Paso y Troncoso rejected the Spanish text of the Florentine in favor of the Códice Castellano de Madrid. He considered the Spanish of the Florentine "grotesco a veces," and summarily stated: "For the Spanish texts it is necessary to definitively reject those from Florence and prepare the edition according to the text of the Códice Castellano de Madrid."[85]

Paso y Troncoso altered his original plan as he began preparing the Sahagún material for publication. In an *Infome* to the Sr. Secretario de Estado y del Despacho de Instrucción Pública y Bellas Artes, dated August 31, 1909, he outlined his revised edition and explained why the published texts became Vols. VI–VIII. At the outset, during the administration of Sr. Lic. Baranda, the funds committed to the Sahagún enterprise sufficed only for the publication of the Florentine MS. Since the colored illustrations are dispersed throughout the MS, it became apparent that the cost of a facsimile reproduction of the entire MS in color would be prohibitive. Therefore, it was decided to group the illustrations together in plates (*estampas*). Vols. I–IV were to contain the Florentine text and Vol. V the plates. Since the location of each individual illustration on the plate could not be anticipated, the illustrations were lithographed to form Vol. V and each illustration assigned to the corresponding text volume. Thus the plates of Vol. V were prepared before Vols. I–IV because of the problems inherent in reproducing the illustrations and, once the plates of the illustrations were prepared, the Florentine text, Vols. I–IV, was, in effect, locked into position. Paso y Troncoso finally decided to start with the Madrid manuscripts as Vols. VI–VIII because he considered them early drafts that could be related later to the Florentine text.[86]

---

78. Daniel G. Brinton, *Rig–Veda Americanus. Sacred Songs of the Ancient Mexicans, with a Gloss in Nahuatl*, p. ix.

79. *Ibid.*, p. 18.

80. Zavala, *Francisco del Paso y Troncoso*, p. 75.

81. *Ibid.*, pp. 6, 240.

82. ". . . y pasando en seguida yo mismo a Italia para hacer la copia del texto, personalmente; operación que duró dos años (porque se hizo a plana y renglón) y que realicé a mis expensas, dado que, por todo ese tiempo, estuve suspenso de sueldo, a causa de la crisis de la plata, y viviendo con estrechez de mis propios recursos." *Ibid.*, p. 75. Three volumes of Paso y Troncoso's personal copy are in the Biblioteca del Instituto Nacional de Antropología e Historia, Mexico. They are: Vol. I, Books I–V; Vol. II, Book VI; Vol. III, Books VII–IX.

83. Cf. n. 57. Although published in 1926, it is dated "Moscou, 7–19 de octubre de 1896."

84. Jesús Galindo y Villa, *Don Francisco del Paso y Troncoso. Su vida y sus obras*, Memorias y Revista de la Sociedad Científica "Antonio Alzate," Vol. 42 (1923), p. 543.

85. Zavala, *Francisco del Paso y Troncoso*, p. 72: "*para los textos castellanos hay que desechar absolutamente los de Florencia, y hacer la edición según el texto del códice castellano de Madrid.*"

86. *Ibid.*, pp. 71–75.

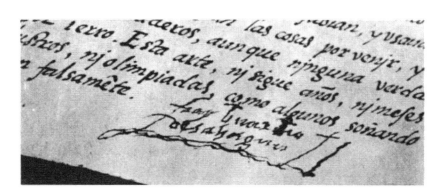

Fig. 1. Sahagún's signature from *Book IV*, Fol. 81[r].

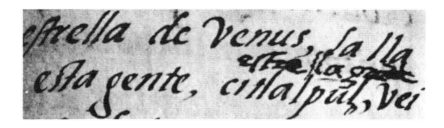

Fig. 2. Sahagún's handwriting from *Book VII*, Fol. 8[r].

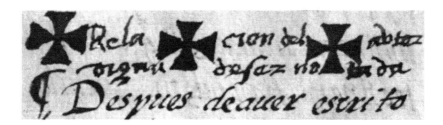

Fig. 3. Sahagún's handwriting from *Book X*, Fol. 70[v].

As late as September 1912 Paso y Troncoso was actively pursuing his publication labors. The colored plates for the Florentine were nearing completion and the edition of the Madrid manuscripts was, likewise, nearly finished. He was preparing to move rapidly to the publication of the Florentine text.[87] Its not being published was due to the uncertainty of adequate funds, his reduced activities by 1914,[88] and his untimely death in 1916. At the time of his passing, 185 plates had been prepared in Florence by Alessandro Ruffoni; 27 plates are from the Academy and Palace manuscripts and the remaining 158 from the Florentine MS.[89] Four of the plates reproduce calendrical charts from Books IV and VII; the remaining 154 plates contain the 1,842 illustrations of the Florentine MS.

As presently preserved in the Medicea–Laurenziana Library in Florence, Italy, the Florentine MS is bound in three volumes. Volume I (Palat. 218) contains Books I–V, Volume II (Palat. 219) contains Books VI–IX, and Volume III (Palat. 220) contains Books X–XII. The Prologue to Book IX gives indication that the work was originally bound in four volumes: Books I–V made up the first volume, Book VI alone comprised the second volume, Books VII–X occupied the third volume, and Books XI and XII were in the fourth volume.[90] The separate entity of Book VI is further verified by Sahagún's dedication to Sequera at the beginning of the Book.[91]

Evidence for the rebinding into three volumes is found in Book VII, fol. 14ᵛ. A part of the Spanish text is written on the left margin of the page, filling the margin. The trimming and rebinding removed a portion of twenty-two lines from the text. The Spanish text, however, can be reconstructed from fol. 197 (page 391) of the Tolosa MS. As will be noted, the Tolosa MS is considered a copy of the *Florentine Codex* and hence the rebinding occurred after the making of the Tolosa copy.[92]

When the Florentine MS was written, the folios of each Book were numbered separately — the folio number being placed in the upper right-hand corner. These are the folio numbers in the indices of each Book. When the four volumes were rebound into three volumes the folio numbers of each volume were written in the lower right-hand corner. Volume I (Palat. 218) contains 353 folios; Volume II (Palat. 219) contains 375 folios; Volume III (Palat. 220) contains 495 folios. The three volumes thus total 1,223 folios or 2,446 pages.

The *Florentine Codex* is generally considered to be the Sequera copy, as suggested by García Icazbalceta in 1886.[93] As Sahagún wrote in the 1585 version of the Conquest, the copy of the *Historia* was illustrated, as is the Florentine.[94] Furthermore, two dedications were directed to Fr. Sequera. The dedication in Book VI documents the transmitting of the Book and his indebtedness to Sequera. A second dedicatory letter to Sequera at the beginning of Book I transmits Books I–V.[95] Although found only in the Tolosa MS, it was conceivably separated from the Florentine at the time of rebinding.

The manuscript can be safely dated between 1577 and 1580. The entry at the end of Book VI verifies that the Spanish translation was not completed before 1577. Sahagún's signature appears on Fol. 81ʳ of Book IV (Fig. 1). Short entries in his unmistakable handwriting appear in the Spanish text, especially in Book VII (Fig. 2), Book IX, and Book X (Fig. 3). This would date the MS prior to 1590, the year of his death. Writing in 1585 Sahagún recorded its completion and lamented its whereabouts.[96] The dedications to Sequera wish him Godspeed and since Sequera embarked for Spain on February 26, 1580,[97] it provides a terminal date for the delivery of the manuscript. As will be noted, the watermarks would tend to substantiate the 1577–1580 period for the MS.

The steps in the production of the Florentine can be discerned from a study of the MS itself. First the Nahuatl text was written in the right column. When

87. *Ibid.*, p. 96.

88. Galindo y Villa, *Don Francisco del Paso y Troncoso*, p. 171–72.

89. *Ibid.*, pp. 549–50.

90. See prologue to Book IX this volume.

91. See Sahagún, *Florentine Codex, Book VI.*

92. Cf. Paso y Troncoso MS copy of Florentine Codex in Biblioteca del Instituto Nacional de Antropología e Historia, Mexico, D.F., Vol. III: "*llego á estas dos conclusiones: 1° que la obra MS de Sahagún fue dos veces empastada: 2° que la pasta que*

*se ve hoy en el ejemplar en de Florencia se puso despues de haber sido copiado el* MS. *Castellano que conserva en Madrid la Real Acada. de la Historia.*" See also Paso y Troncoso, "Estudios sobre el códice mexicano," pp. 318–20.

93. See García Icazbalceta, *Bibliografía mexicana*, p. 353.

94. See n. 50.

95. Sahagún, Garibay ed., Vol. I, pp. 25–26.

96. See n. 50.

97. See n. 53.

minor spaces occurred, a floral design filled these spaces. With the exception of the appendix of Book I and minor occurrences in Books X, XI, and XII, the Nahuatl column is devoid of illustrations.

As a second step, the Spanish text was written in the left column. Spaces occurred at the end of chapters or paragraphs because of the lesser space occupied by the Spanish text. For various reasons, Sahagún left sections of the Nahuatl text without a corresponding translation or paraphrasing. In Chapter 27, Book X, he wrote regarding native education, and in Book XI he inserted extended comments on Christianity.[98] The hymns to the gods he considered occult and the work of the devil, wherefore they remained untranslated.[99] He considered the content of Chapter 16 in Book IX on goldsmiths of little import for the faith or the virtues.[100] Likewise, at the end of Chapter 17 in Book IX, dealing with the working of stone, he stated the Nahuatl text was not translated because the working of stone was easily observable.[101] Also, the Nahuatl text of Chapters 20 and 21, which deals with feather working, was not translated into Spanish.[102] Elsewhere, especially in Books XI and XII, Sahagún measurably compressed the Spanish version and in some instances gave only a summary paragraph, thus leaving many folios available for illustrations. This may partially account for the many illustrations in these two Books.

The spaces provided by the shorter Spanish texts, the summary statements in Spanish, or the absence of Spanish translations, enabled the artist to add illustrations or floral designs. The size, shape, and number of illustrations depended on the dimensions of the available spaces. In parts of Books X and XI, the absence of adequate spaces forced the artist to reduce the size of the illustrations and, in some instances, place them in the Nahuatl column. The fact that the illustrations are numerous where the Spanish texts are absent would suggest that the artist relied on the terms or descriptions in the Nahuatl column to prompt the composition of the illustrations.

In the appendix of Book I, the pattern varied and the illustrations were interspersed in the Nahuatl text because the procedure was reversed: the original texts in Spanish and Latin were translated into Nahuatl. In one instance, Book IX, illustrations applicable to the entire Book were placed at the end of the chapter summaries.

The function of the pictorial material changed as the *Historia* passed through its several stages and modifications. In the Tepepulco period the pictorial material served to elicit the verbal explanations that became the Nahuatl text. By the Tlatelolco period the Nahuatl text had become standardized with less dependence on the pictures. The pictorial material in the Florentine became illustrative of the texts rather than the pictorial source of the texts.

The art style of the Florentine illustrations reflects both native and Spanish traditions. When compared with the drawings of the Tepepulco period they reveal more of the Colonial tradition. A limited number of representations are readily recognizable as very much akin to their pre-Hispanic prototypes. They include: cotton, paper flags, down feathers, obsidian swords, water, speech scrolls, rocks, reed mats, musical instruments, and name glyphs. However, viewed collectively, Spanish influence is clearly visible. Robertson, considering the illustrations in detail, concludes that they show the presence of many hands and many styles.[103] Elsewhere he observes:

> The rendering of the colonial forms and shapes representing the Spanish traditions in New Spain shows us that the artist knew them intimately. They were a part of his daily life, and thus there are few lapses when they are painted. Not only the forms but the technical skills of the Spanish artist are used with assurance. Perspective, light and shade, the ability to show space, mass, and volume, and the ability to place

---

98. See these texts in this volume.

99. See this text in Sahagún, *Florentine Codex, Book II*, p. 207 (221).

100. *La sentencia deste capitulo no importa mucho, nj para la fe, nj para las virtudes, porq es pratica meramête geometrica: si alguno, para saber vocablos, maneras de dezir, exqujsitas: podra preguntar a los officiales, que tratan este officio, q̃ en toda parte, los ay.*

101. *En esta letra se pone la manera que tenjan los lapidarios de labrar las piedras: no se pone en romance, porque como es cosa muy vsada, y siempre se vsa, en los pueblos principales desta nueua españa, qujn qujsiere entender los vocablos, y esta manera de hablar podralo tomar de los mesmos officiales.*

102. [Chapter 20] *En esta letra, se ponen todos los instrumentos, que vsauan estos officiales, de la pluma: y tambien agora los vsan; donde qujera, que estan: por esso no se declara, en la lengua española: qujen qujsiere verlos, y saber sus nombres, de los mesmos officiales, lo podra saber, y verlos con sus ojos.*

[Chapter 21] *En esta letra, se pone la manera, de obrar, que tienen los officiales de la pluma dõde se ponen por menudo, todas las particularidades deste officio: qujen qujsiere verlas, y entenderlas, podralo ver, con sus ojos, en las casas de los mesmos officiales; pues que los ay, en todas las partes, desta nueua españa y hazen sus officios.*

103. Robertson, *Mexican Manuscript Painting*, p. 178. See also Robertson's "Commentary," in *Investigaciones contemporáneos sobre historia de Mexico*, pp. 91–95.

the human figure convincingly in an interior or an exterior space all show how "Spanish" the background of Sahagún's artists was.

The native component in the illustrations of the manuscript, on the other hand, shows knowledge of pre-Hispanic forms in widely varying degrees of proficiency. At times the artist seems to be working from drawn or painted models; at other times he seems to have abandoned the model and struck out on his own, and the results demonstrate how minimal the understanding of native forms can be.[104]

The Prologues were probably from several sources and were written over a period of time. We have previously suggested the Prologue to Book II is an extension of the 1570 Prologue in the *Breve compendio*.

The first 19 chapters of Book II are in Spanish without a corresponding Nahuatl text. Copied from the *Breve compendio* or a similar MS, with only minor differences, they are summaries in Spanish of the month rituals that follow. In the earlier *Memoriales en tres columnas* MS (fols. 126ʳ–129ʳ, Palace MS) they appear in outline form with short Nahuatl texts as the concluding section of Book II, and Sahagún certified their position at the end of Book II with his signature. In the Florentine, the Spanish and Nahuatl chapters of the month rituals were copied first and later the chapter numbering was changed to accommodate the summary chapters at the beginning. The major portion of Chapter 19, the movable feasts, is out of place. As a Spanish summary of the chapters of Book IV, it belongs properly with them.[105]

From 1906 until 1916, the Florentine MS was inaccessible to scholars in anticipation of Paso y Troncoso's facsimile edition.[106] In the early 1970s the Laurentian Library withdrew study privileges to assure the continued preservation of the MS. In 1979 the Mexican government, under the supervision of the Archivo General de la Nación, edited a facsimile edition of the MS in dimensions corresponding to the original. This edition is of such excellence that an equivalent of the original MS has become accessible to all interested scholars.[107]

# THE TOLOSA MANUSCRIPT

The Tolosa MS, known as *Códice Castellano de Madrid* or *Manuscrito de Tolosa*, is presently in the Royal Academy of History (Madrid). It is catalogued as A–77 or 9–4812. All the published Spanish editions of the *Historia* derive directly or indirectly from copies of this MS.

In 1867 Ramírez made a study of the Sahagún manuscripts in the Royal Academy. The study, published in 1885, included a description and some information on the Tolosa MS.[108] From the Ramírez study we learn that the MS was first mentioned by Fr. Juan de San Antonio in his *Bibliotheca Universa Franciscana*, Madrid, 1732–1733. He described a MS of 12 Books bound in four volumes that was in the Franciscan convent of Tolosa in the province of Cantabria.[109] The Juan de San Antonio reference was cited by Juan José de Eguiara y Eguren in his *Bibliotheca Mexicana*, Mexico, 1755; by Francisco Javier Clavijero in his *Historia antigua de México*, published in 1780–1781; and by José Mariano Beristáin de Souza in his *Biblioteca Hispano–Americana Septentrional*, Mexico 1816–1821.

An inserted page at the beginning of the Tolosa MS contains a title and includes a *nota* dated 1804, which states that the cosmographer Juan Bautista Muñoz had been commissioned by the crown to write a history of the Spanish Indies. On April 6, 1783, provided with a royal order, he obtained the MS from the Franciscan convent of Tolosa. It remained in his possession until his death in 1799. It then passed to the Secretaría del Despacho de Gracia y Justicia de Indias. In 1804 those of the Order, learning of the king's desire to obtain the MS, surrendered it in lieu of a faithful copy that had been made for them.[110] García Icazbalceta states the MS passed to the private

---

104. Robertson, "The Treatment of Architecture in the Florentine Codex of Sahagún," in *Sixteenth-Century Mexico: The Work of Sahagún*, p. 163.

105. See "To the sincere reader," Books II and IV this volume.

106. Seler, *Einige Kapitel*, p. ix.

107. A detailed study by José Luis Martínez entitled El "Códice Florentino" y la "Historia General" de Sahagún is presently in press to be published by the Archivo General de la Nación, Mexico.

108. Cf. Ramírez, "Códices mejicanos," p. 103.

109. San Antonio, *Bibliotheca universa franciscana*, Vol. I, p. 214: "*Historiam Universalem Nova Hispania in 12 libros distributam. Manuscripta asservatur in Tolosano Conventu Cantabricae Provinciae, tomis 4.*"

110. "*Este libro se hallava en el Conbento de Frayles Franciscos de la Villa de tolosa de Guipuzcoa, de donde lo recojió en Virtud de Rl. orn de 6. de Abril de 1783. por el exmo. Dn. Jph de Galvez, Dn. Juan Bauptista Muñoz Cosmografo mayor de Indias comisionado por S. M. para escrivir la Historia Grãl de aquellos Dominios por cuyo fallecimito. se traxo con otros papeles suyos á esta Sria. del Despacho de Gracia y Justicia de Indias. Haviendolo reclamado dhos Religiosos, se les insinuó que S. M. tendria gusto de tenerlo; en cuya Virtud lo cedieron voluntariamte. dandoles vna copia integra de dho Libro en el año de 1804. como consta del expediente causado sobre el particular qe. existe en esta Secretaria.*"

Royal Library where it was apparently consulted in 1807. The king donated it to the Royal Academy in August 1815, and it was delivered to the Academy in March 1816.[111]

The discrepancy between the present single volume and Fr. Juan de San Antonio's mention of a four-volume work prompted Ramírez to speculate that the monks had made a substitution in response to the royal order.[112] García Icazbalceta, considering the same problem, suggested Fr. Juan had not seen and had not personally examined the work.[113]

The Tolosa MS contains 682 pages. The handwriting is uniform throughout; it is the work of a single copyist. The paper is uniform throughout and clearly from one stock of paper. Only one watermark appears, although repeated many times. In addition to the early Ramírez study in 1867, Ballesteros Gaibrois and his students described it and compared the chapter headings with the Madrid Codices and the *Florentine Codex*.[114]

I have compared the Tolosa text with the Florentine text, and the similarities are such as to justify considering it a copy of the Florentine.[115] In the main it is a loyal copy, the exceptions being where the copyist chose to write the numeral "9" in place of the word "nine," etc., altered the spelling and punctuation to make the Spanish more readable, and employed frequent word abbreviations.

In those Books that were straightforward narrative, the copyist remained extremely loyal to his master copy. In those Books where the text became fragmented, the copyist abridged, omitted, and altered the Spanish text with frequency. This is most apparent in Book VI and Book XI. The disparities are too numerous to document in this study.

Of a more serious nature is the copyist's willingness to editorialize. This has led scholars, editors, and publishers to attribute certain Spanish texts to Sahagún, when in reality they represent the editorial comments of the Tolosa copyist. Sahagún's phrase, *esta muy a la larga en la letra*, is his way of indicating greater detail is contained in the Nahuatl text. However, the phrase, repeated several times in Chapter 6 of Book XI, and elsewhere, represents the copyist's reference to the more expanded Spanish text in the Florentine. Three examples of the copyist's editorializing are cited:

1. In Chapters 41, 42, and 43 of Book VI, which deal with adages, riddles, and metaphors, the copyist abridged and altered many and omitted a great number. In Chapter 41 he copied about half of the adages and then added: "I don't know how many other adages or proverbs there are which should mean something in the Mexican language, according to the hidden meaning of the words or the language. And in our language they are absurdities, very displeasing and annoying, as will be seen from those written here, which are those which can be read with less annoyance. And I don't even know who can endure to read all of them."[116]

2. The Nahuatl text of Chapter 27 of Book X in the Florentine presents a long and detailed consideration of human anatomy. Sahagún left the Nahuatl text untranslated and wrote at length on the Royal College of Santa Cruz. The Tolosa copyist inserted the following comment between the chapter heading and Sahagún's interpolation: "The author did not translate any of this chapter into Castilian for the reason that, in place of the translation, said author placed the following account which is worthy of note and more pleasing than an explanation of the text could be."[117]

3. In Chapter 2 of Book XI the Nahuatl text of paragraph 10 is a lengthy treatment of the anatomy

*Este Libro aunque se llama original. no es sino Copia ni tiene otra Recomendacion que el es estar escrito en letra antigua de la epoca de la conquista de Nueva España. y á pocos años despues de ella.*
Madd. 4. Julio de 1804
*La copia qe. se dió á dhos Religiosos de tolosa costó mil y doscientos rres. /"*

111. García Icazbalceta, *Bibliografía mexicana*, p. 353–54.

112. Ramírez, "Códices mejicanos," p. 104.

113. García Icazbalceta, *Bibliografía mexicana*, p. 352–53.

114. Ballasteros Gaibrois, *Códices matritenses de la Historia general*, Vol. 1, pp. 173–253.

115. Nicolau D'Olwer and Cline, "Sahagún and His Works," p. 199; Baudot, "Fray Rodrigo de Sequera," pp. 67–68. For differing views, see Nicolau D'Olwer, "Fray Bernardino de Sahagún," p. 181; Zavala, "Francisco del Paso y Troncoso," pp. 71–72; Charles Gibson and Glass, "A Census of Middle American Prose Manuscripts," p. 369.

116. "*Otros no se quantos adagios o Refranes ay que en el lenguaje mexicano deuen ser algo. Por la energia de los bocablos o de la lengua y en el nro son disparates y muy desgustosos y enfadosos. como se vera por los que estan aqui escritos los quales son los que con menos enfado se pueden leer y aun no se si abra alguno que sufra a acabarlos de leer.*" Tolosa MS, p. 374 (fol. 189).

117. "*deste capitulo no traduxo en lengua castellana cosa alguna El autor Porque en lugar de la tradución del puso el dho autor la Relación siguiente la qual es digna de ser notada y mas gustosa q pudiera ser la declaración del texto.*" Tolosa MS, p. 510 (fol. 257).

of birds. Sahagún translated the Nahuatl text into Spanish. The copyist failed to record the lengthy Spanish text but substituted the following editorial comment: "The text of the tenth paragraph which deals with the internal and external body parts of birds, is all synonyms. And the same words are placed in the translation as in the [Mexican] language, explaining in Spanish to what part of the bird it refers or to which [bird] it applies. And so I wrote nothing thereof, as it pertains more to the Mexican language than anything else."[118]

For nearly a century and a half, the Tolosa MS has served well. It has been the source of all published versions of Sahagún's Spanish text. The recent publication of the Spanish text of the Florentine will enable scholars to fill the lacunas of the Tolosa text, just as the translation and publication of the Nahuatl text of the Florentine has filled the lacunas of its Spanish text, affording us Sahagún's unabridged *Historia*.

---

118. "*El texto del decimo parrapho que trata de las partes de las aues assi interiores como exteriores todos son sinonimos y en traducion se ponen los mismos que la lengua dizido. en Romance para que parte de la aue se aplican / o a qual dellas siruen y assi no puse del nada porque mas pertenece a la lengua mexicana q a otra cosa.*" Tolosa MS, p. 581, (fol. 293).

# The Watermarks in the Florentine Codex

*by* Charles E. Dibble

Admittedly there are dangers inherent in utilizing watermarks as a means of dating a manuscript or establishing the contemporaneous dates for two manuscripts. Hunter has carefully listed the pitfalls which are ever present in this procedure.[1] Nevertheless, there are unique factors regarding the use of paper in New Spain which make the study of watermarks rewarding and helpful.

First, all paper was imported into New Spain during the sixteenth century.[2] Native *amatl* paper found limited use, and attempts to manufacture European paper in New Spain are recorded for 1533[3] and 1580.[4] Nevertheless, the shipping lanes supplied all the European paper utilized in New Spain during that century.

Secondly, paper was relatively scarce in the New World and often in short supply.[5] Available paper stocks were quickly used, precluding prolonged storage in warehouses. Thus each of the different watermark categories (such as the hand, the caballero, the cross) appears, attains maximum frequency, and disappears in a chronological order.

Studies of sixteenth-century watermarks in New Spain have been made by two Mexican scholars.[6] In both cases they have indicated the date range of

each watermark category, based on the samples at their disposal. Briquet's examples are more numerous and are taken from European samples.[7] The date range of his examples has been tabulated from his study. The three sources are in general agreement and indicate the hand category as being the earliest of the three.

|  | Mena | Lamadrid Ibarra | Briquet |
|---|---|---|---|
| Hand (with star and letter) | 1528–1545 | 1528–1573 | 1493–1590 |
| Caballero-with-staff | 1548–1605 | 1541–1608 | 1510–1600 |
| Heart-Cross | 1540–1594 | 1538–1623 | 1555–1600 |

Photographs of watermarks from the *Florentine Codex* have been provided through the courtesy of Dr. G. B. Pineider, photographer for the Biblioteca Medicea–Laurenziana. Two variants are given of the caballero-with-staff watermarks. Watermark A (Fig. 4) is from Pal. 218, fol. 54, and C (Fig. 6) is from Pal. 220, fol. 151.[8] Three heart-cross variants are given. Watermark E (Fig. 8) is from Pal. 219, fol. 257, G (Fig. 10) is from Pal. 219, fol. 3. Watermark I (Fig. 12) from Pal. 220, fol. 404, and J (Fig. 13) from Pal. 218, fol. 321, appear to be the same watermark. In both the letters are AM; however, the outline of the cross varies slightly. (In such cases, where the watermarks exhibit a slight variation, one from another, they are considered as contemporaneous. As Hunter has observed, the wire

1. Dard Hunter, *Papermaking: The History and Technique of an Ancient Craft*, pp. 264–66.

2. Ramón Mena, *Filigranas o Marcas Transparentes en Papeles de Nueva España, del Siglo XVI*, p. 10.

3. Joaquín García Icazbalceta, *Bibliografía mexicana del siglo XVI*, p. 42.

4. Hunter, *Papermaking*, p. 479.

5. García Icazbalceta, *Bibliografía mexicana*, pp. 24, 39.

6. Mena, *Filigranas o Marcas Transparentes*; María Cristina Lamadrid Ibarra, "Determinación de la Edad de un Papel por Métodos Físicos y Químicos," Tesis que para su Examen Profesional de Químico Farmecéutico Biólogo presenta, Universidad Nacional Autonóma de Méxcio, Facultad de Ciencias Químicas, Mexico, D.F., 1952.

7. C. M. Briquet, *Les Filigranes: Dictionnaire historique des marques du papier*.

8. The fol. references to the watermarks in the Florentine refer to the numbers at the bottom of the page in the manuscript.

Fig. 4. Watermark A.

Fig. 5. Watermark B.

Fig. 6. Watermark C.

Fig. 7. Watermark D.

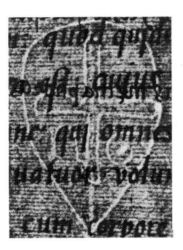

Fig. 8. Watermark E.

Fig. 9. Watermark F.

Fig. 10. Watermark G.

Fig. 11. Watermark H.

Fig. 12. Watermark I.

Fig. 13. Watermark J.

Fig. 14. Watermark K.

Fig. 15. Watermark L.

forms of the watermark often become detached from the mould, and, upon being attached again, a slight variation results.)[9]

In an effort to ascertain the date when paper bearing a specific watermark was available in Mexico, the manuscripts of the *Fondo de la Inquisición* in the Archivo General de la Nación (Mexico) were examined. Since each document bears a date, the watermark can, in effect, be dated. The intent was to encounter watermarks identical or similar to those contained in the Florentine MS. Watermark B (Fig. 5) is considered identical to A (Fig. 4) of the Florentine; it is from *Inquisición* Vol. 83 and bears the date 1577. D (Fig. 7) is considered identical with C (Fig. 6) of the Florentine; it appears in Vol. 83 of the *Inquisición* with the date 1577 and in Vol. 80 with the date 1575. The similarity between E (Fig. 8) of the Florentine and F (Fig. 9) is observable; the letters are the same, although the outline of the cross varies slightly. F (Fig. 9) is from *Inquisición* Vol. 83 and bears the date 1577. Watermark H (Fig. 11) varies in several details from G (Fig. 10)

of the Florentine. However, the similarities seem sufficient to merit its inclusion. H (Fig. 11) is from *Inquisición* Vol. 80, dated 1575. No watermark corresponding to I (Fig. 12) and J (Fig. 13) of the Florentine was encountered in the search.

As noted elsewhere in this volume, the paper of the Tolosa MS is uniform throughout. Only one watermark appears—the caballero-with-staff and the letters IA. K (Fig. 14) is the watermark from the Tolosa MS. A watermark with minor variations, L, (Fig. 15) is taken from *Inquisición* Vol. 83 and is dated 1577.

Provisional conclusions suggest that the Florentine was written on a paper bearing watermarks with a date range reaching to or a little beyond 1600 and that paper bearing watermarks the same as or similar to the Florentine paper was available in Mexico in the 1570s. The watermark evidence would suggest that the Tolosa is also a sixteenth-century MS. It lends feasibility to Baudot's suggestion that the Tolosa MS was copied from the bilingual Florentine under Sequera's direction after his return to Spain in 1580.[10]

---

9. Hunter, *Papermaking*, p. 266.

10. Georges Baudot, "Fray Rodrigo de Sequera, avocat du diable pour une histoire interdite," *Cahiers du Monde Hispanique et Luso-Brésilien*, p. 67.

# Sahagún: Career and Character

*by* Arthur J. O. Anderson

## Background Scene

Sahagún the town, from which Sahagún the Franciscan took his name, was once an important center in the ancient Kingdom of León, Spain. In 1955 when I visited it the town still retained something of the atmosphere it must have had during Fr. Bernardino's boyhood there. Many of the town's monuments showed their centuries of neglect. The monastery, once the heart of the region, was never rebuilt after fire and other calamities razed it during the Napoleonic Wars and in 1835. The Santísima Trinidad Church had survived, bleak and bare, apparently unused, to judge by boarded-up doors and windows; the less pretentious Church of San Juan was still in service. The town's most venerable monument, the Church of San Tirso, was being rebuilt after the collapse of the Romanesque bell tower some years earlier. Said to date from the ninth century, construction on San Tirso may have been begun by priests who fled from the Moors in Córdoba to a refuge in Sahagún.[1]

There were not many trees. Most of the dwelling houses showed their considerable age, although the central plaza, named for Generalísimo Franco, was neat and fresh looking. On the streets most of the loads were carried by donkeys and oxcarts, as at any time in the last five centuries, though there were some trucks. The countryside, once important agriculturally to judge by eleventh-century documents, evidently has become progressively less productive beginning perhaps even before Fr. Bernardino's time. The surrounding landscape looked forbidding and dry compared to other parts of northern Spain.

Although Sahagún had passed its peak of brilliance by the time Fr. Bernardino was born, it had enjoyed centuries of prominence. The name goes back to the persecution of Christians in Roman Spain when the brothers St. Facundus and St. Primitivus were martyred near the present townsite. In time a small church commemorated the event, and the town (Camala in Roman days) derived its name, Sanctus Facundus, from it. The transformations through which the name passed in eleven or twelve centuries —Sanctus Facundus, Sanct Facund, Sant Fagund, San Fagunt, San Fagun, Safagun, and Sahagún—appear consecutively in archival sources.

After the Roman period and the Visigothic invasions, the inundation by the Moors began in 711 and finally subsided after eight centuries when the last Mohammedan was driven from Granada in 1492 only a few years before Fr. Bernardino was born. The Moorish occupation affected every city, town, village, and settlement in Spain. It shows today in Sahagún in a few fine examples of Mudéjar art produced by Moors living under Christian rule. But in the reconquest wars, not only did Christians fight Moors, but Christians, rival kings, and noblemen fought one another, and Mohammedan rival caliphs, emirs, and other potentates contended.

In those troubled times in the eighth century Sahagún was destroyed, then rebuilt in the ninth century by refugees from Córdoba aided by King Alfonso III, and in the tenth century destroyed again.

---

1. This essay, like the others in this volume, was prepared between five and ten years ago. It has been somewhat revised more than once since then, but during this time such studies have appeared as Luis Nicolau D'Olwer and Howard F. Cline's "Sahagún and His Works" and H. B. Nicholson's "Sahagún's 'Primeros memoriales,' Tepepulco, 1559–1561," both in the *Handbook of Middle American Indians*; Georges Baudot's *Utopie et histoire au Mexique: les premiers chroniqueurs de la civilisation mexicaine (1520–1569)*; and Manuel Ballesteros Gaibrois's *Vida y obra de Fray Bernardino de Sahagún*. To these, along with Luis Nicolau D'Olwer's *Fray Bernardino de Sahagún*, published in 1952, the reader should refer for fuller data or for details not touched upon in this essay.

Moors, local noblemen, and the king's forces fought over and ravaged the town for the next century until Alfonso VI's reign brought calmer times.

According to one tradition, the monastery in Sahagún had helped Alfonso in his wars against his brother, Sancho II. Defeated and imprisoned in the monastery, Alfonso escaped, aided by don Pedro Ansúrez and probably some of the monks. On Sancho's assassination, Alfonso gained the crown of Castile and León.

Sahagún flourished quickly. By Alfonso's favor, French Cluniac Benedictines came to introduce ecclesiastical changes, notably the substitution of the Roman for the old Mozarabic rite and administrative and moral reforms. St. Hugo of Cluny was asked to center a Cluniac establishment in Sahagún that would be the model for other reformed Benedictine monasteries. As many as ninety reformed monasteries followed, all subject to the Sahagún monastery.

Abbot Robert led the first contingent of Cluniacs in Sahagún in 1079. However, he was unable to overcome local ecclesiastical and lay opposition and was replaced the next year by Abbot Bernard, who was well educated and experienced in both ecclesiastical and military affairs. Bernard inexorably instituted permanent reforms and began the order's work in Sahagún with such success that after five years he was Archbishop of Toledo on its reconquest from the Moors and became the Primate of Spain. His leadership in Sahagún was so effective that it provided him with priests educated in the reformed pattern.

The first of a number of charters in favor of the monastery date from the time of Abbots Robert and Bernard. While the charters imposed new and severe restrictions on the town, they also brought expansion and prosperity. Influxes of people, adequate housing, good fortifications, and imposing churches developed rapidly in the next few decades. Vineyards, orchards, and fields flourished outside the walls. Records of the time tell of newcomers from Germany, England, Italy, France, and elsewhere settling there, mostly as merchants, for Sahagún was a prominent stopping place along the Camino de Santiago for pilgrims on their way to Compostela. Jewish and Moorish quarters developed. In time the foreigners mingled with the original population. The visitor today may note what appears to be a diversity of physical types in the population, and the late Angel María Garibay K.'s suggestion that Fr. Bernardino de Sahagún had Jewish or Moorish ancestors may have some validity. The most authentic portrait of Bernardino de Sahagún, though probably an early seventeenth-century work, tends to support Garibay's impression.

The abbot of the monastery was dominant over all and enjoyed authority and independence through royal charters that were onerous to the general population and irritating to the nobility. Feudal obligations based on French customs of the time made the abbot overlord with the right to enforce reversion of lands to the monastery under certain conditions; to exact dues, tributes, and fines; to force all to grind grain, press grapes, and bake only in monastery facilities; to forbid sales of agricultural products before those of the monastery; to exempt town and monastery from search and arrest by the king's officers; to excuse townsmen from military service; to administer justice; and to forbid Spanish noblemen residence in Sahagún except by permission and as the abbot's vassals.

These restrictions were so foreign to Spain's customs that reactions were frequent, violent, and destructive. The king intervened; even on occasion the Pope. The monastery's holding and prestige diminished. Finally, after a series of convulsions, revised charters reestablished the king's authority. The monastery, lacking the strong abbots of earlier times, failed even to hold its own and gradually subsided until, in 1496, it was absorbed by the Congregación de San Benito in Valladolid.[2]

Fr. Bernardino was born in Sahagún probably in 1499 or 1500. The family surname may have been Ribeira,[3] but no records of the time have survived to answer even the most elementary personal and family questions.

While still a student in the University of Salamanca he took the vows and assumed the habit of

2. The foregoing account is adapted from my "Sahagún's Sahagún," *El Palacio*, Vol. LXIII, (1956), pp. 195–201, for which the main source of information was Julio Puyol y Alonso's discourse at the time of his election to the Real Academia de la Historia, *El abadengo de Sahagún*.

3. J.–C. Beltrami, *Le Mexique*, Vol. II, pp. 167ff.; Bernardini Biondelli, ed., *Evangelarium, epistolarium et lectionarium aztecum*, p. viiiff.; Alfredo Chavero, *Sahagún*, p. 7; Nicolau D'Olwer, *Fray Bernardino de Sahagún*, p. 1, n. 1; Angel María Garibay K., *Historia de la literatura náhuatl*, Vol. II, p. 64. As to the surname Ribeira (or Ribera), Beltrami evidently found it current in the probably quite inaccurate folklore about Sahagún in early nineteenth–century Mexico; he gives no authority for his statement, for which there is, in fact, some basis. Biondelli reproduced his account verbatim. Chavero, Nicolau D'Olwer, and Garibay apparently accepted Beltrami's account as a matter of course.

the Franciscan order.[4] We know little of Sahagún's early life—his student years, his becoming a mendicant friar, his mission to help spread the Gospel in the New World—until 1529[5] when, with nineteen other friars under Fr. Antonio de Ciudad Rodrigo, he came to New Spain, the forty-third to have arrived in Mexico.[6] We are told that he learned Nahuatl quickly; and it is plain that he eventually gained and undoubtedly deserved the reputation of being the best, or one of the two or three best, *nahuatlatos* or interpreters in New Spain[7] (though there is a contrary possibility referred to by Dibble and Mikkelsen[8] who point out how little Nahuatl there is known to be in Sahagún's handwriting).

## Linguistic Development

There is good reason to consider Sahagún's first phase (1529–1547) in New Spain as a linguistic stage.[9] While Garibay is correct in numbering Sahagún with the "ethnographer-missionaries,"[10] it must be remembered that Sahagun's obligations as a Franciscan, as a priest, and as a missionary were more important to him than his work of genius as a pioneer ethnographer and as a compiler of his *Historia general de las cosas de Nueva España.* Spectacular though that work is from the perspective of the twentieth-century anthropologist or historian, Sahagún did not go to Mexico to study Aztec culture but as a missionary to teach the Aztecs a religious system new to them. The degree to which he may have acquired a sympathetic and anthropological view of the ancient culture is another matter that the student can judge for himself on studying Sahagún's prologues to the *Historia* and related writings in which he expresses his official or personal views.

From Mendieta,[11] who knew Sahagún well, we learn that "In his youth"—he must mean up to 1550 or soon after—"he was *guardián* [local supervisor] of important monasteries," probably in either Spain or Mexico. So a part of Sahagún's first decades in the New World was also devoted to Franciscan routine adapted to conditions much different from what they were in Spain, where

if the religious priest remains cloistered or sometimes goes out for a charitable purpose when necessary, he fulfills his obligations, and solely those matters come under discussion concerning them. But here, considering the shortage of priests, it has always been necessary that the religious serve in the same way as the secular clergy and that His Majesty make use of them to indoctrinate the Indians. Attending to this indoctrination has to be done by walking among all these towns sometimes alone, sometimes in pairs, never staying long. It is a freer life than those of their name and calling ought to lead. Hence there is more controversy over them than over all the rest of the people.[12]

4. Gerónimo de Mendieta, *Historia eclesiástica indiana,* Vol. IV, p. 114. Mendieta is still the ultimate authority.
Documentary evidence exists of a student named Bernardino Ribeira at the University of Salamanca in 1516. I am indebted to Mr. Wayne Ruwet, of the College Library, University of California, Los Angeles, for this information; he will publish it in due course.

5. A logically reconstructed outline of these years, however, may be found in Ballesteros Gaibrois, *Vida y obra,* pp. 33ff.

6. Mendieta, *Historia eclesiástica indiana,* Vol. IV, p. 114; Chavero, *Sahagún,* pp. 8–9, citing a "Becerro general menologico chronologico de todos los religiosos . . ." in a MS of 1746 compiled by Fray Francisco Antonio de la Rosa Figueroa. The dearth of material has been attributed to the ravages of the Napoleonic wars, perhaps more savage and destructive in and about Salamanca and in the province of León than elsewhere in Spain; to the unwillingness of the various orders to open their archives to scholars; to the ideal of anonymity among the religious, particularly in the times we are considering, etc.

7. He is usually paired with Fray Alonso de Molina, whom some considered to be the better of the two.

8. Charles E. Dibble and Norma B. Mikkelsen, "La olografía de Fray Bernardino de Sahagún," *Estudios de cultura náhuatl,* Vol. IX (1971), pp. 232–36. On balance, however, they find no reason to doubt his mastery of Nahuatl. The same statement would apply to Fray Alonso de Molina and Fray Andrés de Olmos, two undoubted masters.

9. My unpublished notes on the advanced Seminar on "La obra de Sahagún," organized by the School of American Research, Santa Fe, N.M. (hereafter referred to as SAR Seminar), Douglas Schwartz, Director, Nov. 13–18, 1972; session of Nov. 16 (development of analyses put forth by Charles E. Dibble and Georges Baudot).

10. Garibay, *Historia de la literatura nahuatl,* Vol. II, Chap. 2 ("Misioneros etnógrafos").

11. Mendieta, *Historia eclesiástica indiana,* Vol. IV, p. 115. He says: "*en su juventud fué guardián de principales conventos; mas después, por espacio de cuasi cuarenta años, se excusó de este cargo. . . .*" That the statement is probably a generalization is indicated by the strong likelihood that Sahagún was *guardián* of San Francisco de México for at least part of 1562.

12. Instructions and advice left by Viceroy don Martín Enríquez (1568–1580) to his successor, the Count of Coruña: "*con estarse el religioso en su cassa o acudir alguna bez a alguna obra de caridad quando se ofreçe cumple con su obligacion y en solo este se encierra lo que ay que dar ni tomar con ellos mas aca con la falta de clerigos a sido forçosso que frailes hagan oficios de curas y que su magd. se ualga dellos para la doctrina de los yndios acudir a esta doctrina a de ser andando por todos estos pueblos vnas veces solos y otras veces de dos en dos donde nunca hacen mucho asiento que es vna vida mas libertada de de [sic] la que havian de tener los de su nonbre e profesion de aqui resulta que con solo ellos ay mas que dar y tomar que con todo el resto de la gente.*" There follows a discussion of some resulting problems from the point of view of viceregal administration and some suggested solutions.—MS in the Biblioteca Nacional, Madrid, Spain, Sig. 2816, fols. 142r–142v.

As to what, how many, where, and when his new obligations may have been, there is scattered, sometimes confusing information. Some precise dates and places are available in the prologues, interpolations, and commentaries in his *Historia.* Much of the Sahagún chronology is speculative. Probably more of it will eventually be deduced, verified, or added. Some data may be exact, like new evidence of his activities about 1535 in the monastery at Xochimilco, where he performed a marriage ceremony.[13] Some will be of indeterminate date, like the occasional references to him in the Oroz papers.[14] Data in Nicolau D'Olwer's biography, *Fray Bernardino de Sahagún,* give an idea of the difficulties involved. Sahagún's early connection with the Royal College of Santa Cruz, Tlatelolco, belongs to this same linguistic stage.[15] For aspects of this enterprise relating to Sahagún's writing of the *Historia,* the reader should refer to Dibble's "Sahagún's *Historia*" (this volume) detailing its inception and preparation, where its place regarding the Franciscan order and the Indians is clearly shown. It was preceded and quite likely inspired by the educational work in monasteries by those accounted among the "first twelve" missionaries who were led by Fr. Martín de Valencia, and probably especially by Fr. Pedro de Gante, the influential lay brother who preceded the twelve. Gante tells[16] of the early introduction of literacy and of Christian doctrine and worship to the sons of leading Indians —five hundred to a thousand at a time—as well as skills useful to them in a European society, such as tailoring, carpentering, shoemaking, ironworking, painting, and sculpturing.[17]

The Royal College of Santa Cruz was established in 1535 mainly through the efforts of Fr. Juan de Zumárraga, Mexico's first bishop, and was opened in 1536 with the encouragement and support of both the bishop and New Spain's newly arrived first viceroy, Antonio de Mendoza.[18] In the early years of the Royal College of Santa Cruz Frs. Bassac, Sahagún, and Olmos successively taught Latin. Data on the college's organization and functioning may be found in Dibble's discussion of the origin and inception of Sahagún's *Historia* and in the translation of Sahagún's interpolation in Book X, Chapter 27 (this volume). Sahagún's remarks in the latter indicate that he and his colleagues contemplated its use in training natives to enter the Church but abandoned the idea after a time because the boys lacked the qualities necessary for priesthood. The benefits of the college to both natives and Spaniards are well summarized by authorities as far apart as Sahagún, in the passages already referred to, and Gibson, in the conclusion to his work on post-Conquest Aztecs.[19] Scorn of and opposition to the curriculum and purposes of the college were more virulent in some quarters, both lay and ecclesiastical, than even Sahagún indicates, as is evident in a number of documents. A dispassionate account of the situation is found in the notes and recommendations directed by Viceroy Mendoza (1535–1550) to his successor, Luis de Velasco:

> In Tlatelolco there is a college of Indians in which they are educated in a Christian manner and instructed in the good learned professions. They have performed well in them, as would be clearly evident if our Lord had not been pleased to take to Himself most of them in the recent plague—the most able ones that there were—though at present there are still some left who are teachers in the study of Latin. Ability for much more than this is to be found in them, but envy and passions have been the reason that this has not increased as it should. Your lordship should favor [this college], for His Majesty sent you principally for the general and individual good of these people; for those who wish to make them out as incapable of any higher learning or of the rest which can be conceded to any others whomsoever, are greatly mistaken. But I do not wish, from what I say, to imply that these people, though they be as wise and virtuous as can be desired, should at present be admitted to the priesthood; for such should be deferred until this nation achieves the same degree of civic development that we have. Until this comes to pass and until Spaniards' sons who know the [native] tongue become

---

13. I am indebted to Prof. James Lockhart, Department of History, University of California, Los Angeles, for this datum, which he found in the Archivo General de la Nación, Mexico, "Tierras" MS 1525, exp. 3 (no foliation).

14. Angelico Chavez, trans. and ed., *The Oroz Codex, passim.*

15. For an overview see the "Indice cronológico," pp. 199ff.

16. Letters to Charles V, 1532, and to Philip II, 1558, Archivo Histórico Nacional, Madrid, Spain, Docs. 13 and 158. Both are published in *Cartas de Indias*; the latter appears also in *Códice Franciscano.*

17. José Gabriel Navarro, *Los franciscanos en la conquista y colonización de América,* p. 72.

18. Joaquín García Icazbalceta, *Fray Juan de Zumárraga,* Vol. I, pp. 286ff.

19. Charles Gibson, *The Aztecs Under Spanish Rule,* pp. 302, 404.

priests, there will never be perfect Christianity, nor is all of Spain enough to fulfill the needs which exist.[20]

Evidence of Sahagún's increasing skill as an interpreter of the native language belongs to this same linguistic phase. His name and signature, with those of Fr. Antonio de Ciudad Rodrigo and Fr. Alonso de Molina, appear in two documents in the *Proceso del cacique de Tetzcoco* of 1539.[21] In that same year he is known to have translated into "elegant Aztec" the sermon Bishop Zumárraga delivered in the Royal College of Santa Cruz.[22] How much more interpreting he may have done is unknown. His association with Molina in the trial of a *cacique* suggests that care was taken to secure the best-qualified interpreters. One statement in the *Códice Franciscano* refers to Molina as the best interpreter in New Spain and another in the same source puts them approximately on the same plane as of about 1569.[23] Significantly Sahagún saw, examined, and approved the 1555 edition of Molina's *Vocabulario en lengua castellana y mexicana*[24] on behalf of the ecclesiastical authorities; probably no one else except Fr. Andrés de Olmos would have been capable.

His early mastery of written Nahuatl belongs in this linguistic phase and was undoubtedly given firm

basis through collaboration with his students in the Royal College of Santa Cruz, as suggested in Dibble's accompanying study and shown in the *Sermonario* and *Santoral* of 1540 (Ayer MS No. 1485). This work, with the corrections, notations, and amplifications made in 1563, is a good example of the way Sahagún collaborated with his students[25] and of his command of the written language. It may be of some significance in the history of Sahagún's growing awareness of the difficulties of persuading the natives to abandon their pre-Conquest religious ways.

To this first stage may be added his use of one of the various compilations of *Huehuetlatolli* (discourses of the elders). It eventually appeared in Book VI of the *Historia*, whose concluding statement—that in 1577 Sahagún had translated what had been written in Nahuatl thirty years earlier, in 1547—provides a link to the work of Fr. Andrés de Olmos, whose *Arte para aprender la lengua mexicana* is dated 1547[26] and ends with some of the best known of the Huehuetlatolli.[27] But previously Olmos had engaged in the compilation of historical-ethnographical information, using methods that Sahagún may well have adopted and improved.

Whether Sahagún depended more or less upon Olmos for the groundwork for the *Historia* and the accumulation of the *Huehuetlatolli*,[28] they appear to have shared similar views about the conversion of the natives. Baudot[29] argues strongly for the occurrence of a crisis in 1545–1547 due to a growing feeling that the conversions of the first two decades after the Conquest had been ineffective. Expressions of disillusionment are strong in Sahagún's later writings[30] (for example, in his appendix to Book IV or some of the interpolations in Book XI, or in much of the discussion in his "Kalendario Mexicano, Latino y

20. Relacion y apuntamientos que dio el virey Don Antonio de Mendoça que lo fue del Reyno de nueua España a don Luis de vsco. su suçesor por mdo. de su magestad:

"14 . . . en la parte de tlatelulco ay vn colegio de indios en que se crian xptianamente y se les enseñan buenas letras y ellos am [sic] prouado arto en ellas y mostrarse bien claro si nño señor no fuera seruido en la pestilencia pasada llebarse los mas y mas auiles que hauia aunque al presente no deja de hauer algunos que quedaron que son preceptores en el estudio de latinidad, y allase auilidad para mucho mas, y enbidias y pasiones an sido parte para questo no aia creçido tanto quanto deuiera. V. S. lo fauoresca pues su magd. le enuio principalmente para el bien gl. y particr. de estas gentes, porque es grande hierro de los que los quieren haçer incapaçes para todas letras ni para lo demas que se puede conceder a otros qualesquiera hombres. Y no por lo que digo quiero sentir que estos al presente aunque sean quan sauios y virtuosos se pueda desear. Se admitan al saçerdocio porque esto se deue de reseruar para quando esta naçion llegue al estado de puliçia en q nosotros estamos y asta que esto sea. y que los hijos de Spañoles que sauen la lengua sean sacerdotes nunca abra xptianidad perfecta ni basta toda Spaña a cumplir la necesidad que ay. . . ." —MS in the Biblioteca Nacional, Madrid, Spain, Sig. 2816, fols. 128v–129r.

21. *Proceso criminal del Santo Oficio de la Inquisición*. . . . García Icazbalceta, in *Fray Juan de Zumárraga*, Vol. I, pp. 203f., mentions that the bishop was censured by his Spanish superiors for his severity.

22. Ballesteros Gaibrois, *Vida y obra*, p. 44.

23. *Códice Franciscano*, pp. 29, 60–61. The date of about 1569 is Nicolau D'Olwer's (*Fray Bernardino de Sahagún*, p. 75, n. 62).

24. Joaquín García Icazbalceta, *Bibliografía mexicana del siglo XVI*, pp. 121–23.

25. Dibble and Mikkelsen, "La olografía," pp. 232–33.

26. Andrés de Olmos, *Grammaire de la langue nahuatl ou mexicaine*.

27. Comparison suggests two bodies of *Huehuetlatolli*, those associated with commoners, with which Olmos was mainly concerned, and those associated with the nobility, which correspond to Sahagún's Book VI. See Garibay, *Historia de la literatura náhuatl*, Vol. I, pp. 407, 439. Olmos was Sahagún's almost exact contemporary: born ca. 1500; took his vows 1520; came to New Spain 1528, with Zumárraga; died 1571 (*ibid.*, Vol. II, p. 29).

28. *Ibid.*, Vol. II, pp. 29–32; Vol. I, pp. 425–27.

29. SAR Seminar, session of Nov. 16.

30. Ballesteros Gaibrois, *Vida y obra*, pp. 37ff., thinks his doubts as to the effectiveness of conversion date to his first few years in New Spain.

Castellano"[31]). They are also reflected in a writing between 1550 and 1560 (in Olmos's *Tratado de hechicerías y sortilegios*[32]) indicating that Sahagún had some support among his colleagues; though, from his insistence upon the point, one suspects that there still remained some to be convinced.

Another of Sahagún's writings of about this time was the Nahuatl text of the native version of the Conquest. Probably this was the account forming the basis for both Book XII of the *Historia*, as published in the complete Spanish-language editions and in the *Florentine Codex*, and the later rewritten Spanish version (1585) that Sahagún mentions.[33] If this native version of the Conquest dates to between 1545 and 1551, as Luis Leal suggests,[34] then it, too, is a part of Sahagún's linguistic phase. In fact, Sahagún's linguistic phase. In fact, Sahagún's "Al lector" preceding the account states his interest in the words and manners of speech appropriate to the waging of war.

### *The* Historia general

All of the foregoing, which accounts for about the first half of Sahagún's life, serves as prelude to and preparation for the second and, to us, most important half, which can be subdivided roughly into two main activities: (1) the compiling, refining, revising, and organizing of Nahuatl texts and (2) the providing of these with a Spanish counterpart culminating (as far as we definitely know) with the one we call the *Florentine Codex*. The reader is referred to Dibble's discussion of the Codex for a full and balanced treatment of this phase. It was followed by additional activities in Sahagún's last decade (1580–1590) on a reduced though still important scale.

What Sahagún accomplished in his *Historia* is neatly summarized in an evaluation of his work by León-Portilla. In producing

the first integral ethnohistorical investigation in the New World, Fray Bernardino knew full well, as all social anthropologists today know, that in order to introduce the processes of change in a human group it is an indispensable requirement to start with the most complete possible investigation of its various institutions and cultural patterns, of its antecedents and historical evolution, and also of the environment in which it has developed, with special emphasis as to its resources and possibilities. This, which today seems self-evident, was Sahagún's point of departure more than four centuries ago. With these criteria he put himself in direct contact with the human and cultural realities of the Nahuatl-speaking communities, as he searched for a firm basis which without violence would permit directing the processes of change and acculturation that, from the time of the conquest, had been inevitably affecting the native societies. Only by knowing their language, their mentality, and their way of life would it be possible to bring them the message of Christianity in their own cultural context, as was the main object of the friars' activities.[35]

Whether the general approach was molded after encyclopedic works known to the educated in Sahagún's time (Pliny's *Natural History* or Bartholomaeus Anglicus's *De Proprietatibus Rerum* have been prominently named; it could have been St. Isidore of Seville's compilations[36]), the manner in which the *Historia* developed is known, and its ultimate form is obvious, as Dibble's study shows. It is possible to discern details of the questionnaire (or *minuta*, as Sahagún called it) on which each Book of the *Historia* was developed, the degree to which the approach must have been either cut and dried or creative, the

31. Bernardino de Sahagún, "Kalendario Mexicano, Latino y Castellano," Biblioteca Nacional, Mexico, D.F., MS No. 1628 *bis*, fols. 86–142; written in 1585.

32. Georges Baudot, "Apariciones diabólicas en un texto náhuatl de Fray Andrés de Olmos," *Estudios de cultura nahuatl*, Vol. X (1972), pp. 349–57. See also his complete translation of *Tratado de hechicerías y sortilegios de fray Andrés de Olmos*.

33. Luis Leal, "El libro XII de Sahagún," *Historia Mexicana*, Vol. V, No. 2 (Oct.–Dec. 1955), *passim*; see esp. pp. 186–87.

34. *Ibid.* Dibble, however, discussing the writing of the *Historia* in this volume sets the date as 1555.

35. Miguel León-Portilla, "Significado de la obra de Fray Bernardino de Sahagún," *Estudios de Historia Novohispana*, Vol. I (1966), p. 21. "... *Tuvo clara conciencia fray Bernardino, como la tiene hoy todo antropólogo social, de que para introducir procesos de cambio en un grupo humano, es requisito indispensable partir de una investigación lo más completa posible de sus diversas instituciones y patrones culturales, de sus antecedentes y evolución histórica y también del medio ambiente en que se ha desarrollado, con especial énfasis en lo que concierne a los recursos y posibilidades del mismo. Esto que hoy parece verdad evidente, fue punto de arranque en el pensamiento de Sahagún hace más de cuatro siglos. Con este criterio se puso en contacto directo con la realidad humana y cultural de los pueblos de idioma náhuatl en busca de una base firme que permitiera encauzar sin violencia los procesos de cambio y aculturación que, a partir de la conquista, inevitablemente estaban afectando a las poblaciones indígenas. Solamente conociendo su lengua, su mentalidad y modo de ser, sería posible hacerles llegar, en su propio contexto cultural, el mensaje cristiano, objetivo principal de la acción de los frailes.*"

36. See discussion in Garibay, *Historia de la literatura náhuatl*, Vol. II, p. 68, and Alfredo López Austin, "The Research Method of Fray Bernardino de Sahagún: The Questionnaires," in *Sixteenth-Century Mexico: The Work of Sahagún*, p. 120, both of whom also mention Flavius Josephus and Aristotle as possibilities, as well as Donald Robertson's complete analysis in his *Mexican Manuscript Painting*, pp. 167–72.

way in which informants showed extraordinary trust in or liking for Sahagún, the depth or superficiality of his understanding of the native culture, or perhaps the bias, and so on.[37]

It is clear from the prologues and other guides that Sahagún left that there was bias and a main purpose in the compilation. Sahagún, and a number of colleagues, had become convinced that the evangelization was failing and the attainment of the order's design for the creation of an ideally Christian Indian society was in danger of disappearing. On the premise that the conversions of the first two or three decades after the Conquest had been superficial, that idolatry presisted unchecked because it went undetected, and that it must be recognized before it could be combated, Sahagún, supported by his superiors in the order, produced the "twelve Books of the divine, or rather, idolatrous, human, and natural things of this New Spain."[38] Knowing what to look for, missionaries would consequently know what to combat.

Since native indoctrination was to be effected in Nahuatl, as Dibble has pointed out,[39] (and in practice had to be because the natives had to be addressed, sermonized, catechized, and confessed in their own language), the work had to present not only the ancient customs but also the language in which these ancient and quite possibly dangerous customs probably would unsuspectedly lurk. So Sahagún, an increasingly expert Nahuatl linguist, presented the work as a net sweeping in "all the words of this language with their exact and metaphorical meanings, and all their ways of speaking, and most of their ancient practices, the good and the evil."[40] The texts, which were begun late in the 1550s, remained in Nahuatl until the end of the 1560s. Systematic production of a Spanish version dates to the mid-1570s and represents the last phase of compiling the *Historia*.

In addition to the main purpose there were also supporting subsidiary purposes—for example, helping the missionaries with language difficulties. And there may even have been additional stimuli Sahagún may or may not have been consciously aware of.

Robertson[41] has argued strongly that there were purely classicist motives to reconstruct ancient Mexican culture and history for its own sake in a manner typical of the Renaissance scholar. In this work Sahagún, as one of the leading Nahuatl linguists, was engaged in something unique. He had no Spanish collaborators, and he certainly knew the importance of what he was doing, as his prologues and interpolations in the *Historia* show.

In view of the varying fortunes attending the compilation and refining of the *Historia*, it may be to the point to note some other features of its beginnings, development, and completion. As mentioned, Olmos may have provided impetus as well as suggested approaches to an undertaking that was probably largely self-generated; and the Provincial may indeed have instructed Sahagún to write. In either case, approval would have been necessary to start the project and, no doubt, to incur expenses and use his and his helpers' time to put his increasing information into usable form.

An *historia moral* had been urged by the Spanish crown since at least 1572, presumably following the advice of the Council of the Indies under its president, Lic. Juan de Ovando.[42] Of the several royal *cédulas* asking for such a *historia*, one issued in 1573 in 134 *capítulos* appears to require precisely the kind of data Sahagún had been preparing. *Capítulo* 18 provides that it should describe for each province

> the discoveries and conquests . . . , the nations of the natives who inhabited and inhabit them . . . , the different languages they had; the kind of government and operation of temporal government matters; their religion and worship, the people who taught it and their method, and everything concerning their religion; rites and customs in birth, upbringing, marriage, death, burial, and life-span; principal food and drink; dress and clothing; houses and dwellings; goods held and esteemed, the kind of dominion they hold them in, those they held in common and individually, and how they inherit them; contracts made, their security, and their manner of trade; their punishable crimes and their penalties; kings and lords they have had and have, the jurisdiction and rule kings and lords exercise over their vassals, and means of governing them; tributes and services they gave

37. López Austin, "Research Method," *passim*.

38. Prologue, Book I. All citations are from sections of the *Florentine Codex* published in this volume, unless otherwise noted.

39. Charles E. Dibble, "The Nahuatlization of Christianity," in *Sixteenth-Century Mexico: The Work of Sahagún*, pp. 225–33.

40. Prologue, Book I, this volume.

41. Robertson, *Mexican Manuscript Painting*, pp. 171–72; also SAR Seminar, esp. sessions of Nov. 13 and 16.

42. Georges Baudot, "Fray Rodrigo de Sequera, avocat du diable pour une histoire interdite," *Cahiers du Monde Hispanique et Luso-Brésilien*, pp. 52ff, 61–62.

and give [kings and lords] as to kind and quantity, when and where given, how distributed, how they were and are exacted, why, and what they were and are given for; the main crafts they made use of; their wars, how they organized their drills in order to wage them; their weapons, their skill and valor, and the forms and rules they observe in their wars; their method of counting, the letters, quipus, or other means of knowing the past or the distant, and any other arts and sciences; how they divide time into days, months, and years, suns, or moons, or how they reckon; in short, all that they had in the time of their unbelief, and how much of it should be taken from them and how much of it should be conserved for them.[43]

Other paragraphs require information on natural resources (animal, vegetable, mineral) and data on the native religion and worship. Various admonitions and requirements on the accumulation and disposition of this information are set forth.

In 1570 Sahagún's manuscripts were dispersed among the Franciscan monasteries of the province

for critical examination. After dispersal of the manuscripts and the hiatus in his undertaking, Sahagún renewed his activities in 1575 with recovery of the manuscripts and with the apparently sudden support given him by Fr. Rodrigo de Sequera. Shortly before Juan de Ovando died in 1575, Sequera, who was in high favor with the crown, became commissary and in the same year reached New Spain. Sequera must have taken full advantage of the temporarily favorable circumstances—particularly since there was probably already suspicion of the mendicant orders because of their importance, their liberality toward the natives, and their disposition, despite the decisions of the Council of Trent in 1545 to reduce scriptural passages to the vernacular. He and Ovando were of the same camp. Sequera must have known of Ovando's death soon after it occurred and possibly before many in New Spain knew, but he succeeded in expediting the completion of Sahagún's copying and preparation of the *Historia.* He also probably engineered saving the copy we call the *Florentine Codex* and quite possibly others.[44]

With the impetus of the crown's interest in the history and ethnography of the New World through the series of *cédulas* and Sequera's support, which must have been enthusiastic, two complete copies of the *Historia* were made, only one of which, the Florentine, is known to have survived.[45]

However, circumstances following Ovando's death and the Council of Trent decisions, with their implementation by the Inquisition in Spain (1576–1577), brought about an immediate reversal of crown policies regarding not only the *Historia,* but in effect all writings on pre-Columbian civilizations.[46] New royal orders and *cédulas* commanded the gathering of the manuscripts and their delivery to crown authorities. A decree of April 22, 1577, ends thus:

> We order that, as soon as you receive this Our *cédula,* with great care and diligence you take measures to get these books without there remaining the originals or copies of them, and to send them well guarded at the first opportunity to Our Council of Indies, that they may there be examined. And you will be advised not to permit anyone, for any reason, in any lan-

---

43. Instruccion y discreption de las cosas de las Indias y lo que se a de hacer en ellas ansi en lo espiritual como en lo temporal, dated San Lorenzo, July 3, 1573, in Ordenanzas y cédulas de Indias, fols. 275ff., esp. paragraphs 17, 18, 37, 80–82, 127, 130. The Spanish text of the extract quoted follows:

". . . los descubrimientos y conquistas . . . las naçiones de los naturales que los auitaron y auitan . . . las diferencias de lenguas que tenian la forma de rrepuca. y los officios de las cosas tocantes a su Repuca. temporal la rreligion y adoracion que tenian y las personas que se la enseñauan y la forma que para ello tenian y todas las cosas pertenecientes a su Religion los Ritos y costumbres que tenian en sus nacimientos crianzas y casamientos y muertes y sepulturas y discurso de vidas comidas y beuidas que principalmente se mantienen Vestidos y traxes que vsan cassas y moradas que habian los bienes que tienen y estiman y en que manera de señorio tienen dellos y los poseen en comũ y los que poseen en particularmente [sic] y como subçeden en ellos los contratos que çelebran y seguridad de ellos y manera de contratacion que tienen los delitos que tienen por punibles y las penas dellos. los Reyes y señores que an tendio y tienen y la juridiçion y imperio que tienen los Reyes y señores sobre sus basallos y la forma de gobernallos los tributos y serviçios que se les dauan y da [sic] en que cosas y en que cantidad a que tiempo y en que lugares como se rrepartian como se cobraua y se cobra por que rrazon y para que se daua y da los officios mecanicos de que principalmente se aprobechauan las guerras que tienen para salir a ellas como ordenauan ejercicios las armas de que vsan la destreza y valor que tienen ellos los officios y leyes que tienen en sus guerras la horden que tienen en contar las letras pinturas o quipus o otros artes que tienen para sauer lo passado o ausente y otras qualesquiera artes y ciencias como Reparten el tiempo por dias meses y años soles, o lunas, o como quentan en sumo todo lo que tubieron en su ynfidelidad y de lo que dello se les debria quitar y lo que dello se les debria conseruar. . . ."

One notes also that (1) in 1570 Fray Miguel Navarro and Fray Gerónimo de Mendieta had taken to Spain Sahagún's "Breve sumario" (a summary of all the books and prologues of the *Historia*), and (2) the post of *cronista cosmógrafo de Indias* had been created in 1571 (Nicolau D'Olwer, *Fray Bernardino de Sahagún,* pp. 77, 90, 201). Ballesteros Gaibrois (*Vida y obra,* pp. 74–75) also draws attention to this circumstance.

44. Baudot, "Fray Rodrigo de Sequera," esp. pp. 60ff.

45. The Tolosa MS is a later copy.

46. There may have been contrary influences within the Franciscan order itself, as suggested by Ballesteros Gaibrois (*Vida y obra,* p. 76). Also see Baudot, *Utopie et histoire,* pp. 487, 492–507.

guage, to write concerning the superstitions and way of life these Indians had. Thus it is best for God our Lord's service and for Our own.[47]

Soon afterward, Sahagún, unknowing and naive, wrote to King Philip II on March 26, 1578, saying that he had sent a copy of the *Historia* to him and that he would have it copied anew if it were not delivered so that "this opportunity not be lost and the memorable affairs of this New World remain forgotten."[48] Even stricter orders, in 1578, caused Sahagún to be deprived of any manuscripts still in his possession.[49] In his 1585 version of Book XII ("The Conquest"), Sahagún notes:

> The King our Lord . . . sent for [the books], and I sent them to him through don Martín Enríquez, late viceroy of this land, but I do not know what he did with them nor who has them now. After this, Fray Sequera took them, when he served as commissary in this land, but he has never written me what became of those books which he took, in Spanish and Nahuatl, profusely illustrated. I do not know who has them now.[50]

Notwithstanding, Sequera returned to Spain in 1580 with a manuscript that is presumably the *Florentine Codex*; by confiding in no one, not even Sahagún, he may quite likely have saved that work from destruction or oblivion.[51] Considerable Sahagún material pertaining to the *Historia* remained in New Spain nonetheless, perhaps largely because of the dispersion of his manuscripts in 1570. In 1585 we find him reworking Book XII. To that same decade belong others works—the *Kalendario mexicano, la-tino y castellano* and the *Arte adivinatoria*, which presented anew materials already used in Book IV of the *Historia*. Fragments continued to appear from time to time, often without crediting Sahagún—figures of speech, for instance,[52] or scattered phrases, as, occasionally, in Carochi's *Arte* of 1645;[53] and there must have been considerably more, to judge by references to presumably lost manuscripts made by such historians as Torquemada, Vetancurt, and Clavijero.

## Sahagún's Last Years

Sahagún's last dozen years following the confiscation of his manuscripts were passed in Tlatelolco where he had remained almost exclusively since 1572.[54] Besides works already named, which represent a continuation of what motivated his efforts in compiling the *Historia*, he completed two or three purely devotional books, including the *Psalmodia christiana*, the only Sahagún work to have been printed during his lifetime. Mendieta tells us he devoted as much time as he could to the affairs of the Royal College of Santa Cruz.[55] His last five years appear not to have been tranquil. From 1585 to 1589 he was *primer definidor* (senior member of the governing committee) of the province at a time when friction between Franciscan prelates in Spain and the Province of Santo Evangelio became open conflict and involved, besides important figures in the Franciscan hierarchy, the viceroy, the vicereine, and the Inquisition. In the course of the disagreement, Sahagún was named provincial, resigned and refused to acknowledge the prelate newly arrived from Spain, and was declared excommunicated. His actions have been interpreted as either betraying weakness or characteristically showing firmness beyond what one would expect of an octogenarian.[56]

---

47. *Códice Franciscano*, pp. 249–50: ". . . *os mandamos que luego que recibais esta nuestra cédula, con mucho cuidado y diligencia procureis haber estos libros, sin que dellos quede original ni traslado alguno, los envieis á buen recaudo en la primera ocasión á nuestro Consejo de las Indias, para que en él se vean; y estareis advertido de no consentir que por ninguna manera persona alguna escriba cosas que toquen a supresticiones y manera de vivir que estos indios tenian, en ninguna lengua, porque así conviene al servicio de Dios Nuestro Señor y nuestro. . . .*"

48. MS in Archivo General de Indias (Seville, Spain), Mexico No. 284: ". . . *pa q̃ . . . no se pierda esta coiuntura, y q̃den en oluido las cosas memorables deste nueuo mũdo. . . .*"

49. Nicolau D'Olwer, *Fray Bernardino de Sahagún*, pp. 96ff., 202; Baudot, "Fray Rodrigo de Sequera."

50. Carlos María de Bustamante, ed., *La aparición de Ntra. Señora de Guadalupe de Mexico . . .*, p. 334: ". . . *envió por ellos nuestro señor el rey . . . y se los envié yo por mano del Sr. D. Martín Henríquez, visorey que fué desta tierra, y no sé que se hizo de ellos, ni en cuyo poder están agora. Llevólos despues desto el P. Fr. Rodrigo de Sequera. desque hizo su oficio de comisario en esta tierra, y nunca me ha escripto en que pararon aquellos libros que llevó en lengua mexicana y castellana, y muy historiados, ni sé en cuyo poder están agora.*"

51. Baudot, *Utopie et histoire*, pp. 483–84.

52. Cf. Arthur J. O. Anderson, "Refranes en un santoral en mexicano," *Estudios de cultura náhuatl*, Vol. VI (1966), pp. 55–61.

53. Horacio Carochi, *Arte de la lengua mexicana*.

54. Nicolau D'Olwer, *Fray Bernardino de Sahagún*, pp. 82ff., 201–202.

55. Mendieta, *Historia eclesiástica indiana*, Vol. III, p. 70; Vol. IV, p. 115.

56. García Icazbalceta, *Bibliografía mexicana*, pp. 332–33, regards him as weak. Nicolau D'Olwer's view (*Fray Bernardino de Sahagún*, pp. 128ff.) is apparently similar. Georges Baudot takes the opposite stand in "The Last Years of Fray Bernardino de Sahagún," in *Sixteenth-Century Mexico: The Work of Sahagún*, pp. 165–87. An excellent account of the controversy is given by Fray Angelico Chavez in *The Oroz Codex*, pp. 24ff.

Sahagún survived the two serious epidemics of his time in Mexico. One in 1545 struck him and may have contributed to the trembling that made his handwriting almost completely illegible.[57] The epidemic of 1576, when he was engaged in producing clean copies of the *Historia*, seems to have depressed him even more than the earlier one.[58] A lesser epidemic, which from Mendieta's terminology can be identified no more closely than as a respiratory infection, killed him in 1590 at about the age of ninety.[59]

### Sahagún's Standards

The natives both revered and loved him and sincerely mourned him, as is evident in the notices of his death quoted by Chavero and by García Icazbalceta from the *Anales de México* and in Chimalpahin's *Annales*.[60] Mendieta's opinion that he was "mild, humble, poor, and in his talk sagacious and affable to all"[61] was probably shared by his Spanish contemporaries. And, in fact, this personal evaluation seems to be accurate. Mendieta, for instance, comments on the confiscation of the *Historia* manuscripts with considerably greater asperity than Sahagún ever did:

> One of the previous viceroys took them from him by trickery to send to a certain chronicler who was asking him most insistently for writings about the Indians; they will serve his purpose as much as the ballads of Gaiferos will [i.e., not at all]. . . . A governor of this land craftily took them from him and sent them to Spain to a chronicler who asked for papers on the Indies; they are probably used there as paper to wrap spices.[62]

In matters relating to the propagation of the Faith, however, Sahagún demonstrated little mildness or resignation; instead we see firmness, insistence, and sometimes exasperation. For example, in 1576, in a passage replacing a Nahuatl description of "the varieties and kinds of roads" appearing in Chapter 12 of Book XI of the *Historia*, he writes that even New Spain, the "most populated and best settled [area] of all the Western Indies," is in "a sterile land . . . very laborious to cultivate, where the Catholic faith has very shallow roots, and with much labor little fruit is produced, and from little cause that which is planted and cultivated withers. It seems to me that the Catholic Faith can endure little time in these parts." In a later passage (Book XI, Chapter 13, paragraphs 1 and 2, on maize) he warns that "we can take it for granted that, though preached to more than fifty years, if [the Indians] were now left alone, if the Spanish nation were unable to intercede, in less than fifty years there would be no trace of the preaching which has been given them."

One sees this same sense of insecurity in writings as early as those of, say, Olmos in 1553.[63] Various places in Sahagún's *Historia*, besides those cited, have the same indications; these were set on paper in the late 1570s. By 1585 his suspicions and pessimism had deepened.[64] Not only were supposedly converted Indians accepting God, Christ, and the Saints merely to incorporate them into the ancient pantheon, which they did not abandon, but, for instance, in revering our Lady of Guadalupe, St. Anne, and St. John the Baptist, the Indians were actually continuing the worship of Tonantzin, Toci, and Tezcatlipoca.[65] The early missionaries had been gullible, easily duped by many whom they thought they were firmly converting (though "great care and caution are necessary in trying to cure this hidden cancer without harming those who really believe");[66] and the 260-day calendar, already severely castigated in 1576 in the Appendix of Book IV of the *Historia*, was now

---

57. Dibble and Mikkelsen, "La olografía," p. 235.

58. Sahagún's interpolation in Book X, following Chap. 27.

59. Mendieta, *Historia eclesiástica indiana*, Vol. IV, pp. 115–16: ". . . *la enfermedad del catarro, que el año de mil quinientos y noventa corrió generalmente.* . . ." Juan Bautista, in the prologue to his *Sermonario*, says that his death occurred in 1591 (García Icazbalceta, *Bibliografía mexicana*, p. 334).

60. Chavero, *Sahagún*, p. 97; García Icazbalceta, *Bibliografía mexicana*, p. 333, referring to "*nuestro querido y venerado padre*"; and Domingo Francisco de San Antón Muñón Chimalpahin Quauhtlehuanitzin, *Annales de Domingo Francisco de Antón Muñón* . . . , where, in the "Septième relation," p. 311, the terminology is similar—*totlaçotatzin*—and the reverential forms are used throughout.

61. Mendieta, *Historia eclesiástica indiana*, Vol. IV, p. 115: "*Era manso, humilde, pobre, y en su conversación avisado, y afable a todos.*"

62. *Ibid.*, Vol. III, p. 213: "*Sacólos de su poder por maña uno de los virreyes pasados para enviar a cierto cronista que le pedía con mucha insistencia escrituras de cosas de indias, y tanto le aprovecharán para su propósito, como las coplas de Gaiferos*"; Vol.

IV, pp. 114–15: ". . . *se los sacó con cautela un gobernador de esta tierra y los envió a España a un cronista que pedía papeles de Indias, los cuales allá servirán de papeles para especies.*"

63. Baudot, "Apariciones diabólicas," p. 357.

64. Sahagún, "Kalendario," Al lector and Prologue, *passim*.

65. See also Sahagún's "Note" in Chap. 12 of the *Historia*.

66. Sahagún, "Kalendario," Al lector: ". . . *Por tanto es menester con gran cordura y cautela procurar de sanar este cancer solapado sin hazer daño a los que de verdad creen.* . . ."

claimed to have been recently invented for the purpose of secretly stimulating and perpetuating the ancient idolatry. In short, the practice of the old rites and the inculcation of the old beliefs continued surreptitiously. The missionaries' weapons were full knowledge of and unrelenting attack against such practices, for by preventing practice of the ancient superstitions and profanation of the Sacraments, the missionaries showed their true love of the Indians.

It is evident from Mendieta's remarks, and even more so from Sahagún's own narrative, that Sahagún was solicitous of the Indians' welfare and the Indians appreciated his solicitude. Regard for the physical welfare of the Indians is notable in an interpolation in Book XI on the plagues of the sixteenth century, especially the one that occurred in 1576, or in the interpretation of the Conquest that one finds in the Prologue to Book I, among others. Likewise there are many indications of his concern over their non-material welfare. Such concerns, and what he and his colleagues did about them, are shown in Book X of the *Historia*[67] (appropriately, since the book was designed to deal with the Indians' vices and virtues). The behavior of the native population and the moral values of both young and old had been under control in pre-Spanish times. There had been no Spaniards, whose ways of life so often set a bad example; and native upbringing and social pressures had provided the necessary severity, austerity, and interdependence. Substitutions for the latter, even those devised by the first missionaries, were insufficient to overcome native inclinations and the unstimulating natural environment (which ruined native and Spaniard alike). Hence though both male and female Indians were intellectually capable, they were morally unequal to the demands of the Christian religious life, as experimentation had shown. But they might eventually become qualified. Meanwhile, though the young converts assisted greatly in the destruction of the outward signs of the ancient idolatry while the alumni of the Royal College of Santa Cruz helped greatly in other ways, the entire structure of evangelization appeared to be falling into ruin. Such was the general situation from the point of view of Sahagún and probably most of the religious priests of New Spain, at a time when their millenary hopes were coming to nothing, the laity were critical of and inimical to their ideals, the increasing numbers of secular clergy encroached upon their influence, and the decisions of the Council of Indies and the Council of Trent both encouraged their critics and blunted their weapons.

Sahagún's insistence upon high standards of observance, belief, and behavior as regards the Indians is evident in the various interpolations in the *Historia general* that replace Nahuatl passages he did not care to translate into Spanish. It is perhaps even more strongly indicated in what survives of an appendix to his "Postilla," in a Nahuatl document (the Newberry Library's Ayer MS 1486) dated 1579, especially in a section whose content very closely parallels the admonitions of a nobleman or ruler to his son in Chapter 22 of Book VI of the *Florentine Codex*. Sahagún must have had in mind the sons of native families formerly of the nobility whom the missionaries were educating. He evidently was equally severe with Spaniards who came under his tutelage. While in the monastery of San Francisco de México, in 1562, presumably as *guardián*, he recorded in the book of novices' professions the acceptance or rejection of a number of young men who had applied for admission to the order as choir members or as lay brothers.[68] "This one became a lay brother on May 20 of the same year," 1562, for instance, or "The above-named fooled us; he had many debts and said he had none. We expelled him so that he would go and pay them," and so on, telling of thirteen novices in all.[69] Of these it seems seven were retained and six were dismissed—one of them for sickness, not lapses in behavior. Presumably other Franciscans demanded as high standards as Sahagún did, but among many entries in two of these books of novices' professions in the Bancroft Library, only his recorded what eventually became of the novice.

### Evaluations of His Work

Some conclusions evident from his organization of writings making up the *Historia* may be added to

---

67. "Author's Account Worthy of Being Noted," following the Spanish text of Chap. 27.

68. "Libro de entradas y profesiones de novicios, 1562–84," Bancroft Library, University of California, Berkeley, Mex. MSS 216.

69. *Ibid.*: "Este paso a lego a 20 de mayo del mjsmo año"; "*El sobre dicho nos ēgaño q tenja muchas deudas y dijo q no echamosle para ā las fuese a pagar.*"

the glimpse of personal relationships just recounted. Two circumstances seem equally important and at the same time contradictory, though actually they are not. One is that he was the first American ethnohistorian (using both ethnographers' methods and documentation, though we do not know how much of the latter); he was the first investigator anywhere to start using ethnographers' methods as they are now conceived; and he developed these techniques centuries before their time. His position as Father of American Ethnography is unquestioned. The other circumstance is that he did all this as a priest searching for the best way to spread the faith or at least to prevent the mendicant orders' preferred way of propagating it from failing. If there arose the idea that in any form it was to be other than a priests' reference book, that happened, it would seem, only in the mid-1570s when the king expressed an interest in it. Sahagún does not tell us this explicitly, but it is evident. It would show his colleagues what the enemies of Christianity were by means of a factual account, and how to find out more for themselves by providing them with the linguistic means for probing. It would teach them the requisite Nahuatl. This he does not mention explicitly but it is implicit in various of the forms the manuscript took—tricolumned with glosses, for instance, or passages demonstrating many different ways of saying the same thing, often resembling the parallelistic rhetorical style of the Aztecs.[70] Hence it follows that the device of using eyewitness reports in the native language was adopted not solely for scientific accuracy but also for educational-evangelizing purposes. Besides this, we may admit as more than a possibility that in the interests of diffusing the Gospel Sahagún exploited the device of letting the natives, by fully describing their own former idolatrous practices, become their own most eloquent accusers as well as their own advocates.

When we attempt to assess Sahagún as a sixteenth-century scholar, we note most how he combined the enduring vision of his religious and scholastic goals

with skill in the use of the knowledge and special abilities of the natives. Thus he could draw from their cultural background to make Christianity intelligible to them and he could delve into native thought. Our Mexican colleagues remind us of this quality when they refer to *"Sahagún y sus informantes,"* though we must bear in mind that our present-day anthropological use of the term "informant" robs the phrase of its impact. So many of Sahagún's informants were essentially collaborators. He tells us in his "Author's Account Worthy of Being Noted," in Book X, how he and his colleagues would indoctrinate the boys, who then, with one of the members of the order, would move collectively to destroy some sign or monument of idolatry. Sahagún carried the process a step further: he trained the boys who then moved collectively with him to record Aztec culture in all its violence and beauty. Such is his *Historia.*

As to subject matter, certain inconsistencies and gaps in the *Historia*, some of them rather surprising, may have been deliberate. Some were not, of course. It is evident that the assistants, the young men educated in the Royal College of Santa Cruz, were partly Hispanized. They had a command of Spanish language and ways, and illustrations in the *Florentine Codex* show much Europeanization.[71] They came from Indian families of the former native nobility, who also became Sahagún's older adult informants; there is no evaluation by the commoner of himself or of his betters. Some informants were expert, some were not. Though all appear to have been willing to talk, some may have been reticent, and some may not have been asked the right questions. Though the facts were gathered in three native centers—Tepepulco, Tlatelolco, and Tenochtitlan—and thoroughly collated and worked over by Sahagún and his informant-collaborators, they may, in emphasizing the Tlatelolco–Tenochtitlan view, have given an unbalanced impression of Nahuatl society. Sahagún may have been uninformed or may have chosen to be selective in some points of data covering religious beliefs; data on the pantheon, cosmology, cosmogony, and mythology suggest little understanding of the general scheme, or possibly fear of leaving a

---

70. Cf. Prologue to Book VII: ". . . there are many synonymous terms for [any] one thing, and a mode of expression or a sentence [is] said in many ways. This was done on purpose, to know and record all the vocabulary of each thing, and all the modes of expressing each sentence. And this is not only in this Book but in the whole work. . . ."

71. Robertson, *Mexican Manuscript Painting*, pp. 48–49, 173ff.

reconstruction of former native religion that could successfully be used to resist Christianization.[72]

None of the suggestions put forth above detract from Sahagún's invaluable pioneer ethnographical production. They merely emphasize its unusualness in view of the motives for and the expected results of the undertaking: more complete and permanent evangelization and support of the Franciscan millenary ideal. Hence, any suspected contradiction is apparent, not real.

Something of Sahagún's view of his own writings is indicated in part of his Prologue to Book X. Among preachers' goals,

> . . . the most constant should be urging upon [people] the theological virtues and dissuading them from the vices at variance with them. And of this there is much material in the first six Books of the *Historia* and in the *Apostilla* dealing with the Epistles and the Gospels for all the Sundays of the year, which I prepared, and, more definitively, in the *Doctrina Cristiana* which the first twelve Fathers preached to these native people, which, as an eyewitness, I compiled in this Mexican language.[73]

## Summary

Sahagún produced an unbelievably thorough ethnographic work, precocious in applying today's anthropological methods over four hundred years ago, when humanistic studies, even in great universities like Salamanca, were still confined to philosophy, grammar (Latin), history, and rhetoric, and European scholars on the whole showed little interest in New World phenomena.[74] He obeyed motives and expected results that were always and perhaps exclusively religious; it is exceedingly doubtful that he ever intended his work for general information. That circumstance, the lack of native experts in certain lines of information, perhaps some fundamental ignorance on Sahagún's part, as well as, perhaps, an unwillingness to go into certain aspects of the ancient civilization, or any combination of the foregoing possibilities, make some parts of the *Historia* uneven in the quality of their information. These features also suggest a contradiction, that of the medieval man of God versus the Renaissance man of learning or even of incipient science.

The contradiction is more apparent than real. While Sahagún clearly reflected the views and methods of his time and of his order, he nevertheless stands absolutely unique as a missionary and absolutely unique as an ethnographer. Even when compared with his ablest contemporaries he excelled any of them in his ability to organize, train, use, and direct effectively a team of emerging native scholars. We cannot say to what degree his doing so reflected his genius or was dictated by his inability to write legibly. Nevertheless, for over fifty years he worked with his assistants toward a comman goal. His skill in coordinating their efforts and combining their strengths, whether in grammar, in art, in penmanship, or in other skills, is attested to by the results of their mutual endeavor.

Sahagún freely and frequently acknowledged the contributions and strengths of student collaborators and of experienced adult informants. This he did to a much greater degree than any of his contemporaries. He not only anticipated the use of informants in ethnographic fieldwork by four centuries but used them so effectively that his achievement was not approached, much less equaled, until the time of Franz Boas. Sahagún developed these techniques perhaps partly as a result of his wish to know and reconstruct the ancient culture, but his overwhelming purpose was to aid in the propagation of the Christian faith. If he feared that in the end the results of his labors and the hope of Christianizing the New World had been lost, he has been proved wrong on both counts.

---

72. SAR Seminar, Nov. 17, 1973, discussion by López Austin, León-Portilla, Baudot, Dibble, and others: Whereas data are superior in Books II, V, VI, IX, XI, and Book XII is unique, especially for its time, there is some question as to Books VIII and X; the materials found in Books I, II, IV, and VII are the weakest. From another point of view, much description is superb: cf. rites, ceremonies, folk superstitions, etc.; medical information is conscientiously given; the possibilities inherent in the language are obviously well shown; the characteristics and activities of the upper classes are adequately reported, together with the ideals which motivated them; the ecological setting is well presented; so are methods of war. Gaps appear in data as to the organization of family, society, and the state, and are even more marked in astronomy and in the pantheon, cosmology, cosmogony, and mythology. What Sahagún calls astrology—soothsaying based on the 260-day calendar—bears little resemblance to what the "official" *tonalamatl* tells us (for example, the *Borbonicus*). See also Nicolau D'Olwer and Cline, "Sahagún and His Works," and Nicholson, "Sahagún's 'Primeros memoriales,'" esp. pp. 189 and 217–18.

73. I have omitted parentheses.
Referring to his closing reference to the *Colloquios y doctrina christiana*, since it is dated 1524, he could not have been an eyewitness.

---

74. See Ballesteros Gaibrois's interesting discussion in his *Vida y obra*, pp. 95ff.

# SAHAGUN'S PROLOGUES AND INTERPOLATIONS

translated from the Spanish by Charles E. Dibble

# Book I: The Gods

## PROLOGUE[1]

The physician cannot advisedly administer medicines to the patient without first knowing of which humour or from which source the ailment derives. Wherefore it is desirable that the good physician be expert in the knowledge of medicines and ailments to adequately administer the cure for each ailment. The preachers and confessors are physicians of the souls for the curing of spiritual ailments. It is good that they have practical knowledge[2] of the medicines and the spiritual ailments. For him who preaches against the evils of the State, in order to marshal his teachings against them, and for the confessor, in order to know how to ask what is proper and understand what they may say pertaining to his work, it is very advisable to know what is necessary to practice their works. Nor is it fitting that the ministers become neglectful of this conversion by saying there are no sins among this people other than orgies, thievery, and lustfulness, because there are many other, much graver sins among them which are in great need of remedy. The sins of idolatry, idolatrous rituals, idolatrous superstitions, auguries, abuses, and idolatrous ceremonies are not yet completely lost.

To preach against these matters, and even to know if they exist, it is needful to know how they practiced them in the times of their idolatry, for, through [our] lack of knowledge of this, they perform many idolatrous things in our presence without our understanding it. And, making excuses for them, some say they are foolishness or childishness, not knowing the source from whence they spring (which is pure idolatry). And the confessors neither ask about them, nor

## PROLOGO

El medico no puede Acatadamente aplicar Las medicinas al enfermo sin que primero conozca: de que humor, o de que causa proçede la enfermedad. De manera que el buen medico conuiene sea docto en el conocimiento de las medeçinas y en el de las enfermedades para aplicar conueniblemente a cada enfermedad la mediçina contraria. Los predicadores, y confesores, medicos son de las animas para curar las enfermedades espirituales: conuiene tengã esperitia de las mediçinas y de las enfermedades espirituales. El Predicador de los Viçios de la Republica para endereçar contra ellos su doctrina, y el confessor para sauer preguntar lo que conuiene y entender lo que dixeren tocante a su officio: conuje mucho que sepan lo neçessario para exerçitar sus officios. Ni conuiene se descuyden los ministros desta conuersion con dezir que entre esta gente no ay mas peccados, de borrachera, hurto y carnalidad. Porque otros muchos peccados ay entre ellos muy mas graues y que tienen gran necessidad de Remedio. Los peccados de la ydolatria, y ritos ydolatricos, y suprestiçiones ydolatricas y agueros, y abusiones, y cerimonias ydolatricas: no son aun perdidas del todo.

Para predicar contra estas cosas y aun para sauer si las ay: menester es, de saber como las vsauã en tiempo de su ydolatria: que por falta, de no saber esto en nr̃a presencia hazen muchas cosas ydolatricas: sin que lo entendamos. Y dizen algunos escusandolos: que son bouerias o niñerias por ygnorar la Raiz de donde salen: (que es mera ydolatria.) Y los confesores ni se las preguntan ni piensan que ay tal cossa: ni sauen lenguaje para se lo preguntar ni aun

---

1. In the *Florentine Codex* manuscript the text of the prologues is continuous. In translation the longer prologues have been divided into paragraphs.

2. In the Spanish read *experiencia* for *esperitia*.

think that such a thing exists, nor understand the language to inquire about it, nor would even understand them, even though they told them of it. In order that the ministers of the Gospel, who will follow those who have come first in the cultivation of this new vineyard of the Lord, may not have reason to complain of the first ones for having left the facts about these natives of this New Spain undivulged, I, Fray Bernardino de Sahagún, a professed monk of the Order of Our Seraphical Father San Francisco de la Observancia, a native of the town of Sahagún en Campos, by order of the very Reverend Father, Father Fray Francisco Toral, Provincial of this Province of the Holy Gospel, and later Bishop of Campeche and Yucatán, wrote twelve Books of the divine, or rather idolatrous, human, and natural things of this New Spain — the first of which treats of the gods and goddesses these natives worshipped; the second, of the feasts with which they honored them; the third of the immortality of the soul and of the places they said the souls went after they left the bodies, and the suffrages and obsequies they provided for the dead, etc. The fourth Book deals with the astrological divination which these natives employed to know the good and bad fortune of those who were born. The fifth Book deals with the auguries which these natives possessed to foretell future matters. Book six deals with the rhetoric and moral philosophy which these natives practiced. The seventh Book deals with the natural philosophy which these natives achieved. The eighth Book treats of the lords, their customs and ways of governing the State. Book nine deals with the merchants and other artisan occupations and their practices. Book ten deals with the evils and virtues of this people, typical of their way of life. Book eleven treats of the animals, birds, fish and the species[3] which exist in this land, and of the trees, herbs, flowers, fruits, metals, stones and other minerals. Book twelve is entitled "The Conquest of Mexico."

A clean copy of these twelve Books, with the grammar and vocabulary as an appendix, has just been made in this year of fifteen hundred and sixty-nine. It has not yet been possible to put them in Spanish nor provide them with the scholia, according to the outline of the work. I do not know what could have been done in the year seventy which follows

lo entenderan aunque se lo digan: pues porque los ministros del euangelio que subçederan a los que primero binieron en la, cultura desta nueua viña del señor no tengan ocassion de quexarse de los primeros por haber dexado a escuras las cosas destos naturales desta, nueua españa, yo fray bernardino de saagun frayle professo de la ordē de nño seraphico padre san francisco de la obseruancia. natural de la, villa de sahagun en canpos por mandado del muy R.ᵈᵒ P.ᵉ el P.ᵉ frai fran.ᶜᵒ toral prouinçial desta prouinçia del santo evangelio y despues obispo de campech. y yucatā: escriui doze libros de las cosas diuinas o por mejor dezir ydolatricas y humanas y naturales desta nueua españa. El primero de las quales trata de los dioses y diosas que estos naturales adorauan. El segundo de las fiestas con que los honrrauan. El terçero de la immortalidad del anima y de los lugares a donde dezian que yban las almas desque salian de los cuerpos y de las sufragias y obsequias que hazian por los muertos, etc. El quarto libro tracta de la astrologia judiçiaria que estos naturales vsauan para sauer la fortuna Buena o mala que tenian los que nacian. El quinto libro trata de los agueros que estos naturales tenian para adiuinar las cosas por venir. El libro sesto trata de la Rectorica, y philosophia moral que estos naturales vsauan. El septimo libro trata de la philophia [*sic*] natural que estos naturales alcançauan. El octauo libro trata de los señores y de sus costumbres y maneras de gouernar la Republica. El libro nono trata, de los mercaderes y otros officiales mechanicos y de sus costumbres. El libro dezimo trata de los Vicios y virtudes destas gentes al proprio de su manera de viuir. El libro vndezimo trata de los animales y aues y peçes y de las generaciones que ay en esta tierra y de los arboles yeruas y flores y frutas metales y piedras y otros minerales. El libro duodecimo se intitula la conquista de mexico.

Estos doze libros con el arte y vocabulario appendiz, se acabaron de sacar en blanco este año de mill e quinientos y sesenta y nueue aun no se an podido Romançar ni ponerlas escolias segun la traça de la obra no se lo que se podia hazer en el año de setenta que se sigue. Pues desde el dicho año hasta casi el fin deste año de 1575 no se pudo mas entender en

---

3. The phrase, "*y de las generaciones que ay en esta tierra,*" appears to belong with the description of Book X. Compare with the description of the Books in the Prologue of Book IX: "*y diuersidades, de generaciones de gẽtes, que en esta tierra avitan.*"

because, from said year until nearly the end of 1575,[4] it has been impossible to deal with this work because of the great disfavor that existed on the part of those who should have favored it. However, when our most reverend Father Fray Rodrigo de Sequera, Commissary General of all these Provinces of this New Spain, Guatemala, etc., of the Order of Our Seraphic Father San Francisco de la Observancia, arrived in this land, he ordered that all these Books be put in Spanish, and that they be written in a clear hand in Spanish as well as Mexican.

This work is like a dragnet to bring to light all the words of this language with their exact and metaphorical meanings, and all their ways of speaking, and most of their ancient practices, the good and evil. It will be a source of great satisfaction, because, with much less effort than it costs me here, those who may so desire will be able to know many of the ancient practices and all the language of this Mexican people in a brief time. All this work will be very useful to learn the degree of perfection of this Mexican people, which has not yet been known, because there came over them that curse which Jeremiah, in the name of God, thundered upon Judea and Jerusalem in the fifth chapter, saying: "I will cause to come upon you, I will bring against you a people from afar, a very vigorous and brave people, a very ancient people skillful in battle, a people whose language ye will not understand, nor hast thou ever heard their manner of speech, all powerful and courageous people, lusting to kill. This people will destroy you and your women and children and everything ye possess, and will destroy all your villages and buildings." This has literally happened to these Indians by way of the Spaniards. They and all their possessions were so trampled underfoot and destroyed that no vestige remained of what they were before. Thus they are considered as barbarians, as a people at the lowest level of perfection, when in reality (excluding some injustices their mode of governance contained) in matters of good conduct they surpass many other nations which have great confidence in their administrations. In this little which has been gleaned with great effort, there seems to be much profit. What might it be if everything could have been done?

Regarding the antiquity of this people, it is con-

esta obra por el gran disfauor que hubo de parte de los que la debieron de fauoreçer. pero como llego a esta tierra nr̃o R.ᵐᵒ P.ᵉ fray R.º de Sequera, comissario general de todas estas prouinçias desta nueua espa. guatimala etc. de la orden de nr̃o Seraphico P.ᵉ san fran.ᶜᵒ de la obseruancia: mando que estos libros todos se Romançasen: y ansi en Romançe como en lengua mexicana se escribiesen de buena letra.

Es esta obra como vna red barredera para sacar a luz todos los vocablos desta lengua con sus propias y methaphoricas significaçiones y todas sus maneras de hablar y las mas de sus antiguallas buenas y malas es para Redemir mill canas porque con harto menos trauajo de lo que aqui me questa podran los que quisieren saber en poco tiempo muchas de sus antiguallas y todo el lenguaje desta gente mexicana. aprouechara mucho toda esta obra para conoçer el quillate desta gente mexicana el qual aun no se a conoçido: porque vino sobre ellos aquella maldicion: que Jeremias de parte de dios fulmino contra Judea y Jerusalen diziendo en el capitulo qujnto. Io hare que venga, sobre vosotros: yo traere contra vosotros, vna gente muy de lexos: gente muy robusta, y esforçada: gente muy antigua, y diestra en el pelear, gente cuyo lenguaje no entenderas, nj jamas oyste, su manera de hablar: toda gente fuerte, y anjmosa, condiciosissima de matar. Esta gente os destruyra a vosotros, y a vr̃as mugeres, y hijos: y todo quanto posseys: y destruyra todos vr̃os pueblos, y edificios. Esto a la letra a acontecido, a estos indios, con los españoles: fueron tan atropellados, y destruydos, ellos y todas sus cosas: que njnguna apparentia les quedo, de lo que eran antes. Ansi estan tenjdos por barbaros, y por gente de baxissimo qujlate: como segun verdad, en las cosas de politia, echan el pie delante, a muchas otras naciones: que tienen gran presuntion, de politicos: sacando fuera algunas tyranjas, que su manera de regir contenja. En esto poco, que con gran trabajo se a rebuscado: parece mucho la ventaja: que hiziera, si todo se pudiera auer.

En lo que toca, a la antiguedad desta gente: tie-

---

4. The date may be 1579, although there are no additional ciphers in the Prologue for comparison. The Tolosa MS scribe read 1575.

sidered certain that they have dwelt in this land now called New Spain for more than two thousand years. For according to their ancient paintings there is information that that famous city called Tula was destroyed a thousand years or so ago. And before it was built many of those who built it were settled in Tollantzinco where they left many very remarkable buildings. As to how long they were there, how long it took to build the city of Tula and how long their prosperity lasted before it was destroyed, it is likely that more than a thousand years went by; from which it follows that at least five hundred years before the incarnation of our Redeemer, this land was populated. This renowned and great city of Tula, very wealthy and with very wise and brave people, had the misfortune of Troy. The Cholulans, who are those who escaped from [Tula], have had the legacy of the Romans, and like the Romans they built their capitol as their fortress. Thus the Cholulans built that mound, which is near Cholula, by hand. It is like a mountain or a large hill and is full of mines or caves within. Many years later the Mexicans built the city of Mexico, which is another Venice. In knowledge and conduct they are as the Venetians. The Tlaxcallans seem to have followed the fate of the Carthaginians. There are large vestiges of the antiquities of this people as they nowadays appear in Tula, Tollantzinco, and a structure called Xochicalco, which is near Quauhnauac. In almost this whole land there are vestiges and traces of buildings and very ancient jewels.

It is certainly a matter of great wonderment that, for so many centuries, our Lord God has concealed a forest of so many idolatrous peoples whose luxuriant fruits only the demon harvested and holds hoarded in the infernal fire. Nor can I believe that the church of God would not be successful where the synagogue of Satan has had so much success, in accordance with that [phrase] of St. Paul's: "Grace will abound where transgression abounded." It is said the knowledge or wisdom of this people was considerable, as appears in Book X, in Chapter 29, where it speaks of the first settlers of this land; where it asserts they were perfect philosophers and astrologers and very skilled in all the crafts. Regarding fortitude, which among them was more esteemed than any other virtue, wherefore they raised it to the

nese por aueriguado, que a mas de dos mjll años, que abitan en esta tierra: que agora se llama, la nueua españa. Porque por sus pinturas antiguas, ay noticia: que aquella famosa ciudad, que se llamo tulla: a ya mjll años, o muy cerca dellos, que fue destruyda: y antes que se edificasse, los que la edificaron, estuujeron muchos poblados, en tullantzinco: donde dexaron muchos edificios, muy notables: pues en lo que alli estuujeron, y en lo que tardaron en edificar, la ciudad de tulla: y en lo que duro, en su prosperidad: antes que fuesse destruyda, es consono a verdad, que passaron, mas de mill años: de lo qual resulta, que por lo menos, qujnjentos años, antes de la encarnacion, de ñro Redemptor: esta tierra, era poblada. Esta celebre, y grã ciudad, de Tulla: muy rica, y de gente muy sabia, y muy esforçada, tuuo la aduersa fortuna, de troya. Los chololtecas, que son los que della se escaparon: an tenjdo la succession de los Romanos: y como los Romanos edificaron el capitolio, para su fortaleza: ansi los chololanos, edificaron a mano: aquel promontorio, que esta junto a cholula, que es como vna sierra, o vn gran monte, y esta todo lleno, de mjnas, o cueuas por de dentro. Muchos años despues, los Mexicanos edificaron, la Ciudad de mexico: que es otra venecia, y ellos en saber, y en pollicia, son otros venecianos. Los tlaxcaltecas, parecen aver succedido, en la fortuna de los cartaginenses. Ay grandes señales, de las antiguallas destas gentes, como oy dia parece en tulla, y en tullantzico: y en vn edificio, llamado xuchicalco: que esta en los termjnos, de quauhnaoac. I casi en toda esta tierra, ay señales, y rastro, de edificios, y alhajas antiquissimos.

Es cierto cosa, de grande admjration: que aya ñro señor dios, tantos siglos occultada, vna silua de tantas gentes ydolatras: cuyos frutos vberrimos, solo el demonjo los a cogido: y en el fuego infernal, los tiene atesorados. Ni puedo creer, que la yglesia de dios, no sea prospera: dõde la synagoga de sathanas, tanta prosperidad a tenjdo: conforme a aquello, de sanct Pablo. Abundara la gratia adonde abundo el delicto. Del saber, o sabiduria desta gente ay fama: que fue mucha como parece en el libro decimo: donde en el capitulo. 29: se habla, de los primeros pobladores, desta tierra: donde se affirma, que fueron, perfectos philosophos, y astrologos, y muy diestros, en todas las artes mechanjcas. De la fortaleza, la qual entre ellos, era mas estimada, que ninguna otra virtud: y por la qual subian, hasta el sumo

highest level of worth: they conducted impressive training in this as appears in many parts of this work. As to the religion and the adoration of their gods, I do not believe there have been in the world idolaters to such a degree venerators of their gods, nor at such great cost to themselves as these of this New Spain. Not even the Jews nor any other nation had such a heavy yoke, nor as many ceremonies as these natives have had for many years, as appears throughout this work.

The account of the origin of this people, which the old people give, is that they came over the waters from the north. And it is certain that they came in some vessels. It is not known in what manner they were constructed, but it is conjectured, it is said among all these natives, that they came forth from seven caves, that these seven caves are the seven ships or galleys in which the first settlers of this land came. As is inferred from likely conjectures, the first people who came to settle this land came from the direction of Florida, came sailing along the coast, and disembarked in the port of Panuco, which they call Panco and which means, "the place where those who crossed the waters arrived." This people came in search of the terrestrial paradise, and they brought as watchword "Tamoanchan," which means, "We seek our home." And they settled near the highest mountains they found. In coming southward in search of the terrestrial paradise they did not err, for it is the opinion of the writers that it is below the equinoctial line. Nor did they err in thinking it is some very high mountain, for the writers say so: that the terrestrial paradise is below the equinoctial line and that it is a very high mountain, that its summit reaches near to the moon. It seems that they or their ancestors possessed some oracle regarding this subject, either from God, or the demon, or from the tradition of the elders, which was handed down to them. They sought that which cannot be found by mortal means. And our Lord God intended the depopulated land be settled so that some of their descendants might go to settle the celestial paradise, as we now witness through experience. But why do I pause to relate riddles? It is most certain all these people are our brothers, stemming from the stock of Adam, as do we. They are our neighbors whom we are obliged to love, even as we love ourselves.

Whatever it may be that they were in times past, we now see through experience, that they are capable

grado, del valer: tenjan desto grandes exercitios: como parece en muchas partes, desta obra. En lo que toca, a la religion y cultura, de sus dioses: no creo a aujdo en el mundo, ydolatras tan reuerenciadores, de sus dioses: nj tan a su costa: como estos, desta nueua españa, Ni los Judios, nj njnguna otra nation, tuuo iugo, tan pesado: y de tantas cerimonjas, como le an tenjdo, estos naturales: por espacio de muchos años, como parece, por toda esta obra.

Del origen desta gente, la relacion que dan los viejos: es, que por la mar vinjeron, de hazia el norte. Y cierto es, que vinjeron, en algunos vasos: de manera no se sabe, como eran labrados: sino que se conjectura, que vna fama que ay, entre todos estos naturales: que salieron de siete cueuas: que estas siete cueuas, son los siete naujos, o galeras, en que vinjeron, los primeros pobladores, desta tierra. Segun se colige, por coniecturas, verisimjles: la gente que primero vino, a poblar a esta tierra: de hazia la florida vino, y costeando vino: y desembarco en el puerto de panuco, que ellos llaman panco, que quiere dezir, lugar donde llegaron, los que passaron el agua. Este gente, venja en demanda del parajso terrenal: y trayan por apellido, tamoanchan: que qujere dezir, buscamos nr̄a casa: y poblauan cerca de los mas altos montes que hallauan. En venjr, hazia el medio dia a buscar el parayso terrenal, no herrauan: porque opinjon es: de los que escriuen, que esta debaxo de la linea equjnoctial: y en pēsar, que es algun altissimo monte: tampoco hierran: porque asi lo dizen los escritores, quel parayso terrenal, esta debaxo de la linea equjnoctial, I que es vn monte altissimo, que llega su cumbre, cerca de la luna: parece que ellos, o sus antepassados, tuujeron algun oraculo: cerca de esta materia: o de dios, o del demonjo, o tradicion de los antiguos, que vino de mano en mano hasta ellos. Ellos buscauan, lo que por via humana, no se puede hallar: y nr̄o señor dios pretendia, que la tierra despoblada se poblasse: para que algunos, de sus descendientes, fuessen a poblar, el parayso celestial: como agora lo vemos por esperiencia. Mas para que me detengo, en contar adeujnanças? Pues es certissimo, que estas gentes todas, son nr̄os hermanos: procedientes, del tronco de Adam, como nosotros: son nr̄os proximos, a quien somos obligados a amar, como a nosotros mjsmos.

Qujdqujd sit, de lo que fueron los tiempos passados, vemos por esperiencia agora, que son abiles:

in all the crafts and they practice them. They are also capable in learning all the liberal arts and sacred theology, as has been seen through experience of those who have been taught in these sciences. As to how they are in the matters of warfare, there is experience of them in the Conquest of this land as well as other specific conquests which have subsequently been achieved here. How strong they are in enduring the hardships of hunger, thirst, cold and sleeplessness! How willing and ready they are to undertake all kinds of dangerous missions! They are no less capable of our Christianity; besides, they have been duly indoctrinated therein. It certainly seems, in our times, in these lands and with this people, that our Lord God has willed to restore to the Church that which the demon robbed her of in England, Germany, France, Asia, and Palestine. Wherefore we are much constrained to give thanks to our Lord and to labor faithfully in this, His New Spain.

## TO THE SINCERE READER

When this work began, it began to be said by those who knew of it, that a dictionary was being made. And, even now, many keep on asking me: "How does the dictionary progress?" Certainly it would be very beneficial to produce so useful a work for those who desire to learn this Mexican language, just as Ambrosio Calepino prepared one for those who desire to learn the Latin language and the meaning of its words. But, assuredly, there has not been an opportunity, because Calepino drew the words, their meanings, their equivocals and metaphors from reading the poets, orators, and other authors of the Latin language, verifying everything said with the expressions of the authors; which source I have lacked, there being neither letters nor writing among this people. And, so, it was impossible for me to prepare a dictionary. But I have laid the groundwork in order that whosoever may desire can prepare it with ease, for, through my efforts twelve Books have been written in an idiom characteristic and typical of this Mexican language, where, in addition to its being a very pleasing and profitable writing, also are found therein all the manners of speech and all the words this language uses, as well verified and certain as that which Virgil, Cicero, and other authors wrote in the Latin language.

para todas las artes mechanjcas, y las exercitan: son tanbien abiles, para deprender, todas las artes liberales, y la sancta theologia: como por esperiencia, se a visto: en aquellos, que an sido enseñados, en estas scientias. Porque de lo que son, en las cosas de guerra, esperientia se tiene dellos: ansi en la conqujsta desta tierra, como en otras particulares conquistas, que despues aca se an hecho: quan fuertes son, en sufrir trabajos, de hambre, y sed, frio, y sueño: quan ligeros y dispuestos, para acometer, qualesqujera trances peligrosos. Pues no son menos abiles, para nr̄o christianjsmo: sino en el deujdamente, fueren cultiuados. Cierto parece, en estos nr̄os tiempos, y en estas tierras, y cõ esta gente: a querido nr̄o señor dios: restituyr a la yglesia, lo que el demonjo la a robado, en inglaterra, alemanja, y francia: en asia, y palestina. De lo qual quedamos muy obligados: de dar gracias, a nr̄o señor, y trabajar fielmente, en esta su nueua españa.

## AL SINCERO LECTOR

Quando esta obra se començo, començose a dezir, de los que lo supieron: que se hazia vn calepino: y aun hasta agora, no cesan muchos, de me preguntar, que en que termjnos anda el calepino? Ciertamente, fuera harto prouechoso, hazer vna obra tan vtil: para los que qujeren deprender esta lengua mexicana: como Ambrosio Calepino la hizo: para los que qujerẽ deprender, la lengua latina: y la signjficacion de sus vocablos. Pero ciertamente, no a aujdo oportunjdad: porque Calepino saco los vocablos, y las significationes dellos, y sus equjuocationes, y methophoras, de la lection, de los poetas, y oradores, y de los otros authores, de la lengua latina: autorisando todo lo que dize, con los dichos de los authores: el qual fundamento, me a faltado a mj: por no auer letras, nj escriptura entre esta gente: y ansi me fue impossible hazer calepino. Pero eche los fundamẽtos, para qujen qujsiere, con facilidad le pueda hazer: porque por mj industria, se an escripto doze libros: de lenguaje propio y natural, desta lengua mexicana: donde allende de ser muy gustosa, y prouechosa escriptura: hallarse han tambien en ella, todas las maneras de hablar, y todos los vocablos, que esta lengua vsa: tambien authorizados, y ciertos: como lo que escriujo Vergilio, y Ciceron, y los demas authores, de la lengua latina.

These twelve Books are arranged in such a way that each page contains three columns, the first in the Spanish language, the second in the Mexican language; the third is the explanation of the Mexican words — with their numbers in both columns.[5] A clear copy of that in the Mexican language has just been finished — all twelve Books.[6] That in the Spanish language and the glosses are not finished. It has not been possible to do more because of lack of aid and help. If the necessary aid were given me, in a year or a little more, all could be finished. And, certainly, if it were finished, it would be a treasury for the knowledge of many things worthy of being known, and for the easy knowledge of this language with all its secrets. And it would be a thing of much value in New Spain and Old Spain.

Van estos doze libros, de tal manera traçados, que cada plana, lleua tres colunas: la primera, de lengua española: la segunda, de la lengua mexicana: la tercera, la declaracion, de los vocablos mexicanos: señalados con sus cifras, en ambas partes: lo de la lengua mexicana se a acabado, de sacar en blanco, todos doze libros: lo de la lengua española, y las escolias, no esta hecho: por no auer podido mas, por falta de ayuda, y de fauor. Si se me diese la ayuda necessaria, en vn año, o poco mas, se acabaria todo: y cierto si se acabase, seria vn tesoro, para saber muchas cosas: dignas de ser sabidas. Y para con facilidad, saber esta lengua, con todos sus secretos, y seria cosa de mucha estima, en la nueua, y vieja españa.

---

5. Sahagún is here referring to the three-column organization which appears in *Memoriales con Escolios*. Therein he noted: "The whole work is to go in the manner of this notebook" (*de la manera que esta este quaderno a de ir toda la obra*).

6. This would be the finished copy of 1569 referred to in the Prologue.

# Book II: The Ceremonies

## PROLOGUE[1]

As best they can, all writers endeavor to authenticate their writings, some with credible witnesses, others by other writers who have written before them, whose testimonies are taken as true; others by witness of the Holy Bible. I have lacked all these proofs to authenticate that which I have written in these twelve Books. And I find no other proof to authenticate it except to place here the account of efforts I made to know the truth of all that I have written in these Books.

As I have said in other Prologues in this work, I was ordered, by the holy command of my highest prelate, to write in the Mexican language that which seemed to me useful for the indoctrination, the propagation and perpetuation of the Christianization of these natives of this New Spain, and as a help to the workers and ministers who indoctrinate them. Having received this command I made an outline or summary in Spanish of all the topics to be considered. This is that which is written in the twelve Books and the *Apostilla* and Canticles that were drafted in the village of Tepepulco, which is in the province of Acolhuacan or Texcoco. It was done in this way.

In the aforementioned village I assembled all the leaders with the lord of the village, named Don Diego de Mendoza, an old man of great distinction and talent, very expert in all things courtly, military, governmental, and even idolatrous. Having assembled them, I presented that which I intended to do and requested that they afford me capable and ex-

## PROLOGO

Todos los escriptores trabaxan de autorizar, sus escripturas, lo mejor que pueden: vnos con testigos fidedignos: otros con otros escriptores, que ante dellos an escripto, los testimonjos de los quales son aujdos por ciertos: otros con testimonjo de la sagrada escriptura: a mj me an faltado, todos estos fundamentos, para autorizar, lo que en estos doze libros, tengo escripto: y no hallo otro fundamento, para autorizarlo: sino poner aqui, la relation, de la diligentia que hize: para saber la verdad, de todo lo que en estos libros, he escripto.

Como en otros prologos, desta obra he dicho: a mj me fue mandado, por sancta obediencia, de mi prelado mayor: que escriujese en lengua mexicana, lo que me pareciese, ser vtil: para la doctrina, cultura, y manutenencia, de la cristiandad, destos naturales, desta nueua españa: y para ayuda, de los obreros, y minjstros, que los doctrinan: rescebido este mandamjento, hize en lengua castellana, vna mjnuta, o memoria, de todas las materias, de que auja de tratar: que fue lo que esta escripto, en los doze libros: y la postilla, y canticos: lo qual se puso de prima tigera, en el pueblo de tepepulco, que es de la proujncia, de aculhuacã, o tezcucu: hizose desta manera.

En el dicho pueblo, hize juntar, todos los principales, con el señor del pueblo, que se llamaua don diego de mendoça, hombre anciano, de gran marco, y habilidad, muy esperimentado, en todas las cosas curiales, belicas, y politicas, y aun ydolatricas. Aujendolos juntado, propuseles, lo que pretendia hazer: y pediles, me diesen personas habiles, y esperimenta-

---

1. The prologues from Books II, IX, XI, and XII of the *Florentine Codex* have been published by Howard F. Cline. He provides the palaeographic texts and an English translation. See *Estudios de*

*Cultura Náhuatl*, Instituto de Investigaciones Históricas, Universidad Nacional Autónoma de México, vol. 9 (Mexico, 1971), pp. 237–52.

perienced persons with whom I could confer and who would know how to give me the information regarding that which I should ask of them. They replied that they would consult one another regarding the proposition and that they would answer me the next day. And thus they took their leave of me. The next day the lord came with the leaders. And, having made a very solemn speech, as they were wont to do at that time, they assigned me as many as ten or twelve leading elders. They told me I could communicate with them, and they would give me answers to all that I should ask them. As many as four Latinists, whom I had taught grammar a few years earlier in the College of Santa Cruz in Tlatilulco, were also there.

With these leaders and grammarians, who were also leaders, I conferred many days, close to two years, following the sequence of the outline which I had prepared.

They gave me all the matters we discussed in pictures, for that was the writing they employed in ancient times. And the grammarians explained them in their language, writing the explanation at the bottom of the painting. I still have these originals. Also at this time I dictated the *Apostilla* and the *Cantares.* The Latinists wrote them in the same village of Tepepulco.

At the time of the Chapter meeting in which Father Fray Francisco Toral, who assigned me this task, completed his term, they transferred me from Tepepulco. Taking all my writings I went to dwell in Santiago del Tlatilulco, where, gathering the leaders, I presented the matter of my writings to them, and requested that they assign me some capable leaders with whom to examine and discuss the writings which I brought recorded from Tepepulco. The governor with his councilmen assigned me as many as eight or ten leaders, selected from among all, very capable in their language and in their ancient customs. Cloistered in the College with them and with four or five students of the College, all trilingual, for a year or more, all I brought written from Tepepulco was amended, explained and expanded. And all was re-written in a poor hand, because it was written in great haste. Of all the students of the College it was Martín Jacobita, then rector of the College, a native of the district of Santa Ana in Tlatilulco, who worked most in this scrutiny or examination.

Having acted as mentioned in Tlatilulco, I came

das con qujen pudiese platicar: y me supiesen dar razon, de lo que los preguntase: ellos me respondieron, que se hablarian, cerca de lo propuesto, y que otro dia, me responderian: y ansi se despidieron de mj. Otro dia vinieron, el señor, con los principales: y hecho vn muy solenne parlamento, como ellos entonce le vsauan hazer: señalaronme, hasta diez, o doze principales ancianos: y dixeronme, que con aquellos, podia comunjcar, y que ellos me darian razon, de todo lo que les preguntase. Estauan tanbien alli, hasta quatro latinos: a los quales, yo pocos años, antes auja enseñado, la gramatica, en el colegio de santa cruz, en el tlatilulco.

Con estos principales, y gramaticos, tambien principales, platique muchos dias, cerca de dos años, sigujendo la orden, de la mjnuta, que yo tenja hecha:

todas las cosas que conferimos, me las dieron por pinturas, que aquella, era la escriptura, que ellos antiguamente vsauan: y los gramaticos las declararon en su lengua, escrjujendo la declaration, al pie de la pintura: tengo aun agora estos originales. Tambien en este tiempo, dicte la postilla, y los cantares: escrjujeronlos, los latinos, en el mjsmo pueblo, de tepepulco.

Quando al capitulo donde cumplio, su hebdomada, el padre fray francisco toral, el qual me inpuso esta carga: me mudaron de tepepulco, lleuando todas mjs escrituras, fuy a morar a santiago, del tlatelulco: donde juntando los principales, los propuse el negotio, de mjs escrituras, y los demande, me señalasen algunos principales, habiles, con qujen examjnase, y platicase las escripturas, que de tepepulco traya escriptas. El gouernador con los alcaldes, me señalaron, hasta ocho, o diez principales, escogidos entre todos, muy habiles en su lengua, y en las cosas de sus antiguallas: con los quales, y con quatro, o cinco colegiales, todos trilingues: por espacio de vn año, y algo mas encerrados, en el colegio: se emendo, declaro, y añadio, todo lo que de tepepulco truxe escripto: y todo se torno, a escriujr de nueuo, de ruyn letra, porque se escrjuio, cõ mucha priesa: en este escrutinjo, o examen el q̃ mas tabaxo, de todos los colegiales, fue martin Jacobita, que entonce era rector, del colegio, vezino del tlatilulco, del barrio de sanctana.

Aujendo hecho lo dicho, en el tlatilulco: vine a

to dwell, with all my writings, in San Francisco de Mexico, where for three years, alone, I examined and re-examined all my writings. And I again amended them and divided them into Books, into twelve Books, and each Book by chapters, and some Books by chapters and paragraphs. After this, Father Fray Miguel Navarro being Provincial and Father Fray Diego de Mendoza being guardian of the convent, with their support, all twelve Books were put in final form in a clear hand. And the *Apostilla* and the *Cantares* were amended and a clear copy made. A grammar of the Mexican language, with a vocabulary as appendix, was also prepared. The Mexicans amended and added many things to the twelve Books when they made a clear copy. Thus the first sieve through which my works were sifted was the people of Tepepulco; the second, the people of Tlatilulco; the third, the people of Mexico. And in all these scrutinies there were grammarians from the College. The principal and wisest one was Antonio Valeriano, a native of Azcaputzalco; another, a little less so, was Alonso Vegerano, a native of Quauhtitlan. Another was Martín Jacobita, of whom I made mention above; another was Pedro de San Buenaventura, a native of Quauhtitlan. All were expert in three languages: Latin, Spanish, and Indian. The scribes who copied all the works in a good hand are Diego de Grado, native of the district of La Concepción in Tlatilulco; Bonifacio Maximiliano, native of the district of San Martín in Tlatilulco; Mateo Severino, native of Xochimilco, near Ullac.

After a clear copy of these writings was made, for which a goodly number of *tomines* were spent for scribes, and with the support of the Fathers named above, the author thereof requested of the Father Commissary, Fray Francisco de Ribera, that three or four members of the Order inspect them so that, in the provincial Chapter meeting which was pending, they might say how they appeared to them. Said persons saw them and gave a report thereof to the governing assembly in the same Chapter meeting, stating how they appeared to them. And they stated in the governing assembly that they were writings of much worth and should be supported so that they might be completed. It seemed to some of the members of the governing assembly that it was contrary to the vows of poverty to spend monies in recording those writings. And so they ordered the author to dismiss the scribes and that he alone should write

morar, a sanct francisco, de mexico, con todas mjs escripturas: donde por espacio, de tres años, pase, y repase, a mjs solas todas mjs escripturas: y las torne a emendar: y diujdilas por libros, en doze libros, y cada libro, por capitulos: y algunos libros, por capitulos, y parraphos. Despues desto, siendo proujncial, el padre fray miguel nauarro: y guardian del conuento de mexico, el padre fray diego de mendoça, con su fabor, se sacaron en blanco, de buena letra, todos los doze libros: y se emendo, y saco en blanco la postilla, y los cantares: y se hizo vn arte, de la lengua mexicana, con vn vocabulario apendiz: y los mexicanos emendaron, y añadieron muchas cosas, a los doze libros, quando se yua sacando en blanco. De manera que el primer cedaço, por donde mjs obras se cernjeron, fueron los de tepepulco: el segundo, los del tlatilulco: el tercero, los de mexico: y en todos estos escrutinjos, vuo gramaticos colegiales. El principal y mas sabio, fue antonjo valeriano vezino de azcaputzalco: otro poco menos, que este fue alonso vegerano, vezino de quauhtitlan: otro fue martin Jacobita, de que arriba hize mencion: otro pedro de san buenauentura, vezino de quauhtitlan: todos espertos en tres lenguas, latina, española y indiana. los escriuanos, que sacaron de buena letra, todas las obras, son: Diego de grado, vezino del tlatilulco, del barrjo de la conception. Bonifacio maximjliano, vezino del tlatilulco, del barrjo de sanct martin. Matheo seuerino, vezino de suchimjlco, de la parte de vllac.

Desque estas escrituras, estuujeron sacadas en blanco: con el fauor de los padres, arriba nombrados: en que se gastaron, hartos tomjnes, con los escriujentes: el autor dellas, demando al padre comissario, fray francisco de ribera, que se viesen, de tres, o quatro religiosos: para que aquellos dixessen, lo que les parecia dellas, en el capitulo proujncial, que estaua propinquo: los quales los vieron, y dieron relacion dellas, al difinjtorio, en el mismo capitulo: diziendo lo que los parecia, y dixeron en el difinjtorio, que eran escrituras, de mucha estima, y que deujan ser fauorecidas: para que se acabasen. Algunos de los difinjdores les parescio, que era contra la pobreza, gastar dineros en escriujesse aquellas escrituras: y ansi mandaron al autor, que despidiese a los escriuanos: y que el solo escriujesse de su mano, lo que qujsiese en ellas. El qual como era maior de setenta años, y por temblor de la mano, no puede

in his own hand what he might desire in them. Because he was over seventy years old and because of the trembling of the hand, he was unable to write anything, nor did he achieve the dispensation of this mandate. For more than five years the writings remained without anything being done on them.

During this time, in the subsequent Chapter meeting, Father Fray Miguel Navarro was elected as General Custodian of the general Chapter, and Fray Alonso de Escalona as Provincial. At this time the author prepared a summary of all the Books and of all the chapters of each Book and the Prologues wherein all that contained in the Books is briefly stated. Father Fray Miguel Navarro and his companion, Father Fray Gerónimo de Mendieta, took this summary to Spain. And thus, that which was written about the things of this land was known in Spain. In the meantime, the Provincial Father took all the Books from said author and they were dispersed throughout all the Province, where they were seen by many of the Order and adjudged as very valuable and useful. After some years, returning from a general Chapter, Father Fray Miguel Navarro came as Commissary of these parts. By threat of censure, he again collected said Books at the request of the author. And, more or less a year after they were collected, they came into the possession of the author. At this time nothing was done on them, nor was there anyone to support the translation into Spanish until the Father Commissary General Fray Rodrigo de Sequera came to these parts and saw them. He was very pleased with them and ordered said author to translate them into Spanish. And he provided everything necessary to write them anew, the Mexican language in one column and Spanish in the other, to send them to Spain because the most Illustrious Señor Don Juan de Ovando, President of the Council of the Indies, wanted them. He had news of these Books by way of the summary that said Father Fray Miguel Navarro had taken to Spain, as mentioned above.

All the above is said in order that it be understood that this work has been examined and verified by many over many years. It has suffered many travails and misfortunes until it has been put into the form it is now in.

End of the Prologue.

escreujr nada, nj se pudo alcançar dispensacion deste mandamjento: estuujeronse las escrituras, sin hazer nada en ellas: mas de cinco años.

En este tiempo, en el capitulo sigujente, fue elegido por custos custodum, para el capitulo general: el padre fray miguel nauarro: y por proujncial fray alonso descaluna. En este tiempo, el autor, hizo vn sumario, de todos los libros, y de todos los capitulos de cada libro, y los prologos: donde en breuedad se dezia, todo lo que se contenja, en los libros. Este sumario, lleuo a españa, el padre fray Miguel nauarro, y su compañero, el padre fray hieronymo de mendieta: y ansi se supo en españa, lo que estaua escrito, cerca de las cosas desta tierra. En este medio tiempo, el padre proujncial, tomo todos los libros, al dicho autor, y se esparzieron, por toda la proujncia: donde fueron vistos de muchos religiosos, y aprouados, por muy preciosos, y prouechosos. Despues de algunos años, bolujendo de capitulo general, el padre fray Miguel nauarro: el qual vino por comissario destas partes: en censuras, torno a recoger, los dichos libros: a peticion del autor, y desque estuujeron recogidos, day a un año poco mas, o menos: vinjeron a poder del autor. En este tiempo, ninguna cosa se hizo en ellos: nj vuo qujen fauoreciese para acabarse, de traduzir en romance: hasta que el padre comissario general, fray Rodrigo de sequera: vino a estas partes, y los vio, y se contento mucho dellos: y mando al dicho autor, que los traduxese en romance: y proueyo de todo lo necessario, para que se escriujesen de nueuo, la lengua mexicana, en vna coluna, y el romance en la otra, para los embiar a españa: porque los procuro el Illustrissimo señor, don Juan de ouando, presidente del consejo de indias: porque tenja noticia destos libros: por razon del sumario, que el dicho padre fray Miguel nauarro, auja lleuado a españa, como arriba se dixo.

Todo lo sobre dicho, haze al proposito, de que se entienda, que esta obra a sido examjnada, y apurada por muchos, y en muchos años, y se an passado muchos trabajos, y desgracias, hasta ponerla en el estado, que agora esta.

fin del prologo.

## TO THE SINCERE READER

It is to be observed, for the understanding of the calendar which follows, that the months are unlike ours in number and in days because the months of these natives are eighteen and each one of them has only twenty days. And thus all the days contained in these months are three hundred and sixty. The last five days of the year do not occur in the count of any month; rather, they leave them outside of the count as unused.

At the beginning of the calendar the months of these natives go indicated according to their reckoning and by the letters of the alphabet, and on the other side our months go indicated by letters of the alphabet and according to [our] reckoning. And so it can be easily understood in what day of our months each of their feasts falls.[2]

The movable feasts, which are compiled at the end of the calendar, derive from another way of reckoning which they used in soothsaying, which contains two hundred and sixty days, in which there are feasts. And since this count does not coincide with the year-count, nor contain as many days, the feasts vary, falling on different days from one year to the next.

## EXCLAMATION OF THE AUTHOR[3]

I believe there is no heart so hard as not to be moved, stirred to tears, horror, and fear upon hearing of a cruelty like the one set forth above, so inhuman, more than bestial and diabolical. And certainly it is a lamentable and horrible thing to see that our human nature had come to such degradation and infamy that the parents, through the prompting of the devil, would kill and eat their children, without thinking that they thereby committed any offense, but rather thinking they thereby performed a great service to their gods. The blame for this cruel[4] blindness perpetrated[5] on these unfortunate children should not be imputed so much to the parents, who practiced it shedding many tears and with great sorrow in their hearts, as to the most cruel hate of our most ancient enemy, Satan, who with most perverse cunning moved them to such an infernal deed. O Lord God, do justice upon this cruel enemy who does

## AL SINCERO LECTOR.

Es de notar, para la intelligencia, del calendario, que se sigue: que los meses, son desiguales, de los nuestros, en numero, y en dias: porque los meses, destos naturales, son diez y ocho, y cada vno dellos, no tiene mas de veynte dias, y asi son; todos los dias, que se contienen, en estos meses, trezientos y sesenta. Los cinco dias postreros del año, no vienen en cuenta de ningun mes, mas antes los dexan fuera de la cuenta, por baldios.

Van señalados, los meses destos naturales, al principio del calendario, por su cuenta, y letras del abece: de la otra parte contraria, van señalados los nuestros meses, por letras del abece, y por su cuenta. Y ansi se puede facilmente entender, cada fiesta de las suyas, en que dia caya, de los nuestros meses.

Las fiestas moujbles, que estan al fin del calendario recopiladas: salen de otra manera de cuenta; que vsauan en el arte adiujnatoria: que contiene dozientos y sesenta dias: en la qual ay fiestas, y como esta cuenta, no va con la cuenta del año, nj tiene tantos dias: vienen las fiestas a uariarse, cayendo en dias diferentes, vn año de otro.

## EXCLAMACION, DEL AUTOR.

No creo, que ay coraçon tan duro, que oyendo, vna crueldad, tan inhumana, y mas que bestial y endiablada, como la que arriba queda puesta: no se enternezca, y mueua a lagrimas, y orror y espanto. Y ciertamente, es cosa lamētable, y orrible, ver que nřa humana naturaleza, aya venjdo a tanta baxeza, y oproprio: que los padres por sugestion del demonjo, maten y comã a sus hijos (sin pensar, que en ello hazian offensa njnguna) mas antes con pensar, que en ello hazian, gran serujcio a sus dioses. La culpa desta tan gruel ceguedad: que en estos desdichados njños, se esecutaua, no se deue tãto imputar a la crueldad de los padres: los quales derramando muchas lagrimas, y con gran dolor de sus coraçones la exercitauan: quanto al cruelissimo odio, de nuestro antiquissimo enemjgo satanas: el qual con malignissima astucia, los persuadio a tan infernal hazaña. O señor dios, hazed justicia deste cruel enemigo, que

---

2. See *Florentine Codex*, Book II, pp. 1–34.

3. This discussion follows the Spanish text of the first month and laments the rituals therein described.

4. In the Spanish read *cruel* for *gruel*.

5. In the Spanish read *exercitaua* for *esecutaua*.

and would do us so much evil! Lord, take from him all power to harm!

## [COMMENT ON THE SACRED SONGS][6]

Consistent with [the passage] in the Holy Gospel which says, "He who does evil detests the light," it is a very ancient practice of our adversary, the devil, to seek hiding places in order to perform his works. Consistent with this, our enemy planted, in this land, a forest or a thorny thicket filled with very dense brambles, to perform his works therefrom and to hide himself therein in order not to be discovered, even as do the wild beasts and the very poisonous serpents. The songs which, in this land, he contrived to be prepared and utilized in his service and for his divine worship, his songs of praise, in the temples as well as beyond them, are this forest or brambled thorny thicket. Said songs contain so much guile that they say anything and proclaim that which he commands. But only those he addresses understand them. It is well established that the songs and psalms he has composed are the cave, the forest, the thorny thicket where this accursed adversary now hides. And they are sung to him without its being understood what they are about, other than by those who are natives and versed in this language, so that, certainly, all he desires is sung, be it of war or peace, of praises to himself, or of scorn of Jesus Christ, without being understood by the others.

tãto mal nos haze, y nos desea hazer: qujtalde [*sic*] señor, todo el poder de empecer.

Costumbre muy antigua es, de ñro aduersario el diablo: buscar escondrijos, para hazer sus negocios: conforme a lo del sancto Euangelio, que dize. Quien haze mal, aborrece la luz: conforme a esto, este ñro enemigo, en esta tierra planto, vn bosque, o arcabuco, lleno de muy espesas breñas, para hazer sus negocios, desde el, y para absconderse en el; para no ser hallado: como hazen las bestias fieras, y las muy ponçuñosas serpientes. Este bosque, o arcabuco breñoso, son los cantares, que en esta tierra el vrdio, que se hisiessen, y vsasen, en su serujcio: y como su culto diujno y psalmus de su loor, ansi en los templos, como fuera dellos: los quales lleuan tanto artificio, que dizen lo que quieren, y apregonan lo que el manda: y entiendenlos solamente aquellos, a qujen el los endereça. Es cosa muy aueriguada, que la cueua, bosque, y arcabuco, donde el dia de oy, este maldito aduersario se absconde, son los cantares, y psalmus, que tiene compuestos: y se le cantan, sin poderse entender, lo que en ello se trata, mas de aquellos que son naturales, y acostumbrados a este lenguaje. De manera, que seguramente se canta, todo lo que el qujere, sea guerra o paz, loor suyo, o contumelia de xp̄o, sin que de los demas se pueda entender.

---

6. This discussion appears without title at the beginning of the Songs to the Gods in Book II. The Spanish text was also published in the *Florentine Codex, Book II*, p. 207, note 14, 2nd rev. ed., p. 221, note 1.

# Book III: The Origin of the Gods

The divine Augustine did not consider it superfluous or vain to deal with the fictitious theology of the gentiles in the sixth Book of the City of God, because, as he says, the empty fictions and falsehoods which the gentiles held regarding their false gods being known, [true believers] could easily make them understand that those were not gods nor could they provide anything that would be beneficial to a rational being. For this reason, the fictions and falsehoods these natives held regarding their gods are placed in this third Book, because the vanities they believed regarding their lying gods being understood, they may come more easily, through Gospel doctrine, to know the true God and to know that those they held as gods were not gods but lying devils and deceivers. And if one thinks that these things are so forgotten and lost and the belief in one God is established and rooted among these natives so that there will be no need at any time to speak of these matters, such a person I believe piously, but I know of a certainty that neither does the devil sleep nor is the reverence these natives render him forgotten; and that he is awaiting an opportunity, that he may return to the dominion he has held. And it will then be an easy matter for him to awaken all things pertaining to idolatry that are said to be forgotten. And for that time it is good that we have weapons on hand to meet him with. And to this end not only that which is written in this third Book but also that which is written in the first, second, fourth and fifth Books will serve. Nor will there be opportunity for his followers to deceive the faithful and the preachers then by gilding with lies and dissimulations the vanities and degradations they held concerning the belief in their gods and their worship, for

No tuuo por cosa superflua, nj vana el diujno Augustino, tratar, de la theologia fabulosa de los gentiles, en el sexto libro de la ciudad de Dios. Porque, como el dize; conocidas las fabulas y ficciones vanas que los gentiles, tenjan cerca de sus dioses fingidos pudiesen facilmẽte darles a entender, que aquellos no erã dioses, nj pudian dar cosa njnguna que fuesse prouechosa a la criatura racional. A este proposito, en este tercero libro, se ponẽ las fabulas, y ficciones que estos naturales tenjã, cerca de sus dioses, porque entendidas las vanjdades: que ellos tenjan por fe, cerca de sus mẽtirosos dioses: vengan mas facilmẽte, por la doctrina euangelica, a conocer el verdadero dios: y que aquellos, que ellos tenjan por dioses: no eran dioses, sino diablos mentirosos, y engañadores, y si alguno piensa, que estas cosas, estan tan olujdadas, y perdidas: y la fe de vn dios, tã plantada, y arraygada, estre estos naturales: que no aura necesidad en njngũ tiempo, de hablar en estas cosas: al tal, yo le creo piadosamente, pero se de cierto que el diablo nj duerme, ni esta olujdado de la honrra, que le haziã estos naturales, y que esta esperando coyuntura, para si podiesse boluer al señorio que a tenjdo: y facil cosa le sera para entonce despertar todas las cosas, que se dizen estar olujdadas, cerca de la ydolatria. Y para entonces bien es, que tengamos armas guardadas, para salirle al encuentro: y para esto, no solamẽte aprouechara, lo que esta escrito en este tercero libro, pero tambien lo que esta escrito, en el primero, y segundo, y quatro y qujnto. Ni tanpoco aura oportunjdad, para que sus satelites, entonce engañen a los fieles, y a los predicadores, cõ dorar, con mentiras y disimulationes, las vanjdades, y bajezes que tenjan cerca de la fe de sus dioses, y su cultura; porque parecerã las verdades,

the pure and clear truths will appear which declare who their gods were and what services they required, as contained in the Books mentioned above.

End of Prologue

puras, y limpias, q̃ declaran, qujenes erã sus dioses, y que serujcios demandauã, segun se contienen, en los libros arriba dichos.

fin del prologo

# Book IV: The Soothsayers

## PROLOGUE

It is well known that the astrologers called genethliacs are careful to know the hour and instant of birth of each person. Such being known, they foretell and prognosticate the natural inclinations of men through a consideration of the sign in which they are born and the position and aspect that the planets then have one with another and with respect to the sign. These astrologers or soothsayers base their prophecies on the influence of the constellations and planets. And for this reason their prophecies are tolerated and permitted in the almanacs which the common people utilize, provided that no one thinks that the influence of the constellations does more than incline one to sensuality and that it has no power over the free will. These natives of all New Spain took and take great care to know the day and hour of birth of every person to foretell the attributes, the life and death of those who were born. Those who held this office were called *tonalpouhque*; to them went, as to prophets, anyone who had given birth to a boy, to a girl, to be informed of their attributes, life and death. These soothsayers were not governed by the signs nor the planets of the heavens but by a formula which, as they say, Quetzalcoatl left to them, which contains twenty characters repeated thirteen times in the manner contained in the present Book. This manner of soothsaying can in no way be valid, because it is based neither on the influence of the stars, nor on any natural thing. Neither is its cycle in accordance with the year cycle, as it contains only two hundred and sixty days; which, ended, begin again. This trick of reckoning is either a necromantic craft or a pact and invention of the devil which should be uprooted with all diligence.

## PROLOGO.

Cosa muy sabida, es: que los astrologos, llamados Genethliaci: tienen solicitud, en saber la hora, y punto del nacimjento de cada persona: lo qual sabido, adiujnan, y pronostican, las inclinaciones naturales de los hombres: por la consideracion del signo, en que nacen, y del estado, y aspecto: que entonce tenjan las planetas entre si, y en respecto del signo. Estos astrologos, o adiujnos: fundan su adiujnança, en la influencia de las constelaciones y planetas: y por esta causa tolerase su adiujnança, y permjtese en los reportorios, que el vulgo vsa: con tal condicion, que nadie piense, que la influencia de la constelacion, haze mas, que inclinar a la sensualidad, y que njngun poder tiene, sobre el libre aluedrio. Estos naturales, de toda nueua españa: tuujeron, y tienen gran solicitud en saber el dia, y hora, del nacimjento de cada persona: para adiujnar las condiciones, vida, y muerte de los que nacian: los que tenjan este oficio, se llamauan tonalpouhque: a los quales acudian como a prophetas, qualqujer que le nacia hijo, hija: para informarse de sus condiciones, vida, y muerte. Estos adiujnos, no se regian: por los signos, nj planetas del cielo: sino por vna instruccion, que segun ellos dizen: se la dexo quetzalcouatl: la qual contiene veynte caracteres, multiplicados treze vezes: por el modo, que en el presente libro se contiene. Esta manera de adiujnança: en njnguna manera, puede ser licita: porque nj se funda en la influencia de las estrellas, nj en cosa njnguna natural, nj su circulo: es conforme al circulo del año: porque no contiene, mas de dozientos, y sesenta dias: los quales acabados, tornan al principio. Este artificio de contar, o es arte de njgromantica, o pacto, y fabrica del demonjo: lo qual, con toda diligencia, se deue desarraygar.

[The Appendix to Book IV, also written in Spanish, has already appeared in our translation of the *Florentine Codex*, Book IV, pp. 137–46.]

## TO THE SINCERE READER

You have in the present volume, friend reader, all the movable feasts of the year in their order and the ceremonies, sacrifices, festivities and superstitions which were observed in them, where it will be possible to detect and to take warning, to know if they are now practiced in their entirety or in part, although, from not knowing the time when they are held, since they are movable, it will be difficult to hit upon them. You also have a great abundance of terms dealing with this subject, very familiar to them and very occult to us. There is an opportunity in this material to judge the capacity of this people, for there are contained in it very refined things, as in the table which appears at the end of the Book.[1]

## AL SINCERO LECTOR.

Tienes en el presente volumen: amjgo lector, todas las fiestas moujbles, del año, por su orden: y las cerimonjas, sacrificios, y regozijos, y supersticiones: que en ellas se hazian: donde se podra tomar indicio, y aujso: para conocer, si agora se hazen del todo, o en parte: aunque por no saber el tiempo, en que se hazen, por ser moujbles: sera dificultuoso, de caer en ellas. Tienes tambien mucha copia de lenguaje: tocante a esta materia: entre ellos bien trillada, y a nosotros bien occulta. Ay occasion en esta materia, de conjecturar la abilidad desta gente: porq̄ se contiene en ella, cosas bien delicadas: como en la tabla, que esta al fin del libro se parece.

---

1. See Figs. 102, 103, and 104 in the *Florentine Codex*, Book IV.

# Book V: The Omens

## PROLOGUE

Since, desirous of more knowledge, our first parents deserved to be deprived of the original knowledge that was given them and to fall into the very dark night of ignorance in which they left all of us, not having, as yet, lost that accursed desire, we do not cease to persist in wanting to investigate, rightly or wrongly, that which we do not know concerning the natural things as well as the supernatural.

And although, to understand many of these things, we have many paths, and very true ones, we do not content ourselves with this, but rather we try through illicit and forbidden ways to know of the things which our Lord God has not willed that we should know, such as the things of the future and secret things.

And this is [done] sometimes by way of the devil, sometimes guessing by the howls of the animals or the cries of the birds or by the appearance of some vermin.

Bad is this which has spread into all the lineage of man, and, since these natives are a good part of it, a good share of this sickness befell them.

And in order that, at the time when, wounded with this sore, they go in search of remedy, and [in order that] the doctor can easily understand them, many of the omens these natives heeded are set forth in the present Book. And at the end the different apparitions which appeared to them at night are treated of.

## PROLOGO.

Como con apetito de mas saber, nuestros primeros padres, merecieron: ser priuados, del original saber, que les fue dado: y caer en la noche muy escura, de la ignorancia: en que a todos nos dexaron. No auiendo aun perdido, aquel maldito apetito: no cesamos, de porfiar: de querer investigar, por fas o por nefas, lo que ignoramos: ansi cerca de las cosas naturales, como cerca de las cosas sobrenaturales.

Y aunque para saber, muchas cosas, destas: tenemos caminos muchos, y muy ciertos: no nos contentamos, con esto: sino que por caminos no licitos, y vedados: procuramos de saber: las cosas, que nuestro señor dios, no es seruido, que sepamos: como son, las cosas futuras: y las cosas secretas.

Y esto a las vezes, por via del demonio: a las vezes, coniecturando, por los bramidos de los animales: o garridos de las aues o por el aparecer de algunas sauandijas.

Mal es este, que cundio en todo el humanal linaie: y como estos naturales, son buena parte del: cupolos harta parte, desta enfermedad.

Y porque, para quando, llagados desta llaga, fueren a buscar medicina: y el medico, los pueda facilmente, entender: se poñe en el presente libro: muchos de los agueros, que estos naturales vsauan: y a la postre, se trata de diuersas maneras de estantiguas: que de noche, los aparecian.

## APPENDIX

### PROLOGUE

Although the auguries and the superstitions seem to be of a like nature, yet the auguries, for a greater part, attribute to living things that which is not of

### PROLOGO

Aunque los agueros y abusiones, parecen ser de vn mjsmo linaje: pero los agueros por la mayor parte, atribuyen a las criaturas, lo que no ay en ellas, como

their essence; that is to say, when a serpent or weasel passes in front of someone who travels along the road, they say it is a sign that some misfortune will befall him along the way. And auguries of this kind are told of in this fifth Book.

The superstitions which are treated in this appendix are the opposite. They take as evil the qualities or influences of living things which are good; for instance, the fragrance of the gardenia, which they call *omixochitl*,[1] is the cause of a sickness which is like hemorrhoids. And they also ascribe a false attribute to the flower called *cuetlaxochitl*.[2] When the woman steps over it, it will inflict upon her a sickness also called *cuetlaxochitl*, which occurs in the female organs.

And, because the auguries and the superstitions are very similar, I place this treatment of the superstitions as an appendix to this fifth Book dealing with auguries. And as regards the auguries, there are not as many mentioned as exist in practice, nor are all superstitions which they practice evilly in this appendix, for these things which are evil go ever increasing. And many of one sort or the other will be found which are not placed here.

End of the Prologue.

es dezir, que quando la culebra o comadreja atraviessan por delante de alguno que va camjno: dizen que es senal, de que le a de acontecer alguna desgracia, en el camjno: y desta manera de agueros esta dicho en este libro qujnto.

las abosiones de que en este apendiz se trata, son al reues que tvmã en mala parte, las impressiones o influencias que son buenas en las criaturas, como es dezir, que el olor del jasmjn indiano, que ellos llaman vmjsuchitl, es causa de vna enfermedad, que es como almorranas y tambien a la flor, que llaman cuetlasuchitl, la atribuyen vn falso testimonjo, que quando la muger passa sobre ella le causa vna enfermedad, que tambien la llaman cuetlasuchitl, la qual se causa en el mjembro mugeril.

y porque los agueros, y las abusiones son muy vezinos. pongo este tratado de las abusiones por apendiz deste libro qujnto de los agueros. y en los agueros no esta todo dicho quãto ay en el vso: nj tampoco en este apendiz estan todas las abusiones de que mal vsan: porque siempre van multiplicandose estas cosas que son malas, y muchos allaran ansi del vno, como del otro cosas que no estan aqui puestas.

fin del prologo.

---

1. *Omixochitl*: *Polyanthes tuberosa*, L; *P. mexicana* Zucc. (cf. *Florentine Codex*, Book V, p. 183).

2. *Cuetlaxochitl*: **Euphorbia (poinsettia) pulcherrima** Willd. (ibid.).

# Book VI: Rhetoric and Moral Philosophy

## PROLOGUE

All nations, however savage and decadent they have been, have set their eyes on the wise and strong in persuading, on men prominent for moral virtues, and on the skilled and the brave in warlike exercises, and more on those of their own generation than on those of others. There are so many examples of this among the Greeks, the Latins, the Spaniards, the French, and the Italians that books are full of this subject.

The same was practiced in this Indian nation, and especially among the Mexicans, among whom the wise, superior, and effective rhetoricians were held in high regard. And they elected these to be high priests, lords, leaders, and captains, no matter how humble their estate. These ruled the states, led the armies, and presided in the temples.

In these matters they were certainly extreme: most devout to their gods, most zealous concerning their states, very courteous among themselves, very cruel toward their enemies, humane and cruel to their own. I think that by means of these virtues they achieved dominion, although it lasted[1] little time and now they have lost all, as one will clearly see who will compare that contained in this Book with the life they now lead.

This being very clear, I do not tell the reason for it. In this Book it will be very clearly seen (as to what some rivals have asserted, that all written in these Books, preceding this one and following this one, is invention and lies) that they speak as intolerant and as liars, because the inventing of that which is written in this Book is not within the understanding of human beings, nor is there a living man who could invent the language which is in it.

1. In the Spanish read *duro* for *turo*.

## PROLOGO

Todas las nationes, por barbaras, y de baxo metal que ayan sido: an puesto los ojos en los sabios, y poderosos, para persuadir: y en los hõbres emjnentes, en las virtudes morales: y en los diestros, y valientes, en los exercicios belicos: y mas en los de su generacion que en los de las otras. Ay desto, tantos exemplos entre los Griegos, y latinos, españoles, franceses, y Italianos: que estan los libros llenos desta materia.

Esto mjsmo, se usaua en esta nation indiana: y mas principalmente, entre los mexicanos: entre los quales, los sabios, Rethoricos virtuosos, y esforçados: eran tenjdos en mucho. Y destos, elegian para pontifices, para señores, y principales, y capitanes: por de baxa suerte que fuesẽ: estos regian las republicas, y gujauan los exercitos, y presidian en los templos.

Fueron cierto, en estas cosas estremados: diuotissimos para con sus dioses: zelosissimos de sus republicas entre si muy vrbanos, para con sus enemigos muy crueles: para con los suios, humanos, y severos. Y pienso que por estas virtudes, alcançaron el imperio: aunque los turo poco, y agora todo lo an perdido: como vera claro, el que cotejare, lo contenjdo en este libro: con la vida, que agora tienen.

La causa desto, no la digo por estar muy clara. En este libro se vera muy claro, que lo que algunos emulos an afirmado que todo lo escripto en estos libros ante deste y despues deste son fictiones y mentiras: hablan como apassionados y mentirosos: porque lo que en este libro esta escripto no cabe en entendimjento de hombre humano el fingirlo nj hombre viujente pudiera fingir el lenguaie que en el esta:

And, if they are asked, all the informed Indians will assert that this language is characteristic of their ancestors and the works they produced.

y todos los indios entendidos si fueren preguntados afirmaran que este lenguaie es el propio de sus antepasados y obras que ellos hazian.

# Book VII: The Sun, Moon and Stars, and the Binding of the Years

## PROLOGUE

How foolish our forefathers, the gentiles, both Greek and Latin, had been in the understanding of created things is very clear from their own writings. From them it is evident to us what ridiculous fables they invented of the sun, the moon, some of the stars, water, land, fire, air, and of the other created things. And, what is worse, they attributed divinity to them, and they worshipped them, made offerings, made sacrifices to them, and revered them as gods.

This originated in part from the blindness into which we fell through original sin and in part from the cunning, the long-standing hatred of our adversary, Satan, who always endeavors to incline us toward vile, ridiculous and very culpable things.

So if this happened, as we know, among people of so much discretion and presumption, there is no reason for one to marvel that similar things are found among these people, so innocent and so easy to be deceived.

So, that they be cured of their blindnesses by means of the preachers as well as the confessors, some fables, no less graceless than frivolous, which their ancestors left them of the sun, the moon, the stars, the [four] elements, and things containing the [four] elements are placed in the present Book.

At the end of the Book are set forth the manner of counting the years, the jubilee year, which was every fifty-two years,[1] and the noteworthy ceremonies they then performed.

## TO THE READER

The reader will have reason for displeasure in the reading of this seventh Book, and will have even

## PROLOGO.

Quan desatinados, aujan sido, en el conocimjento, de las criaturas, los gentiles, nuestros antecessores: ansi griegos, como latinos: esta muy claro, por sus mjsmas escripturas. De las quales, nos consta: quan ridiculosas fabulas, inuentaron, del sol, y de la luna, y de algunas, de las estrellas: y del agua, tierra, fuego, y ayre: y de las otras criaturas: y lo que peor es, les atribuyeron diujnidad: y adoraron, ofrecieron, sacrificaron, y acataron: como a dioses.

Esto proujno, en parte, por la ceguedad, en que caymos, por el peccado original: y en parte por la malicia, y enuegecido odio, de nuestro aduersario, satanas: que siempre procura: de abatirnos, a cosas viles, ridiculosas, y muy culpables.

Pues, si esto paso, como sabemos, entre gente, de tanta discrecion, y presuncion: no ay porque, nadie se maraujlle: porque se hallen, semejantes cosas, entre esta gente: tan parbula, y tan facil para ser engañada.

Pues a proposito, que sean curados de sus cegueras, ansi por medio de los predicadores: como le los confessores: se ponen en el presente libro, algunas fabulas, no menos frias que fribulas: que sus antepassados, los dexaron: del sol y de la luna, y de las estrellas: y de los elementos, y cosas elementadas.

Al fin del libro, se pone la manera, del contar los años: y del año del jubileo: que era de cincuenta, en cincuenta y dos años y de las notables cerimonjas: que entonce hazian.

## AL LECTOR.

Razon tendra el lector, de desgustasse en la lection deste septimo libro: y mucho mayor la tendra si

---

1. The corresponding Spanish passage should read: "*de cincuenta y dos, en cincuenta dos años*." The *Tolosa MS* and subsequent edi-tions of Sahagún's *Historia* make the correction.

more if he deals with the Indian language along with the Spanish language, because the style in Spanish is very crude and the subject-matter this seventh Book deals with is treated very crudely. This is because the natives themselves gave the account of the things treated in this Book very crudely, according as they understood them, and in crude style. And so it was translated into the Spanish language in crude style, with little excellence of understanding, with the sole object of knowing and recording what they understood of this subject of astrology and natural philosophy, which is very little and very crude.

There is another thing in the language which will also give displeasure to one who would understand it, and it is that there are many synonymous terms for [any] one thing, and a mode of expression or a sentence is said in many ways. This was done on purpose to know and record all the vocabulary of each thing and all the modes of expressing each sentence. And this is not only in this Book but in the whole work.

Farewell.

[Among the illustrations in our translation of Book VII of the *Florentine Codex*, there appears a paragraph of Spanish text explaining the calendar wheel.]

entiende la lengua yndiana, iuntamẽte con la lẽgua española: porque en lo español el lenguaje va muy baxo, y la materia de que se trata en este septimo libro, va tratada muy baxamente. Esto es porque los mjsmos naturales dieron la relacion de las cosas, que en este libro se tratan muy baxamente, segun que ellos las entienden: y en baxo lenguaje. Y asi se traduxo en la lengua española en baxo estilo, y en baxo qujlate de entendimjento: pretendiendo solamente saber, y escuijr lo que ellos entendian en esta materia, de Astrologia, y Philosophia natural: que es muy poco y muy baxo.

Otra cosa ay en la lengua que tambien dara desgusto al que la entendiere: y es que de vna cosa van muchos nõbres sinonjmos: y vna manera de dezir o vna sentencia va dicha de muchas maneras, esto se hizo aposta, por saber y escreujr, todos los vocablos de cada cosa: y todas las maneras de dezir de cada sentencia: y esto no solamente es en este libro pero en toda la obra.

Vale.

# Book VIII: Kings and Lords

## PROLOGUE

As the old men, in whose possession were the paintings and recollections of ancient things, asserted, those who first came to settle this land of this New Spain came from the north in search of the earthly paradise. They had as [their] watchword *Tamoanchan*. And it is what they now say [as] *tictemoa tochan*, which means, "We seek our native home." Perhaps [they were] influenced by some oracle, which one of the very esteemed among them had received and divulged, that the earthly paradise is to the south, as is true. According to nearly all those who write, it is below the equinoctial line. And they settled near the highest mountains they could find, because of having information that it is a very high mountain; and it is true.

These first settlers, as the very ancient buildings which are now very visible reveal, were a very robust, very wise, very warlike people. Among the very noteworthy things they did, they built a very impregnable city in very fertile lands. There are still abundant indications of its fortune and wealth in the destroyed buildings. They called this city Tullan, which means "place of fertility and abundance." And even now it is a very pleasant and fertile place.

A king named Quetzalcoatl ruled many years in this city. He was a great necromancer and inventor of necromancy, and he left it to his descendants and to this day they practice it. He was consummate in the moral virtues.

Among these natives the activities of this king are like those of King Arthur among the English.

This city was destroyed and this king put to flight. They say he traveled to the east, that he went to the city of the sun called Tlapallan, and that he was

## PROLOGO.

Segun, que affirman los viejos, en cuyo poder, estauan las pinturas, y memorias de las cosas antiguas: los que primeramente, venjeron a poblar, a esta tierra, desta nueua españa: vinieron de hazia el norte, en demanda del parayso terrenal. Traian por apellido, tamoanchan: y es lo que agora dizen, tictemoa tochan: que quiere dezir, buscamos n̄ra casa natural. Por uentura, induzidos de algun oraculo, que alguno de los mui estimados, entre ellos, auia rescibido y diuulgado: que el paraiso terrenal, esta hazia el medio dia: como es uerdad, segun casi todos, los que escriuen; que esta debaxo de la linea equinocial. I poblauan, cerca de los mas altos montes, que hallauan: por tener relation, que es vn monte altissimo, y es ansi uerdad.

Estos primeros pobladores, segū lo manifiestan, los antiquissimos edificios, que agora estan muy manifiestos, fueron: gente robustissima, sapientissima, y belicosissima. Entre otras cosas, mui notables, que hizieron: edificaron vna ciudad, fortissima, en tierra opulentissima: de cuya felicidad y riquezas, aun en los edificios destruydos della, ay grandes indicios. A esta ciudad llamaron Tullan, que quiere dezir: lugar de fertilidad, y abundancia, y aun agora se llama ansi: y es lugar muy ameno, y fertil.

En esta ciudad, reyno muchos años, vn rey, llamado Quetzalcoatl: gran nigromantico, y inuentor de la nigromancia, y la dexo a sus decendientes, y oy dia la vsan: fue estremado, en las virtudes morales.

Esta el negocio deste Rey, entre estos naturales: como el del Rey Artus entre los ingleses.

Fue esta ciudad destruida, y este Rey ahuyentado: dizen, que camino, hazia el oriente: que se fue a la ciudad del sol, llamada tlapallā, y fue llamado del

summoned by the sun. And they say he is still alive and that he is to reign again and rebuild that city which [his enemies] destroyed. And so to this day they await him.

And when Don Hernán Cortés came [the natives] thought it was he. And they received, they took Cortés as such until his behavior and that of those who came with him disabused them.

Those who fled from this city built another very prosperous city which is called Cholula, to which the Spaniards, upon seeing it, gave the name Rome, because of its nobleness, buildings, and grandeur. It seems that the affairs of these two cities went the way of Troy and Rome.

Many years after this the Mexican nation began to settle and in three hundred years, more or less, they gained dominion over most of the kingdoms, the seigniories which there are in all that is now called New Spain. And they founded the city of Mexico, which is another Venice.

Its lords were emperors, especially the last one, who was Motecuçoma, a very brave man, very warlike, skilled in arms, magnanimous, of great ability, splendid, consummate in the affairs of his governance, but cruel.

The Spaniards arrived in his time. He already had many omens that they would come during his time.

The Spaniards having arrived, the empire of the Mexicans ceased and that of the Spaniards began. And, as there are many notable things in the way of governing that these infidels have, I compiled this volume which deals with the lords and all their customs.

sol: y dizen, que es uiuo, y que a de boluer a reinar, y a reedificar aquella ciudad, que le destruyeron: y ansi oy dia le esperan.

I quando vino don hernando Cortes, pensaron: que era el, y por tal le recibieron, tuuieron: hasta que, su conuersacion, y la de los, que con el venian, los desengaño.

Los que desta ciudad huyeron, edificaron otra, muy prospera ciudad, que se llama Cholula: a la qual por su nobleza, edificios, y grandeza: los españoles en viendola, la pusieron nombre: Roma parece que el negocio destas dos ciudades, llevaron el camino de troya, y roma.

Despues desto, muchos años començo a publar, la nacion mexicana, y en trezientos años, pocos mas o menos, se enseñorearon de la mayor parte, de los reynos, y señorios, que ay en todo lo que agora se llama, nueva españa: y fundarõ la ciudad de mexico, que es otra venecia.

Los señores della, fuerõ emperadores, en especial, el vltimo: que fue motecuçoma: varõ muy esforçado, muy belicoso, y diestro en las armas: magnanimo, y de grande habilidad, y magnifico, estremado en las cosas de su policia, pero cruel.

En tiempo deste llegaron los españoles y el tenia ya muchos pronosticos, de que avian de venir, en su tiempo.

llegados los españoles, ceso el imperio de los mexicanos: y començo el despaña. I porque, ay muchas cosas notables, en el modo de regir que estos infieles tenian, copile, este volumen: que trata de los señores y de todas sus Costumbres.

# Book IX: The Merchants

## PROLOGUE

The arrangement which has been maintained in this *History* is that to begin with, in the first Books, the gods, their feasts, their sacrifices, their temples and all pertaining to their worship, were considered. The first five Books were written regarding this. And the last of these was Book Five, which deals with soothsaying; it also speaks of supernatural matters. All these five Books were placed in one volume. The sixth Book, which forms a volume by itself, deals with the rhetoric and moral philosophy which these natives achieved. In it are set forth many forms of very elegant, very moral prayers. And even those that touch upon the gods and their ceremonies can be said to be very theological. The esteem in which the rhetoricians and orators were held is dealt with in this same Book. After this the natural phenomena are dealt with; this in Book Seven. And then the lords, kings, governors, and leaders, and then the merchants, who, next to the lords, captains, and brave men, are the most revered in the State: these are dealt with in Book Eight. And after these are the featherworkers, the goldworkers, the workers of precious stones: these are treated in Book Nine. The qualifications, qualities, and customs of all the trained workmen and persons are dealt with in Book Ten, where also the parts of the body, the ailments, the cures, and also the differences, the diversities of the generations of people who dwell in this land, with their qualities, are dealt with.[1] These four Books comprise the third volume, which is this one. In the fourth volume those of a lesser order are dealt with; these are the animals, birds, plants, and trees, which comprise the eleventh Book. In Book Twelve the wars when this land was

---

1. Cf. Prologue to Book I, note 3 above.

## PROLOGO.

La orden que se a tenjdo en esta historia, es que primeramẽte y en los primeros libros, se trato de los dioses, y de sus fiestas, y de sus sacrificios, y de sus templos, y de todo lo concernjente a su serujcio: y desto, se escriujeron los primeros cinco libros: y dellos el postrero: fue el libro qujnto, que trata de la arte adiujnatoria, que tambien habla de las cosas sobrenaturales: todos estos cinco libros, se pusierõ en vn volumen. El sexto libro, que haze volumen por si: trata de la rethorica, y philosophia moral, que estos naturales alcançauan, donde se pone muchas maneras de oraciones, muy elegãtes y muy morales, y aun las que tocan a los dioses, y sus cerimonjas se pueden dezir muy theologales: en este mjsmo libro, se trata de la estimaciõ, en que se tenjan los rethoricos, y oradores. Despues desto se trata de las cosas naturales: y esto en el septimo libro: y luego de los señores reyes, y gouernadores, y principales personas: y luego de los mercaderes, que despues de los señores, capitanes, y hombres fuertes son los mas tenjdos en la republica; de los quales se trata en el octauo libro: y tras ellos los officiales de pluma, y de oro, y de piedras preciosas: destos se trata en el nono libro. Y las calidades, condiciones, y maneras de todos los officiales, y personas: se trata en el libro decimo, donde tambien se trata de los mjembros corporales, y de las enfermedades, y medicinas contrarias: y tambien de las differencias, y diuersidades, de generaciones de gẽtes, que en esta tierra avitan, y de sus condiciones: estos quatro libros constituyẽ, el tercero volumẽ que es este. En el quarto volumẽ se trata de las cosas mas baxas, que son anjmales, aues, yeruas, y arboles, que constituye, el vndecimo libro. En el libro duodecimo se trata de las guerras, quando

conquered are dealt with as a thing horrible and contrary to human nature. [Both of] these Books constitute the fourth and final volume.

esta tierra, fue conqujstada, como de cosa orrible, y enemiga de la naturaleza humana: todos estos libros, constituyen, el quarto, y postrero volumen.

# Book X: The People

## PROLOGUE

Although preaching is considered to be evangelical and apostolic, it must appear very clear that the preaching of the Catholic preachers should be of virtues and vices, encouraging the one and discouraging the other. And the most constant should be urging[1] upon [people] the theological virtues and dissuading them from the vices at variance with them. (And of this there is much material in the first six Books of the *Historia* and in the *Apostilla* dealing with the Epistles and the Gospels for all the Sundays of the year which I prepared; and more definitively in the *Doctrina Cristiana* which the first twelve Fathers preached to these native people, which, as an eyewitness, I compiled in this Mexican language.) In this volume, to provide more convenience and help to the preachers of this new Church, I have dealt with the moral virtues, according to the understanding, and practices and language these same people maintain regarding them. In this treatise I do not follow the arrangement other writers have followed in dealing with this subject; rather I follow the order of the persons, the ranks, the crafts, and the trades which exist among these people, setting forth the goodness of each person and then the badness, with a multitude of nouns, adjectives and verbs (where among them there is a great abundance of very characteristic and very extensively used terms). In this volume are also contained, in the same pattern, all the parts of the body, the internal and external organs in much detail, and after this the majority of the ailments to which the human body in this land is susceptible, and the cures, and with this nearly all the generations which have come to settle this land.

## PROLOGO

Si bien se considera la predication euangelica y apostolica, hallarse a muy claro, que la predication de los catholicos predicadores, a de ser vicios, y virtudes: persuadiendo lo vno y disuadiendo lo otro, y lo mas continuo a de ser el persuadirlos las virtudes theologales, y disuadirlos los vicios a ellas cõtrarias (y desto ay mucha materia en los seys libros primeros desta historia: y en la postilla sobre las epistolas y euangelios de los domingos de todo el año que hize: y muy mas resolutamente en la doctrina christiana: que los doze primeros predicadores predicaron a esta gente indiana: la qual yo como testigo de vista copile, en esta lengua mexicana) y para dar mayor oportunidad y ayuda a los predicadores desta nueua yglesia en este volumen he tractado de las virtudes morales segun la intelligencia y pratica y lenguaje que la misma gente tiene dellas. No lleuo en este tractado la orden que otros escriptores an lleuado en tratar esta materia, mas lleuo la orden de las personas dignidades y oficio y tractos: que entre esta gente ay poniendo la bondad de cada persona y luego su maldad con copia de nombres sustantiuos, adiectiuos y verbos (donde ay gran abundancia de lenguaje muy proprio y muy comun entrellos) Contienense tambien por el mismo estilo en este volumen todas las partes del cuerpo, interiores, y esteriores, muy por menudo: y tras esto las mas de las enfermedades a que los cuerpos humanos son subjectos, en esta tierra y las medicinas contrarias: y junto a esto casi todas las generationes que a esta tierra an venido a poblar.

---

1. In the Spanish read *persuadirlos a*.

## AUTHOR'S ACCOUNT
## WORTHY OF BEING NOTED[2]

After having written of the talents and skills these native Mexicans possessed in the time of their unbelief and of the vices and virtues which were considered as such among them, it seemed to me consistent with reason to set forth here the skills and talents, vices and virtues which they have subsequently acquired.

As for the first, we know from experience that they are capable of learning and practicing the mechanical skills just as the Spaniards know them and practice them. For instance, they understand and perform the geometric skills, that is, construction, like the Spaniards; also the skill of masonry, and of stone working, and of carpentry; also the skills of the tailors, the shoemakers, the silk workers, the printers, the scribes, the readers, the bookkeepers, the singers of plain song, of descant; the playing of flutes, flageolets, sackbuts, trumpets, organs; the knowledge of [Latin] grammar, of logic, of rhetoric, of astrology, of theology. All this we know from experience: that they have a capacity for it, they learn it, understand it, and teach it. There is no art they do not have the capacity to learn and practice.

With regard to what they were most capable of in times past in the administration of the state as well as in the service of the gods, it is the reason why they held the affairs of their administration in accordance with the need of the people. And, therefore, they reared the boys and girls with great sternness until they were adults. And this was not in the home of their parents, because, each one in his home, they were not effective at rearing them as was fitting. Therefore, they reared them conjointly under very careful and stern teachers, the men by themselves and the women by themselves. There they taught them how they were to honor their gods and how they were to revere and obey the state and its rulers. They had heavy punishments to punish those who were disobedient and irreverent, especially to their teachers. They took great care that they not drink pulque. They occupied people under fifty in many exercises, by night and by day. And they reared them in great austerity so that the carnal activities and

## RELACION DEL AUTOR
## DIGNA DE SER NOTADA

Despues de auer escrito las habilidades, y officios, que estos naturales mexicanos, tenjan en tiempo de su infidelidad, y los vicios, y virtudes, que entre ellos, eran tenjdas por tales: pareciome consono a razon, poner aquj los officios, y abilidades, vicios y virtudes, que despues aca an aqujrido.

Quanto a lo primero: tenemos por experiencia, que en los officios, mecanjcos, son abiles para deprenderlos, y vsarlos segun, que los españoles los saben, y vsan: como son; officios de geumetria, que es edificar, los entienden y hazen, como los españoles tambien el officio de albañeria, y canteria, y carpinteria tambien los officios de sastres y çapateros, sederos, impresores escriuanos, letores, contadores musicos de canto llano, de canto de organo: tañer flautas, cheremjas, xacabuches, trumpetas, organos: saber gramatica logica, y rethorica, astrologia theologia: todo esto tenemos por experiencia, que tienen abilidad para ello, lo deprenden, y lo saben, y lo enseñan: y no ay arte njnguna que no tengan abilidad, para deprēderla, y vsarla.

En lo que toca a que eran para mas en los tiempos pasados, ansi para el regimjento de la republica, como para serujcio de los dioses: es la causa porque tenjan el negocio de su regimjento, conforme a la necesidad de la gente: y por esto los muchachos, y muchachas criauanlos con gran rigor hasta que erã adultos: y esto no en casa de sus padres, porque no eran poderosos para criarlos, como convenja, cada vno en su casa: y por esto criauanlos de comunjdad debaxo de maestros muy solicitos, y rigorosos: los hombres a su parte, y las mugeres de las suya. Alli los enseñauan como aujan de honrrar a sus dioses, y como aujan de acatar, y obedecer a la republica, y a los regidores della: tenjan graues castigos, para castigar a los que no eran obediētes, y reuerentes a sus maestros en especial, se ponjan gran diligencia, en que no beujessen vctli, la gente que era de cincuenta años abaxo, ocupauãlos, en muchos exercicios, de noche, y de dia: y criauanlos en grande austeridad: de manera que los brios, y inclinaciones carnales, no

2. This treatise by Sahagún is in lieu of a Spanish translation or Spanish text for Chapter 27. Although the paragraph headings are translated into Spanish, the Nahuatl text remains untranslated. This treatment by Sahagún is parallel to paragraphs 1 through 9 of the Nahuatl text.

tendencies had no dominion over them, whether men or women.

Those who lived in the temples had so many labors by night and by day and were so abstinent that sensual things did not occur to them.

As for those who were of the military calling, the wars they had one with another were so continuous that there was little time that they ceased war and its works.

This manner of governing was much in conformity with natural and moral philosophy, because the mildness and abundance of this land and the climates which prevail in it considerably aided human nature to be licentious and idle and much given to sensual vices. And moral philosophy taught these natives through experience that, to live morally and virtuously, rigor, austerity, and continuous concern for things beneficial to the state was necessary.

Since this ceased with the coming of the Spaniards, and since these put down and destroyed all the ways of governing these natives had, and tried to convert them to the ways of living of Spain in things divine as well as human, understanding that they were idolaters and barbarians, all the government which they possessed was lost.

It was necessary to destroy idolatrous things and all idolatrous buildings, and even the customs of the state which were mixed with idolatrous rites and accompanied by idolatrous ceremonies which were present in nearly all the customs of the state, by which it was governed. And for this reason it was necessary to destroy all of it and place [the Indians] in another kind of established order which in no way smacked of idolatry.

But now, seeing that this kind of established order produces very licentious people of very evil tendencies and very evil works, which make them odious to God and to men, and even cause them great sicknesses and a short life, it will be necessary to remedy it. And it seems to all of us that the principal cause of this is drunkenness, for that olden rigor of punishing drunken feasts with the death sentence has ceased. Although now there is punishment by whipping them, cutting off their hair, selling them as slaves by the year or by the month, this is not an adequate punishment to stop their becoming drunk. Nor are even the very frequent sermons of the preachers against this vice nor the threats of hell

tenjan señorio en ellos: ansi ē los hombres, como en las mugeres:

los que biujan en los templos, tenjan tantos, trabajos, de noche, y de dia, y erā tan abstinentes, que no se les acordaua de cosas sensuales:

los que eran de el exercicio, mjlitar, eran tan continuas las guerras, que tenjan los vnos con los otros, que muy poco tiempo cesauan de la guerra y de los trabajos della:

era esta manera de regir muy conforme a la philosophia natural, y moral, porque la templança y abastança, desta tierra: y las constelaciones que en ella reynan ayudan mucho, a la naturaleza humana, para ser viciosa, y ociosa, y muy dada a los vicios sensuales: y la philosophia moral enseño por experiencia a estos naturales, que para biujr moralmente, y virtuosamēte era necesario el rigor, y austeridad, y ocupaciones continuas, en cosas prouechosas a la republica.

Como esto ceso, por la uenjda de los españoles, y porque ellos derrocaron, y hecharon por tierra: todas las costumbres y maneras de regir, que tenjan estos naturales; y qujsieron reduzirlos, a las maneras de biujr de españa: ansi en las cosas diujnas, como en las humanas: tenjendo entendido, que eran ydolatras, y barbaros, perdiose todo el regimjento que tenjan:

necesario fue destruyr las cosas ydolatricas, y todos los edificios idolatricos: y aun las costumbres de la republica, que estauan mezcladas con ritos de idolatria, y acompañadas con cerimonjas ydolatricas, lo qual auja casi en todas las costumbres que tenja la republica con que se regia, y por esta causa fue necesario desbaratarlo todo, y ponerlos en otra manera de policia, que no tuujesse njngun resabio de cosas de idolatria:

pero viendo agora que esta manera de policia cria gente muy viciosa de muy malas inclinaciones, y muy malas obras: las quales los haze a ellos odiosos a dios, y a los hōbres: y aun los causan grādes enfermedades, y breue ujda sera menester, poner remjdio y parecenos a todos que la principal causa desto; es la borrachera, que como ceso aquel rigor antiguo de castigar cō pena de muerte las borracheras; aunque agora se castiga, con açotarlos, trasqujlarlos, y venderlos por esclauos, por año, o por meses, no es suficiente castigo este para cesar de emborracharse, y aun tampoco las predicaciones, de los predicadores, muy frequentes contra este vicio, nj las amenāças del infierno bastan para refrenarlos: y sō estas borrache-

enough to restrain them. And these drunken feasts are so immoderate and injurious to the state and to the health and salvation of those who indulge in them that many deaths are caused by them. Being drunk they kill each other and abuse each other by deeds and by words; and great dissensions in the state are caused. And those who govern it dishonor and defame themselves and commit great faults in their work, and [Spaniards] judge them to be unworthy of [their works]. And, further, because of this vice, they are considered unworthy and unfit for the priesthood, as well, also, because they, especially the drunkards, are incapable of maintaining the continence or chastity necessary to priests.

In the beginning a trial was made of making religious of them, for it seemed to us then that they would be capable in ecclesiastical matters and for the religious life. And so the habit of Saint Francis was given two Indian youths, the most able and unworldly there were at that time, who preached with great fervor on matters of our Catholic Faith to their [fellow] natives. And it appeared to us that if they, clothed in our habit and adorned with the virtues of our holy Franciscan Order, should preach with that fervor with which they were preaching, they would reap the greatest harvest of souls. But when they possessed the habit and made use of it in the affairs of this holy Order, it was discovered through experience that they were not equal to such a calling. And so [the friars] deprived them of their habits and never since has the Indian been received in the Order, nor are they even considered capable of the priesthood.

At this time, as even the religious did not know the language of these natives, they instructed as best they could those Indians who seemed capable and unworldly, that they might preach to the people in the presence of the religious. But after the religious knew the language and began to preach, they relieved [the Indians] of the preaching because of the faults they discovered in them, in appearing decent and unworldly in the presence of the religious [though] not being so — a thing they knew very well how to do.

And I do not wonder so much at the faults and absurdities of the natives of this land, because the Spaniards who dwell in it and, much more, those born in it, acquire these evil tendencies. Those who are born in it, much like the Indians, resemble the

ras, tan destempladas, y perjudiciales, a la republica, y a la salud, y saluacion, de los que las exercitã que por ellas se causan muchas muertes, que se matan los vnos a los otros, estando borrachos, y se maltratan de obras, y de palabras, y se causan grandes disensiones en la republica: y los que la rigẽ se deshonrran, y se amẽguã y hazen grandes faltas en sus officios, y los juzgan por indignos dellos; y aun por este vicio son tenjdos por indignos, y inabiles, para el sacerdocio, y tãbien porque la continencia, o castidad, que es necesaria a los sacerdotes, no son abiles para guardarla, en especial los borrachos.

A los principios se hizo experiencia de hazerlos religiosos, porque nos parecia entonce, que serian abiles para las cosas eclesiasticas, y para la vida religiosa: y ansi se dio el abito de sanct francisco a dos mancebos indios los mas abiles, y recogidos, que entonce auja, y que predicauã con gran feruor las cosas de nr̃a fee catholica a sus naturales. y parecionos, que si aquellos vestidos de nuestro abito, y adornados con las virtudes de nr̃a sancta religion franciscana, predicassen con aquel feruor, que predicauan; harian grandissimo fruto, en las anjmas: y como tuujessẽ el abito, y los exercitasen en las cosas desta sancta religion: hallose por experiencia, que no eran suficientes para tal estado: y ansi les quitaron los abitos, y nunca mas se a recibido indio a la religion: nj aun se tienen por abiles para el sacerdocio.

En este tiempo como aun los religiosos, no sabian la lengua destos naturales, como mejor podian, instruyan a los indios, que parecĩa abiles, y recogidos para que ellos predicassen, delante de los religiosos, al pueblo: pero despues que los religiosos supieron la lengua y comẽçaron a predicar qujtarõlos de la predicacion, por bajos que hallaron en ellos, en mostrarse, en presencia de los religiosos honestos, y recogidos, no siendo tales, cosa que ellos saben muy bien hazer.

Y no me maraujllo tanto de las tachas, y dislates, de los naturales desta tierra: porque los españoles, que in ella abitan, y mucho mas, los que en ella nacen, cobran estas malas inclinaciones; los que en ella nacẽ muy al propio de los indios, en el aspectu

Spaniards in appearance, but in character are otherwise. Those who are native Spaniards, if they are not very careful, become different a few years after reaching this land, and I think the clime or climates of this land bring [the difference] about.

But it is to our great disgrace that the native Indians, prudent and wise old men, knew how to remedy the harm this land impresses on those who dwell in it, hindering the natural conditions with opposing practices. And we drift with our evil tendencies. And certainly a people, Spanish as well as Indian, is reared which is unbearable to control and very difficult to save. Neither the fathers nor the mothers can control their sons and daughters to free them from the vices and lewdnesses which this land breeds.

The ancient inhabitants of this land showed good judgment rearing their sons and daughters through the efforts of the state and not letting their parents rear them. And, if this manner of administration had not been so corrupted by idolatrous rites and superstitions, it seems to me it was very good. And if, cleansed of all idolatry which it possessed and made completely Christian, it were introduced in this Indian and Spanish state, it would be the means of freeing the one state as well as the other of great ills and the rulers of great hardships.

Now we too cannot cope with those who are reared in the schools, for they do not have the fear and submission which they had in times past. We rear them with neither the rigor nor the austerity with which they were reared in the time of their idolatry. They do not control themselves, nor school themselves, nor abide by what [the friars] teach them as [they would] if they had been under the past system of the elders of old.

At the beginning, because we discovered that in their ancient state they reared the boys and girls in the temples and there disciplined them and taught them the adoration of their gods and submission to their state, we adopted that manner of rearing the boys in our houses. And they slept in the house which was built for them next to ours, where we taught them to arise at midnight. And we taught them to repeat the matins of our Lady and then in the morning the prayer book. And, furthermore, we taught them to flagellate themselves by night and to hold silent prayers. But, since they engaged in no physical labors, as used to be customary and as the

parecen españoles, y en las condiciones no los son: los que son naturales, españoles, si no tienen mucho aujso, a pocos años andados, de su llegada a esta tierra, se hazen otros. y esto pienso que lo haze el clima, o consdelaciones desta tierra:

pero es gran verguença nuestra; que los indios naturales cuerdos, y sabios antiguos: supieron dar remedio a los daños, que esta tierra imprime, en los que en ella biuen: oviando a las cosas naturales, con contrarios exercicios; y nosotros nos vamos el agua abaxo de nuestras malas inclinaciones, y cierto se cria vna gente ansi española, como india, que es intolerable de regir, y pesadissima de saluar: los padres, nj las madres, no se pueden apoderar cõ sus hijos, y hijas, para apartarlos de los vicios, y sensualidades y que esta tierra cria:

buẽ tino tuujeron los abitadores desta tierra antiguos en que criauan sus hijos, y hijas con la potencia de la republica y no los dexauan criar a sus padres: y si aquella manera de regir, no estuujera tan inficionada, con ritos, y suprsticiones ydolatricas. pareceme que era muy buena, y si limpiada de todo lo idolatrico que tenja, y haziendola del todo xp̃iana, se introduxesse en esta republica indiana, y española: cierto seria gran bien, y seria causa de librar ansi a la vna republica, como a la otra de grandes males, y de grandes trabajos, a los que las rigen.

Ia tampoco nosotros, no nos podemos apoderar con los que se crian en las escuelas: porque como no tiene aquel temor, y subjection que antiguamẽte tenjan: nj los criamos, cõ aquel rigor, nj austeridad, que se criauan en tiempo de su idolatria, no se subjectan, nj se enseñan, nj toman lo que les enseñan, como si estuujeran en aquella imprensa pasada de los viejos antiguos.

A los principios, como hallamos que en su republica antigua criauã los muchachos, y las muchachas en los templos, y alli los disciplinauã y enseñauã la cultura de sus dioses, y la subjection a su republica: tomamos aquel estilo, de criar los muchachos, en nuestras casas, y dormjan en la casa que para ellos estaua edificada, junto a la nuestra donde los enseñauamos a leuantarse a la media noche: y los enseñauamos a dezir los maytines de nuestra señora: y luego de mañana las horas: y aun les enseñauamos a que de noche se açotassen, y tuujessẽ oracion mental. Pero como no se exercitauan en los trabajos corporales, como solian, y como demanda la condicion

state of their active sensuality requires, [and since] also they ate better than they were accustomed to in their ancient state, for we treated them with the tenderness and mercy usual among ourselves, they began to feel a strong sensuality and to practice lascivious things. And so we expelled them from our dwellings, that they go to sleep in the dwellings of their parents and come of a morning to the schools to learn to read and write and sing. And this is what we still do now.

But since these practices have slowly slackened with them, there is hardly anyone who has the pride and energy to teach these things of his own volition, if we ourselves do not attend to them. There is no one in the schools of our dwellings who correctly teaches reading and writing and singing nor the other musical things. Almost everything declines.

Since, in the time of idolatry, there were convents for the women who served in the temples and maintained chastity, trials were also made to see if they were capable of being nuns and sisters of the Christian religion and of maintaining constant chastity. And to this end convents and sisterhoods of women were created. And they were instructed in spiritual matters. And many of them knew how to read and write. And those who seemed to us to be well instructed in the Faith, and those who were matrons of good judgment, we made Mother Superiors of the others that they might direct them and teach them Christian matters and all good practices.

And certainly, at the beginning, we were of the opinion that the men would be capable as priests and monks, and the women as nuns and sisters. But our opinion deceived us. From experience, we learned that, at the time, they were not capable of such perfection. And so the sisterhoods and convents, which we had planned in the beginning, ceased. Nor do we see even now indications that this can be brought about.

Also, at the beginning, a measure was undertaken in some villages of this New Spain where the religious reside, such as Cholula, Huexotzinco, etc., that [the religious] settled those who married apart, by the monasteries. And there they lived; from there they all came every day to the monastery for mass. And [the religious] preached Christianity and the ways of marital cohabitation to them. And this was a very good way to free them of the infection of idolatry and other evil practices which they could

de su briosa sensualidad. tambien comjan mejor, de lo que acostumbrauan en su republica antigua: porque exercitauamos con ellos la blandura, y piedad, que entre nosotros se usa: comēçaron a tener brios sensuales y a entender, en cosas de lacivia: y ansi los echamos de nr̄as casas, para que se fuessen a dormjr a las casas de sus padres, y venjā a la mañana a las escuelas a deprēder a leer, y a escreujr, y a cantar: y esto es lo que aun agora se vsa.

pero como se an venjdo relaxando de poco, en poco estos exercicios y entre ellos, casi no ay qujen tenga orgullo, y industria, para por si enseñar estas cosas: si nosotros mjsmos, no entendemos en ellas, no ay, ya en las escuelas de nuestras casas, qujen a derechas enseñe a leer, y a escreujr, y a cantar, nj a las otras cosas de musica, casi todo se va cayendo.

Tambien se hizo esperiencia en las mugeres para ver si como en el tiempo de la idolatria auja monasterios dellas, que serujan en los templos, y guardauan castidad serian abiles, para ser monjas y religiosas, de la religion christiana, y guardar perpetua castidad, y a este proposito se hizieron monasterios, y congregaciones de mugeres: y fueron instruidas en las cosas espirituales, y muchas dellas supieron leer, y escreujr, y las que nos parecian que estauā bien instruidas en la fe, y eran matronas de buen juyzio; las hizimos perladas de las otras, para que las regiessen, y enseñassen, en las cosas de la Christiandad, y de todas buenas costumbres.

I cierto a los principios tuujmos opinjon que ellos serian abiles, para sacerdotes, y para religiosos: y ellas para monjas, y religiosas. Pero engañonos nuestra opinjon: por experiencia; entendimos, que por entonce no erā capaces, de tanta perfeccion: y ansi ceso, la congregacion y monasterios, que a los principios intentauamos; nj aun agora vemos indicios, que este negocio se pueda effectuar.

Hizose tambien a los principios, vna diligencia en algunos pueblos desta nueua españa: dōde residen los religiosos, como fue en chulola, y en vexocinco, etc. que los que se casauan, los poblaron por si, junto a los monasterios, y alli morauan: y de alli venjā todos a mjsa cada dia al monasterio, y los predicauan el christianjsmo, y el modo de la quoabitacion matrimonjal, y eran muy buen medio este, para sacarlos, de la inffection de la idolatria, y otras malas costumbres, que se les podia apegar de la conuersa-

contract through association with their parents. However, it endured little because they gave most of the religious to understand that all idolatry, with all its ceremonies and rituals, was already so forgotten and abhorred that there was no reason to have this caution, since all were baptized and servants of the true God. And this was very false, as since then we have witnessed very clearly. Not even now do there cease to be many dregs of idolatry and drunkenness and many evil practices, which would have been considerably avoided if that procedure had continued as it began, and if it were everywhere as it was in a few places, and if it had persisted until today. Now it is almost hopeless to correct.

Great were the labors and perplexities we had in the beginning in marrying those who were baptized and who had many women, so as to give them those whom the law requires them to take; for in investigating the relationships and knowing which was the first, in order to give her to him, we found ourselves in a labyrinth of great difficulty, for they lied in saying which was the first, and they committed fraud in order to marry those for whom they had greater affection. And, to know with whom they had performed the ceremony which they practiced when they took a legitimate wife, it was necessary to review and understand many idolatrous ceremonies and rituals of the time of their unbelief. And as we knew little of the language, hardly ever did we gain the insight as we have now learned it.

Regarding the other Sacraments such as confession and communion, there has been so much difficulty in placing them on their right course that even now there are very few who proceed the correct way to receive these Sacraments, which brings us much weariness and much awareness of the little they have availed themselves of Christianity.

At the beginning the boys we reared in the school, as well as those taught in the courtyard, helped us considerably, for, as [they] were wont to do in olden times, we reared the sons of the noblemen in our schools. There we taught them to read and write and sing. And we taught Christian doctrine to the sons of the commoners in the courtyard. A great number of them assembled and after they had been taught a short time one or two friars went with them, and they ascended a pyramid-temple and demolished it in a few days; and thus in a short time they demolished all the pyramid-temples so that no vestige of

cion de sus padres: pero duro poco. Porque ellos hizierõ entender a los mas de los religiosos, que toda la idolatria, con todas sus cerimonjas, y ritus, estaua ya tan olujdada, y abomjnada, que no auja para que tener este recatamjento: pues que todos eran baptizados, y sieruos del verdadero dios, y esto fue falsissimo, como despues aca lo hemos visto muy claro, que nj aun agora cesa de auer muchas hezes de idolatria, y de borracheria, y de muchas malas costũbres: lo qual se vujera mucho remediado, si aquel negocio fuera adelante, como se començo y como fue en pocas partes, fuera en todas, y perseuerara hasta agora, ya casi esta imposibilitado de remediarse.

fueron grãdes los trabajos, y perplexidades que tuujmos a los principios, para casar a los baptizados; y que tenjã muchas mugeres, para darles aquellas, que el derecho manda que tomen, porque para examjnar los parentescos, y saber qual fue la primera, para darsela: nos vimos en vn laberinto de gran difficultad, porque ellos mentian en dezir qual fuesse la primera, y hazian embustes para casarse con aquellas que ellos tenjan mas affection y para saber con qual avian hecho la cerimonja, que vsauã quando tomavan muger legitima: fue necesario reboluer, y saber muchas cerimonjas, y ritus idolatricos de su infidelidad, y como sabiamos poca lengua, casi nunca bien caymos en la cuenta, como agora lo auemos entendido.

Cerca de los otros sacramentos, como fue el de la confession, y comunjon ha avido tanta dificultad, en ponerlos en el camjno derecho dellos, que aun agora ay muy pocos, que vayan via recta a recibir estos sacramẽtos, lo qual nos da gran fatiga, y mucho conocimjento de lo poco que han aprouechado en el christianjsmo.

A los principios ayudaronnos grandemente los muchos [sic], assi los que criauamos en la escuela, como los que se enseñauan en el patio: porque como al tono de lo antiguo, criauamos los hijos de los principales, dentro de nuestras escuelas: alli los ensenauamos a leer, y a escreujr, y cantar: y a los hijos de los plebejos, enseñauamoslos, en el patio, la doctrina christiana: juntauanse gran copia dellos, y despues de auerse, enseñado vn rato, yba vn frayle con ellos, o dos: y subianse en vn cu, y derrocauanlo en pocos dias: y ansi se derrocaron en poco tiempo, todos los cues que no quedo señal dellos, y otros edi-

them remained. And [they demolished] other buildings dedicated to the cult of the idols.

These boys were very useful in this task. Those from within the house helped much more in uprooting the idolatrous rituals which were held at night, and the orgies and celebrations which they secretly performed at night in honor of the idols, for these boys, by day, spied out where something of this sort was to be performed at night. And at night, at the suitable hour, sixty or a hundred of these who had been brought up in the house went with one or two friars and secretly fell upon those who held some affair as mentioned above, idolatry, orgy or feast. And they seized all of them, bound them and led them to the monastery, where they punished them, [made them] do penance, and taught them the Christian doctrine. And they made them go to matins at midnight and discipline themselves — and this for some weeks until they were finally repentant of what they had done and of a mind to do it no more. And so they came forth therefrom instructed in the Christian doctrine and punished, and the others learned a lesson from them and dared not do anything similar. And if they did it, then they were entrapped and punished as is said.

The fear which the common people felt of these boys who were reared with us, was so great that, after a few days, it was not necessary to go with them, nor to send many of them when some feast or orgy took place at night. For if we sent ten or twenty of them, they seized and bound all those of the feast or orgy, even though there might be a hundred or two hundred. And they led them to the monastery to do penance. And in this way idolatrous practices were destroyed so that no one publicly, nor even in any conceivable manner, dared to do anything which would be idolatrous or an orgy or a feast. And when they wished to undertake some feast for their temporal pleasure or entertain their relatives and friends, they did it with the consent of the religious, assuring them first that there would be nothing of idolatry, nor other offense to God in the affair.

Since then, that solicitude which the religious had in the matters just mentioned has ceased, because nothing which was worthy of punishment appeared publicly. And [the natives] lost the fear they had at the beginning because also those reared in the [convent] ceased to sleep and eat within the [convent]

ficios de los idolos dedicados a su serujcio.

Estos muchachos serujeron mucho en este officio: los de dentro de casa ayudarõ mucho mas, para destirpar los ritus idolatricos, que de noche se hazian, y las borracheras, y areytos, que secretamente, y de noche hazian, a honrra de los idolos: porque de dia estos espiauan, a donde se auja de hazer algo desto de noche, y de noche a la hora convenjente, yvan con vn frayle, o con dos sesenta, o ciento destos criados de casa, y dauan secretamẽte sobre los que haziã alguna cosa de las arriba dichas ydolatria, borrachera o fiesta: y prendianlos a todos: y atauanlos, y lleuauanlos al monesterio, donde los castigauan, y hazian penjtencia, y los enseñauan la doctrina christiana, y los hazian yr a maitines a la media noche, y se açotauan: y esto por algunas semanas, hasta aquellos estauan ya arrepentidos, de lo que aujan hecho, y con proposito, de no lo hazer mas: y assi salian de alli catetizados, y castigados: y dellos tomauan exemplo los otros: y no osauã hazer semejante cosa, y si la hazian luego cayan en el lazo: y eran castigados como dicho es.

Fue tan grãde el temor, que toda la gente popular cobro destos muchachos, que con nosotros se criauan, que despues de pocos dias, no era menester yr con ellos, nj embiar muchos, quãdo se hazia alguna fiesta, o borrachera de noche, que embiando diez, o veinte dellos, prendian, y atauan todos los de la fiesta, o borrachera: aunque fuessen ciento, o dos cientos, y los trayan al monasterio, para hazer penjtencia. Y desta manera se destruyeron las cosas de la idolatria, que nadie en publico: nj de manera que se pudiesse saber, vsaua hazer nada, que fuesse de cosas de idolatria, o de borracheria o fiesta: y quando ellos querian hazer alguna fiesta, para su regocijo temporal, o combidar a sus parientes, y amjgos, haziãlo con licencia de los religiosos, protestando primero, que njnguna cosa de idolatria, nj de otra offensa de dios auja de auer en el negocio.

Despues aca, ceso aquella solicitud, q̃ los religiosos tenjan en las cosas ya dichas: porque publicamẽte no parecia cosa ninguna que fuesse digna de castigo: y ellos perdieron el temor, que a los principios tenjan, porque tãbien los que se criauan en casa, dexarõ de dormjr, y comer, dentro de casa: y duermen, y

and [now] sleep and eat in the houses of their parents. And, although they see and know of some idolatrous matters or orgies, they dare not mention them. And also the religious are forbidden to imprison or punish anyone in their houses for any infraction.

In this way they [now] sing when they wish and become drunk when they wish and celebrate their feasts as they wish and sing the ancient songs they were wont to sing in the days of their idolatry — not all of them but many of them. And no one understands what they say as their songs are very obscure. And if, after their conversion here, they sing some songs they have composed, which deal with the things of God and His saints, they are surrounded by many errors and heresies. And even in the dances and celebrations many of their ancient superstitions and idolatrous rituals are practiced, especially where no one resides who understands them. This happens most frequently among the merchants when they hold their feasts, entertainments, and banquets.

This continues; every day it grows worse. And there is no one who strives to remedy it because it is not understood, except by a few, and they do not dare tell. Matters of drunkenness grow worse every day, and the punishments which are meted out are not such as to remedy the situation but rather such as to worsen it.

It is quite true that because some of the boys, who were reared in our houses at the beginning, told us of the idolatrous things their parents did, having been baptized, and because we punished them therefor, their parents killed them and others punished [their boys] severely. And even now when, having learned that things happen worthy of reproach and punishment, we criticize these things from the pulpits, they begin to seek out those who do these things, to discover who it was who informed of that which was criticized from the pulpit. And they almost always discover the person. And they punish [informers] evilly, deceitfully, and slyly, keeping after them in their private tasks, and inflicting other vexations on them which the sufferers neither can complain of nor are able to remedy. They complain to us secretly and, having entreated us not to say anything of what they tell us lest they suffer greater injuries, we thus must be silent and commend the matters to God that He may solve them.

comẽ en casa de sus padres: y aunque veen, y saben algunas cosas idolatricas, o de borracherias, no las osan dezir. y tambien se a prohibido, a los religiosos, que a njnguno encierren, nj castiguen en sus casas por njngun delicto.

Desta manera ellos canctan [*sic*] quando qujeren, y se emborrachan, quando qujeren, y hazẽ sus fiestas como qujeren, y cãtan los cantares antiguos, que vsauan en el tiempo, de su idolatria, no todos, sino muchos: y nadie entiende lo que dizen, por ser sus cantares muy cerrados. Y si algunos cantares vsan, que ellos han hecho, despues aca de su conuertimjento, en que se trata de las cosas de dios, y de sus sanctos; van enbueltos cõ muchos errores, y heregias: y aun en los bayles, y areitos se hazen muchas cosas, de sus supersticiones antiguas, y ritus ydolatricos: especialmente donde no reside qujen los entiende; y entre los mercaderes mas comunmente pasa esto, quando hazen sus fiestas, combites, y banquetes.

Esto va adelante, cada dia se empeora, y no ay qujẽ procure de lo remediar: porque no se entiende, sino de pocos, y ellos no lo osan dezir las cosas de la borracheria, cada dia se empeoran, y los castigos, que se hazen no son de manera, que el negocio se remedie, mas antes, de manera que se empeora.

Bien es verdad, que algunos de los muchachos, que se criauã en nuestras casas a los principios, porque nos dezian las cosas, que sus padres haziã de idolatria, siendo baptizados: y por ello los castigauamos, los mataron sus padres, y otros los castigauã reciamente: y aun agora, quãdo aviendo sabido, que pasan algunas cosas dignas de reprehension, y de castigo: y las reprehendemos, en los pulpitos: comjençan a rrastrear, los que las hazen, para saber qujen fue, el que dio noticia de aquello, que se reprehendio en el pulpito, y casi siempre caen con la persona, y los castigan malamente, con solapacion, y disimulaciõ cargandoles la mano, en los servicios personales, y haziendoles otras vexaciones de que los pacientes, nj se pueden quexar, nj se saben remediar, quexansenos en secreto, y cõ auernos se conjurado, que njnguna cosa digamos, de lo que nos dizen, por no padecer maiores agraujos: ansi tenemos necesidad de callar, y encomẽdar a dios los negocios, para que el, los remedie.

In the implanting of the Faith in these parts we have received and still receive great help and much light from those we have taught the Latin language. This people did not have letters nor any characters. They could neither read nor write. They communicated with one another by means of representations and paintings. And all their ancient customs and books they had about them were painted with figures and representations in such a way that they knew and had records of the things their ancestors had done and had left in their annals more than a thousand years ago, before the Spaniards had come to this land. Most of these books and writings were burned when the other idolatrous things were destroyed. But many remained hidden, for we have seen them. And, even now, they are kept; through them we have understood their ancient customs.

After we came to this land to implant the Faith, we assembled the boys in our houses as is said. And we began to teach them to read, write, and sing. And, as they did well in this, we then endeavored to put them to the study of grammar. For this training, a college was formed in the city of Mexico, in the Santiago de Tlatilulco section, in which [college] were selected from all the neighboring villages and from all the provinces the most capable boys, best able to read and write. They slept and ate in the same college, not leaving except on rare occasions.

The Spaniards, and the other religious who knew this, laughed much and made fun, taking it very much for granted that no one would have such ability as to succeed in teaching grammar to so incapable a people. But on our working with them for two or three years, they came to understand all the subjects of the grammar book and to speak Latin, and understand it, and to write Latin, and even to compose hexametric verses.

When the Spanish laity and clergy saw this from experience they marveled much that that could be done. I was the one who worked with them the first four years and gave them understanding in all subjects of the Latin language. The laity as well as the clergy, when they saw that this progressed and that [the boys] had even greater capabilities, therefore began to oppose this activity and to raise many objections against it to prevent it. Because I was a witness to all these things, for I lectured to the Indians of the college on [Latin] grammar, I can

hemos recebido, y aun recebimos, en la plantacion de la fe, en estas partes grande ayuda, y mucha lumbre, de aquellos, a qujen hemos enseñado la lengua latina. Esta gente no tenja letras, nj caracteres algunos, nj sabian leer, nj escreujr, comunjcauãse por imagines, y pinturas, y todas las antiguallas suyas, y libros que tenjan dellas, estauan pintados, con figuras, y imagines: de tal manera que sabian, y tenjan memorias de las cosas, que sus antepassados, aujan hecho, y aujan dexado en sus anhales, por mas de mjll años atras, antes que vinjessen los españoles, a esta tierra. De estos libros, y escrituras los mas dellos se quemaron al tiempo que se destruyeron las otras idolatrias, pero no dexarõ de quedar muchas ascondidas que las hemos visto, y aun agora se guardan por donde hemos entendido sus antiguallas.

luego que venjmos a esta tierra a plantar la fe, juntamos los muchachos en nuestras casas como esta dicho, y los començamos a enseñar, a leer, y escreujr, y cantar, y como salieron bien con esto, procuramos luego de ponerlos, en el estudio de la grãmatica, para el qual exercicio, se hizo vn collegio, en la ciudad de Mexico, en la parte de santiago del tlatilulco: en el qual de todos los pueblos comarcanos, y de todas las proujncias se escogieron los muchachos mas abiles, y que major sabiã leer, y escreujr, los quales dormjan, y comjan en el mjsmo collegio, sin salir fuera, sino pocas vezes:

los españoles, y los otros religiosos, que supieron esto, reianse mucho, y hazian burla, tenjendo muy por aueriguado, que nadie seria poderoso, para poder enseñar gramatica, a gente tan inabil, pero trabajando con ellos, dos o tres años, vinjeron a entender todas las materias del arte de la gramatica, y a hablar latin, y a entenderlo, y a escreujr en latin, y aun a hazer uersus heruicus.

como vieron esto, por experiencia: los españoles seglares, y ecclesiasticos espantaronse mucho, como aquello, se pudo hazer. Yo fuy, el que los primeros quatro años, trabaje con ellos, y los puse en la intelligencia de todas las materias, de la latinidad: Como vieron, que esto yva adelante, y aun tenjã abilidad, para mas; començaron ansi los seglares, como los ecclesiasticos, a contradezir este negocio, y a poner muchas objecciones contra el para impidirle. Porque yo me halle presente en todas estas cosas porque leya la grãmatica, a los indios del collegio: podre dezir

accurately tell the objections they raised and the answers they were given.

They said that inasmuch as these were not to be priests, what would be the purpose of teaching them [Latin] grammar? It would place them in danger of becoming heretics. And also, seeing the Holy Writ, they would discover in it that the ancient patriarchs had many wives simultaneously, which is in accordance with what was their custom, and that they would not wish to believe what we now preach to them, that no one may have more than one wife when married *in facie ecclesiae.* They raised other objections of this sort. To these it was responded that, admitting that they were not to be priests, we wished to know how far their capabilities might be expanded. Knowing this from experience we could bear witness what was in them, and, in accordance with their capabilities, there would be done with them what would seem to be just, as nearly as possible.

To their saying that we gave them opportunity to become heretics, it was replied that there was no expectation of that; but rather the opposite [would happen]; that is that they would be better able to understand matters of the Faith, and, being subject to a Most Christian Prince, it was very easy to remedy it, should something of this sort appear. Regarding the wives, since the correction which our Redeemer made concerning what anciently was customary as to a man's having many wives is in the Gospel, they are to believe this — [the priests] preaching it as they ordinarily preach to them, and if they should be rebels in this, punishing them as heretics, since there is the authority of clerical and lay power to do it. They had many other controversies regarding this matter which would be tedious to place here.

This college has persisted for over forty years and its collegians have transgressed in nothing, neither against God, nor the Church, nor the king, nor against his state. Rather they have helped and still help in many things in the implanting and maintaining of our Holy Catholic Faith, for if sermons, *Apostillas* and catechisms have been produced in the Indian language, which can appear and may be free of all heresy, they are those which were written with them. And they, being knowledgeable in the Latin language, inform us to the properties of the words, the properties of their manner of speech. And they correct for us the incongruities we express in the

con verdad las objecciones, que ponjan, y las respuestas que se les dauan;

dezian, que pues estos no aujan de ser sacerdotes, de que seruja enseñarles, la grammatica, que era ponerlos en peligro, de que hereticassen. y tambien, que viendo la sagrada escritura, que entenderian en ella; como los patriarchas antiguos, tenjan juntamente muchas mugeres, que es conforme, a lo que ellos vsauan, y que no querriã creer, lo que agora, les predicamos, que no puede nadie tener mas q̃ vna muger casado con ella in facie ecclesie. otras objeccion desta calidad, ponjan, a las quales, se les respondia, que puesto caso que no vujessen, de ser sacerdotes, queriamos tener sabido, a quanto se estiende su abilidad; lo qual sabido por esperiencia, podriamos dar fe, de lo que en ellos ay: y que conforme a su abilidad se haria cõ ellos, lo que pareciesse ser justo, segun proximjdad.

A lo que dezian, que les dauamos ocasion de hereticar se respondia, que cõ no pretender aquello, sino lo contrario: conviene a saber, que pudiessen entender mejor las cosas de la fe, y con estar subjectos a principe christianjssimo, estaua muy en la mano; quando algo desto pareciesse remediarlo. A lo de las mugeres, como esta en el evangelio la correciõ que nuestro redemptor hizo, cerca de lo que antiguamẽte se vsaua, de que vn hombre, tenja muchas mugeres; son obligados a creerlo, predicandoselo, como ordinariamente, se les predica, y siendo en esto rebeldes castigarlos, como a hereges; pues ay, oportunjdad de poder ecclesiastico y seglar, para hazerlo. Muchas otras altercaciones se tuujeron cerca deste negocio: las quales seria cosa prolixa ponerlas aquj.

A ya mas de quarenta años que este collegio perseuera: y los collegiales del, en ninguna cosa han delinqujdo, nj contra dios, nj contra la yglesia, nj contra el rey, nj contra su republica: mas antes hã ayudado, y ayudan en muchas cosas a la plantacion, y sustẽtacion de nuestra sancta fe catholica. Porque si sermones y postillas, y doctrinas, se hã hecho en la lengua indiana, que puedan parecer, y sean limpios, de toda heregia, son los que con ellos, se han compuesto y ellos por ser entendidos en la lengua latina, nos dan a entender las propriedades de los vocablos, y las propriedades de su manera de hablar, y las incongruidades, que hablamos en los sermones, o

sermons or write in the catechisms. And whatever is to be rendered in their language, if it is not examined by them, if it is not written congruently in the Latin language, in Spanish, and in their language, cannot be free of defect. With regard to orthography, to good handwriting, there are none who write it other than those reared here.

The friars taught the collegians. And they were with them for more than ten years teaching them all the instructions and ways which were to be maintained in the college. And seeing that there were among them those who could lecture and who apparently were capable of governing the college, [the friars] drew up ordinances for them, and they elected among themselves a rector and counsellors that they might govern the college. [The friars] left them by themselves to lecture and to govern themselves for more than twenty years, during which time the entire administration and the good order of the college failed, in part on account of the majordomo who had charge of the college, who was a Spaniard, in part from the negligence and carelessness of the rector and the counsellors as well as from the carelessness of the friars who did not concern themselves with how things went until all collapsed.

Forty years after the founding of the college the condition of the affairs of the college was again examined and discovered to be in ruin. And it was necessary to refit it and make new ordinances superseding the first ones, so that the college might progress, as is apparent from the very ordinances which were newly made.

I, who was present at the foundation of said college, was also present at the reorganization thereof, which was more difficult than the actual founding. The plague which occurred thirty-one years ago gave the college a great blow, and this plague, of this year of 1576, has not given it a lesser one, for there is hardly anyone still in the college. Dead and sick, almost all are gone.

I have great misgivings that this is to be completely ruined, both because they are difficult to govern and are ill-disposed to learn and because the friars tire of expending the effort they require to carry them ahead; again because I see that neither among the laity nor the clergy is there anyone who would favor them, not even with a *tomín*. If Don Antonio de Mendoza, may he be in glory, who was Viceroy of this New Spain, had not provided them

escreujmos en las doctrinas, ellos nos las emjendan y qualqujera cosa que se a de conuertir en su lengua, si no va con ellos examjnada no puede yr sin defecto, [sin] escriujr congruamente en la lengua latina, nj en romãce, nj en su lengua, para lo que toca a la orthographia, y buena letra: no ay qujen lo escriua, sino los que aquj se crian.

Enseñaron los frayles a los collegiales, y estuujeron cõ ellos mas de diez años, enseñandolos toda la disciplina, y costũbres, que en el collegio se aujã de guardar. I ya que avia entre ellos qujẽ leyesse, y qujen al parecer fuessen abiles para regir el collegio: hizieronles sus ordenaciones, y elegieronse rector, y consiliarios, para que regiessen el collegio: y dexaronlos que leyessen, y se regiessen ellos a su solas, por mas de viente años. En el qual tiempo, se cayo todo el regimiento, y buen concierto del collegio: parte por el mayordomo, que tenja cargo del collegio, que era español: parte por la negligencia, y descuydo del rector, y consiliarios: tambien por descuydo de los frayles, que no curauã de mjrar, como yvan las cosas, hasta que todo dio en tierra.

quarenta años, despues de la fũdacion del collegio, tornose a examjnar el estado, en que estauan las cosas del collegio: y hallose estar perdido, y fue necessario dar otro corte y hacer otras ordenaciones de nueuo, sobre las primeras, para que el collegio fuesse adelante, como parece por las mjsmas ordenaciones, que se hizieron de nuevo:

yo que me halle, en la fũdacion del dicho collegio, me halle tambien en la reformacion del, la qual fue mas dificultuosa, que la mjsma fundacion la pestilencia que vuo agora ha treinta y vn años, dio gran bacque al collegio y no le ha dado menor esta pestilencia deste año de mjll, y qujnjentos y setenta y seys, que casi no esta ya nadie en el collegio muertos, y enfermos, casi todos son salidos.

Recelo tengo, muy grande que esto, se ha de perder del todo: lo vno porque ellos son pesados de regir, y mal inclinados a deprender: lo otro porq̃ los frayles, se cansan de poner con ellos, el trabajo de que tienẽ necesidad, para lleuarlos adelante. lo otro porque veo que nj entre los seglares, nj entre los ecclesiasticos, no ay nadie, qujen los fauorezca, nj con solo vn tomjn: si el señor don Antonio de mẽdoça, que en gloria sea, Visorrey, que fue desta

from his estate with the little income which they had, with which a few barely supported themselves, there would now be the memory of neither college nor collegian. It could have provided great good to this entire Indian state, and the king, our lord, would have more subjects than he has or will have in it; for they decrease constantly. And the cause [of the decline], which I have personally witnessed, is that in the plague of thirty[-one] years ago, most of those who died, died because there was no one who knew how to let blood, nor to administer the medicines as required. And [they died] of hunger. And in this present plague the same thing is happening. And in all those which will occur it will be the same until [the natives] are all gone.

And if there had been the care and foresight through which these Indians had been instructed in grammar, logic, moral philosophy and medicine, they could have aided many of those who died, because in this city of Mexico we witness with our own eyes that those whom they visit to bleed and to purge, as is proper, in time recover, and the rest die. And since the Spanish doctors and bloodletters who know how to do these things are few, they help few. And already the bloodletters and doctors are almost exhausted, sick, and dead. And now there is no one who can or will visit and help the poor Indians. And so they die, having neither remedy nor aid.

nueua españa: no los vujera proueido de su hazienda, de vna poca de rentezilla que tienen, con que se sustentan pocos, y mal: ya no vujera memoria de collegio, ni de collegial, y podierase, auer hecho gran bien a toda esta republica indiana, y el Rey nuestro Señor, tuujera mas vasallos en ella, de los que tiene, y tendra: porque siempre van en dimjnucion. y la causa que yo he visto con mjs ojos es. que en la pestilencia de agora ha treinta años, por no auer qujen supiesse sangrar, nj admjnjstrar las medecinas, como conviene, murieron los mas que murieron, y de hambre, y en esta pestilencia presente acontece lo mjsmo: y en todas las que se offrecierẽ, sera lo mjsmo, hasta que se acaben.

y si si vujera tenjdo atenciõ y aduertencia, a que estos indios vujeran sido instruydos en la grãmatica, logica, y philosophia natural, y medicina, pudieran auer socorrido muchos, de los que hã muerto: porque en esta ciudad de Mexico, vemos por nuestros ojos, que aquellos que acuden a sangrarlos, y purgarlos, como conviene, y con tiempo sanan, y los demas mueren: y como los medicos, y sãgradores españoles, que los saben hazer, son pocos, socorrẽ a pocos. I ya casi estan cansados, y enfermos, y muertos los sangradores, y medicos: y no ay ya, qujen pueda, nj qujera acudir, y ayudar a los indios pobres: y ansi se mueren por no tener remedio, nj socorro./.

# Book XI: Earthly Things

## PROLOGUE

In order to give examples and make comparisons, in the preaching of the gospel, a knowledge of the things of nature is certainly not the least noble jewel in the coffer. We see the Redeemer as having used it. And the more familiar these examples and comparisons are to the hearers, the most used are the words and the language, the more effective and beneficial they will be. To this end, with much labor and work, this volume, a compendium, was made. In it, recorded in the Mexican language, are the better known and most utilized animals, birds, fish, trees, herbs, flowers, and fruits which exist in all this land — their characteristic properties and traits, exterior and interior. In it there is a great abundance of words and many current expressions, very correct and very common, very pleasing material. This work will also be timely to inform the natives of the meaning of created things, that they not attribute divinity to them, because whatsoever creature they see as being eminent in good or in evil they called *teotl*, which means god. So, they called the sun *teotl* because of its beauty; likewise the ocean because of its grandeur, its fury; and also they called many of the animals by this name because of their frightening aspect and ferocity. From this it is inferred that this name, *teotl*, is taken as good and as evil. And this is much better recognized when [the term] is in a compound: as in this name *teopiltzintli*, a very handsome child; *teopiltontli*, a very mischievous or bad boy. Many other words are compounded in this same manner, from the meaning of which it can be conjectured that this word *teotl* means a thing consummate in good or in evil. And so the present volume can be held or esteemed as a compendium of the idioms and words of this Mexican language and a

## PROLOGO

No cierto es, la menos noble joia: de la recamara, de la predicacion euangelica: el conocimjento, de las cosas naturales: para poner exemplos, i comparationes. Como vemos, el redemptor, auerlo vsado: i estos exemplos, i comparationes: quanto mas famjliares fuerẽ, a los oientes i por palabras, i lenguage mas vsadas, entrellos, dichas: tanto serã mas efficazes: i prouechosas. A este proposito se hizo, ia tesoro: en harta costa, i trabaxo: este volumen en que estã escriptas en lengua mexicana: las propiedades i maneras exteriores, i interiores que se pudieron alcançar: de los anjmales, aues, i peces: arboles, i ieruas, flores, i frutos mas conocidos: i vsados, que ai en toda esta tierra: donde ai, gran copia de vocablos: i mucho lenguage: muy propio, i mui comũ: i materia mui gustosa. Sera tambien esta obra mui oportuna, para darlos a entender, el ualor de las criaturas: para que no las atribuiã, diujnjdad: porque a qualqujera criatura, que vian ser imjnente: embiẽ o en mal, la llamauan Teutl qujere dezir dios: de manera que al sol, le llamauan teutl: por su lindeza: al mar, tãbiẽ por su grandeza, i ferocidad: i tambien a muchos de los anjmales los llamauã por este nombre: por razõ de su espantable disposition, i braueza. Donde se infiere, que este nombre teutl, se toma, en buena, i en mala parte. I mucho mas se conoce esto, quãdo esta en compositiõ: como en este nombre, teûpiltzintli, njño muj lindo: teuhpiltontli, muchacho muj traujeso, o malo. Otros muchos vocablos, se cõponen desta mjsma manera: de la signjficacion de los quales, se puede conjecturar: que este vocablo, teutl, quiere dezir: cosa estremada en biẽ o en mal. Ansi que, el presente volumẽ, se podra tener, o estimar como vn tesoro, de lenguage i vocablos desta lengua mexicana: i vna recamara, muy rica de las

very rich storehouse of the things which are in this land.

## TO THE SINCERE READER

Friend reader, thou hast in the present volume a forest with a great diversity of mountains, woodlands and cliffs, where thou wilt find all kinds of native trees, wild beasts, and serpents, as many as thou mayest wish for. Thou hast a garden stocked with fruit-bearing trees, with all kinds of herbs, where there are all manner of springs and rivers. It is full of birds, animals, and fish of all kinds. Thou hast a luxuriant woodland filled with all varieties of flowers, those that blossom on the trees, shrubs, and bushes as well as those that blossom on the herbs. In it are birds of pleasing song and rich plumage. There are also exquisite, well-kept parks. Thou hast a diversity of roads and buildings. Likewise, thou hast fields and plains where there are all kinds of food. It is where there are pools and lagoons, where canes, reeds, and rushes grow, and diverse kinds of little animals live, aquatic and terrestrial. It is where there are mines for all kinds of metals and all kinds of precious stones and many other things beneficial to mankind. It is where there are many kinds of lands, rocks, waters, and mountains.

The work follows not the order placed above, but rather the following order:

The first chapter deals with the animals; it contains seven paragraphs. The second deals with the birds; it contains ten paragraphs. The third chapter deals with the aquatic animals, like the fish and other animals that live in the water; it contains five paragraphs. The fourth deals with the wild animals that live in the water; it contains four paragraphs. The fifth deals with serpents and other poisonous animals of the land; it contains fourteen paragraphs. The sixth chapter deals with the trees; it contains nine paragraphs. The seventh chapter deals with the herbs; it contains twelve paragraphs. The eighth chapter deals with precious stones; it contains five paragraphs. Chapter nine, of metals. Chapter ten, of other minerals. Chapter eleven, of the colors; it contains three paragraphs. Chapter twelve, of the diverse waters; it contains ten paragraphs. Chapter thirteen, of maize and the other edible vegetables; it contains six paragraphs.

The door remains open to add that which may seem proper.

cosas que ai en esta tierra.

## AL SINCERO LECTOR.

Tienes, amjgo lector, en el presente volumen: vn bosque con grã diuersidad de mõtañas, mõtes, i riscos: donde hallaras, arboles siluestres, de todo genero: i bestias fieras, i serpientes quantas demandares: tienes vn jardin poblado, de todos arboles fructiferos: i de todas maneras de ieruas: donde ai fuentes, i rios de diuersas maneras. Esta lleno de aues, anjmales, i peces de todo genero: tienes vna floresta, muj deleitosa, llena de todo genero de flores: ansi de las que se hazẽ en los arboles, arbustos, i matas: como de las que se hazen en ieruas: en ella ai aues, de dulces cantos: i de ricas plumas: ai tambien florestas edificadas, a las mjl maraujllas: tienes diuersidades de camjnos i edificios: tienes ansi mjsmo campos, i llanuras, donde ai toda manera de mantenjmjentos: donde ai charcos, i lagunas: donde se crian cañas, espadañas i juncos: i diuersas maneras de anjmalejos, aquatiles i terrestres. Donde ai mjnas, de todas maneras de metales: i todas maneras de piedras preciosas: i de otras muchas cosas prouechosas, a la vida humana. Donde ai, muchas maneras de tierras, i piedras, i aguas, i cerros.

No procede, la obra por la orden arriba puesta: sino por la que se sigue.

El primero capitulo, trata de los anjmales[:] contiene siete parraphos. El segundo, trata de las aues: contiene diez parraphos. El tercero capitulo trata de los animales del agua: como son peces, i otros anjmales, que viuẽ en el agua: contiene cinco parraphos. El quarto, trata de los anjmales fieros: que viuen en el agua: contiene quatro parraphos. El qujnto, trata de serpeintes i otros anjmales ponzoñosos, de tierra: contiene catorze parraphos. El sesto capitulo trata de los arboles: contiene nueue parraphos. El capitulo septimo, trata de las ieruas: contiene doze parraphos. El octauo capitulo, trata de las piedras preciosas: contiene cinco parraphos. Capitulo nueue: de los metales. Capitulo diez de otros mjnerales. Capitulo onze, de las colores: contiene tres parraphos. Capitulo doze, de las diuersidades de las aguas: contiene diez parraphos. Capitulo treze, del mahiz, i de las otras legũbres comestibles: contiene seis parraphos.

Queda la puerta abierta: para añadir, lo que paresciere conuenjr.

# NOTE[1]

Having discussed the springs, waters and mountains, this seemed to me to be the opportune place to discuss the principal ancient idolatries which were practiced and are still practiced in the waters and the mountains.

A very solemn idolatrous act was practiced in this Mexican lagoon in a place called Ayauhcaltitlan, where, they say, there are two large stone statues. And when the lagoon recedes [the statues] stand out of the water and the copal offerings appear, and also many broken pottery vessels which are offered there. Also they offered the hearts of children and other things there.

They say that in the middle of the lagoon, which place they call Xiuhchimalco, there is a whirlpool where the water drains from the lagoon. There they also made sacrifices each year. They placed a child of three or four years in a new small boat and the whirlpool carried it away swallowing it and the child. They say this whirlpool has an outlet toward Tula, which place they call Apazco Santiago, where there is a deep pool, and when the lagoon rises, it rises; and when [the lagoon] recedes, it recedes. And there, they say, many times they have discovered the little boat in which the child had been placed.

There is another body of water, where they were also accustomed to sacrifice, which is in the province of Toluca near the village of Calimanyan. It is a high mountain which has two springs on top which flow nowhere. The water is very clear and nothing lives in it because it is very cold. One of these springs is very deep. A great number of offerings appear therein. And it was a short time ago that certain religious, going to see those springs, discovered that there was an offering there, recently offered, of paper, copal and small straw mats, for little time had passed since it had been offered; it was in the water. This was in the year 1570, or near then. And one of those who saw it was Father Fray Diego de Mendoza who was the then Guardián of Mexico, and he related to me what he had seen there.

There is another very clear and very beautiful body of water or spring in Xochimilco, which is now called Santa Cruz, in which there was a stone idol down in the water, where they offered copal. And I saw this

# NOTA

Aujendo tratado de las fuentes aguas, y montes; pareciome lugar oportuno, para tratar de las ydolatrias principales antiguas, que se hazian, y aun hazen: en las aguas y en los montes,

vna ydolatria muy solemne, se hazia en esta laguna de mexico, en el lugar que se llama Ayauhcaltitlan, donde dizen, que estan dos estatuas de piedra grandes, y quando se mẽgua la laguna, quedan en seco, y parecense, las ofrẽdas de copal, y de muchas baxijas q̃bradas, que alli estan ofrecidas; alli tambien: Alli tanbien, ofreciã coraçones de njños, y otras cosas.

En el medio de la laguna, donde llaman Xiuhchimalco, dizen que esta, vn remolino, donde se sume el agua, de la laguna: alli tanbien, se haziã sacrificios cada año, hechauan vn njño, de tres, o quatro años, en vna canoita nueua; y lleuauala el remolino, y tragauala a ella, y al njño. Este remolino, dizen que tiene vn respiradero hazia Tula, donde llaman apazco Sanctiago, donde esta vn ponzanco profundo: y quando crece la laguna, crece el, y quando mẽgua la laguna, megua el: y alli dizen que muchas vezes an hallado la canoyta donde el njño auja sido hechado.

Ay otra agua, donde tanbien solian sacrificar, que es en la proujncia de tolocan, cabe el pueblo de calimanyan: es vn monte alto, que tiene encima dos fuentes, que por njnguna parte corren: y el agua es clarissima, y njnguna cosa se cria en ella, porque es frigidissima, vna destas fuentes, es profundissima, parece gran cantidad de ofrendas en ella, y poco a, que yendo alli cierto religiosos, a uer aquellas fuentes, hallaron que auja vna ofrenda alli, reciente ofrecida de papel, y copal, y petates pequeñjtos, que auja muy poco, que se auja ofrecido, estaua dentro del agua: esto fue el año de mjll, y qujnjẽtos, y setenta o cerca de por alli: y el vno de los que la vieron, fue el padre Fray Diego de mendoça: el qual era al presente guardian de mexico, y me conto, lo que alli, auja visto.

Ay otra agua, o fuente, muy clara, y muy linda en Xuchmjlco, que agora se llama sancta cruz: ẽ la qual estaua vn ydolo de piedra, debaxo del agua, donde ofrecian copal: y yo vi el ydolo, y copal, y

---

1. This digression by Sahagún is found in place of a Spanish translation or text for paragraphs 6 and 7 of Chapter 12 of Book XI.

The corresponding Nahuatl text describes mountains (§ 6) and rocks (§ 7).

idol and the copal and removed the idol therefrom. And to remove it I went down into the water and I placed a stone cross there which, even now, is there in the same spring.

There are so many other springs and bodies of water where offerings are made, even today, that it would be a good thing to investigate them to discover that which is offered there.

Near the mountains, there are three or four places where they were accustomed to perform very solemn sacrifices and they came to them from very distant lands. One of these is here in Mexico where there is a small mountain they call Tepeyacac. The Spaniards call it Tepeaquilla; now it is called Nuestra Señora de Guadalupe. At this place they had a temple dedicated to the mother of the gods whom they called Tonantzin, which means Our Mother. There they performed many sacrifices in honor of this goddess. And they came to them from more than twenty leagues away, from all the border regions of Mexico, and they brought many offerings. Men and women, youths and maidens came to these feasts. There was a great conflux of people on these days, and they all said: "We are going to the feast of Tonantzin." And now that a church of Our Lady of Guadalupe is built there, they also call her Tonantzin, being motivated by the preachers who called Our Lady, the Mother of God, Tonantzin. It is not known for certain where the beginning of this Tonantzin may have originated, but this we know for certain, that, from its first usage, the word means that ancient Tonantzin. And it is something that should be remedied, for the correct [native] name of the Mother of God, Holy Mary, is not Tonantzin but rather Dios inantzin. It appears to be a Satanic invention to cloak idolatry under the confusion of this name, Tonantzin. And they now come to visit this Tonantzin from very far away, as far away as before, which is also suspicious, because everywhere there are many churches of Our Lady and they do not go to them. They come from distant lands to this Tonantzin as in olden times.

The second place where there were anciently many sacrifices, to which they came from distant lands, is near the mountain range of Tlaxcalla where there was a temple which was called Toci, where a great multitude of people met at the celebration of this feast. Toci means Our Grandmother, and by another name she was called Tzapotlan tenan, which means

saque de alli, al ydolo, y entre debaxo del agua, para sacarle, y puse alli vna cruz de piedra: que hasta agora, esta alli en la mjsma fuente.

Ay otras muchas fuentes, y aguas, donde ofrecen, aun el dia, de oy, que convendria, requerirlas, para ver lo que alli se ofrece.

Cerca de los montes, ay tres, o q̃tro lugares, donde se solian hazer, muy solemnes sacrificios: y que venjan a ellos de muy lexas tierras, el vno destos es, aquj en mexico, donde esta vn montezillo, que se llama Tepeacac: y los españoles llaman Tepeaqujlla, y agora se llama, n̄ra señora de guadalope. en este lugar tenjan vn templo dedjcado, a la madre de los dioses, que la llamauan Tonantzin que qujere dezir, n̄ra madre, alli hazian muchos sacrificios, a honrra desta diosa, y venjan a ellos, de mas de veynte leguas de todas estas comarcas de mexico y trayan muchas ofrendas, venjã hombres, y mugeres, y moços, y moças, a estas fiestas, era grande concurso de gente en estos dias, y todos dezian bamos a la fiesta de tonantzin, y agora que esta alli edificada la yglesia, de n̄ra señora de guadalope, tanbien la llaman Tonantzin, tomada ocasion de los predicadores, que a n̄ra señora la madre de dios llaman tonantzin de donde aya nacido esta fundacion desta Tonantzin, no se sabe de cierto: pero esto sabemos cierto, que el vocablo significa de su primera imposicion, a aquella Tonantzin antigua. y es cosa que se debria remediar, porque el proprio nombre de la madre de dios sancta maria, no es Tonantzin, sino dios ynantzin, parece esta ynvencion satanjca, para paliar la ydolatria, debaxo equjvocacion, deste nombre tonãtzin. Y vienen agora, a ujsitar a esta Tonantzin de muy lexos, tan lexos: como de antes, la qual devocion, tanbien es sospechosa, porque en todas partes, ay muchas yglesias de n̄ra señora, y no van a ellas y vienen de lexos tierras a esta tonantzin, como antiguamente.

El segundo lugar, donde auja antiguamente muchos sacrificios, a los quales venjan, de lexas tierras es cabe la sierra de Tlaxcalla donde auja vn templo que se llamaua Toçi, donde concurrian gran multitud de gente a la celebridad desta fiesta Toçi: q̃ qujere dezir n̄ra avuela y por otro nombre se llamaua Tzapotla Tenan que qujere dezir la diosa de los Te-

the goddess of sweatbaths and medicines. And subsequently they built a Church of Santa Ana there, where there is now a monastery with monks of Our Father Saint Francis. And the natives call her Toci, and people from over forty leagues away attend the feast of Toci. And they name Santa Ana in this manner, being motivated by the preachers who say that, since Santa Ana is the grandmother of Jesus Christ she is also our grandmother, [grandmother] of all Christians. And so they have called her and call her Toci at the pulpit, which means our grandmother. And all the people who come, as in times past, to the feast of Toci, come on the pretext of Saint Ann. But since the word is ambiguous, and they respect the olden ways, it is believable that they come more for the ancient than for the modern. And thus, also in this place, idolatry appears to be cloaked because so many people come from such distant lands without Saint Ann's ever having performed any miracles there. It is more apparent that it is the ancient Toci rather than Saint Ann. In this year of 1576 the plague which prevails began there and, they say, there are no people there now. It seems mysterious for the punishment to have started there where the transgression of cloaking idolatry under the name of Saint Ann started.

The third place where there were anciently many sacrifices, to which they came from distant lands, is at the foot of the volcano, in a village of Calpa, which is called Tianquizmanalco San Juan. At this place they performed a great feast in honor of the god they called Telpochtli which is Tezcatlipoca. And as they heard the preachers say that Saint John the Evangelist was a virgin, and such in their language is called *telpochtli*, they took occasion to perform that feast as they were accustomed to perform it in times past, cloaked under the name of San Juan Telpochtli as it appears on the surface but [performed] in honor of the old Telpochtli, which is Tezcatlipoca. Since Saint John has performed no miracles there, neither is there reason to meet there rather than any other place where he has a church.

## NOTE ALSO

Nowadays great numbers of people from very distant lands come to this feast and they bring many offerings. And with regard to this, it is similar to the ancient ways although they do not practice the sacri-

mascales y de las medicinas: y despues aca edificaron alli vna yglesia de sancta ana donde agora ay monesterio y religiosos de ño padre San Frã.ᶜᵒ y los naturales llamanla Toçi y cõcurren a esta fiesta de mas de quarẽta leguas gente a la fiesta de Toçi, y llaman ansi a sanctana tomado ocasion de los predicadores que dizen que porque sanctana es abuela de Jesu xp̃o es tanbien ñra avuela de todos los xp̃ianos, y ansi la an llamado y llaman en el Pulpito Toçi que qujere dezir ñra abuela: y todas las gentes que vienen como antiguamente, a la fiesta de Toçi vienen so color de sanctana pero como el vocablo es equjvoco y tienen respecto a lo ãtiguo mas se cree que vienen por lo antiguo que no por lo moderno y ansi tanbien en este lugar parece estar la ydolatria paliada porq̃ venir tanta gente y de tan lexos tierra sin aver hecho sanctana alli mjlagros njngunos mas parece que es el toci antiguo que no Sanctana y en este año de mill y qujnjentos y setenta y seys: la pestilencia que ay, de alli comẽço: y dizen que ya no ay gente njnguna alli parece mjsterio de auer comẽçado el castigo donde començo el delicto: de la paliacion de la ydolatria debaxo del nombre de Sanctana.

El tercero lugar donde auja antiguamente muchos sacrificios a los quales venjan de lexas tierras es a la rayz del bulcan en vn pueblo de calpa que se llama tianqujzmanalco San Juan: hazian en este lugar gran fiesta a honrra del dios que llamauã telpuchtli que es tezcatlipuca; y como a los predicadores oyeron dezir que San Juã Euangelista fue virgen: y el tal en su lengua se llama Telpuchtli. Tomaron ocasion de hazer aquella fiesta como la solian hazer antiguamente paliada debaxo del nombre de San Juan Telpuchtli como suena por de fuera: pero a honrra del telpuchtli antiguo que es Tezcatlipuca, porque San Juã alli njngunos mjlagros a hecho nj ay porque acudir mas alli que a njnguna parte donde tiene yglesia.

## JTEM NOTA

Vienen a esta fiesta, el dia de oy, grã cantidad de gente, y de muy lexas tierras, y traen muchas ofrendas: y q̃to a esto, es semejante a lo antiguo, aunque no se hazen los sacrificios, y crueldades, que antigua-

fices and cruelties which they practiced anciently. And [as to] their having practiced this dissimulation in these aforementioned places, I am well assured in my judgment that they do not do it out of love for the idols but rather out of love for avarice and ostentation, so that the offerings which used to be customary should not be lost, nor the glory of ostentation which they received by these places being visited by many strange people from distant lands.

And the attachment which this people adopted anciently to coming to visit these places is [from this]: since these indicated mountains spontaneously produce clouds which constantly rain in certain areas, the people who live in those lands where these clouds which form in these mountains shower, observing that the benefaction of rain comes to them from those mountains, considered themselves obligated to go to visit those places and give thanks to that divinity which resided there, which sent the water, and to take their offerings in appreciation for the benefaction which they received therefrom. And so the dwellers of those lands which were sprinkled by the clouds of those mountains, persuaded or threatened by the demon or his agents, adopted the custom and attachment to come to visit those mountains each year in the feast which was assigned there: in Mexico in the feast of Cioacoatl who is also called Tonantzin, in Tlaxcalla in the feast of Toçi, in Tianquizmanalco in the feast of Tezcatlipoca.

And, in order that they not lose this custom, the villages that enjoyed it persuaded those provinces that they come as usual because they already had Tonantzin and Tocitzin and Telpochtli, who on the surface were like, or whom they made like, Saint Mary, Saint Ann, and Saint John the Evangelist or Baptist. And it is clear that, in the minds of the common people who come there, it is nothing other than the ancient custom. I now know that it comes from ancient custom. And it is not my judgment that they should be denied either the coming or the offering, but it is my judgment that they be undeceived of the error from which they suffer, by giving them to understand, on those days they come there, the ancient falsehood, and that it is not as in times of old. Preachers well versed in the language and the ancient customs which they had, as well as in the Holy Writ, should do this.

I verily believe that there are many other places in these Indies where reverence and offerings to the

mente se hazian: y aver echo esta paliacion. En estos lugares ya dichos: estoy bien certificado de mj opinjon que no lo hazen por amor de los ydolos, sino por amor de la auaricia, y del fausto: porque las ofrēdas que solian ofrecer, no se pierdan nj la gloria del fausto, que recebian en q̃ fuessen visitados: estos lugares de gētes estrañas, y muchas y de lexas tierras.

Y la devocion que esta gente tomo antiguamente de venjr a ujsitar: estos lugares es que como estos montes señalados en producir de si nubes que llueuen por ciertas partes continuamēte: las gentes que residen en aquellas tierras donde riegan estas nubes que se forman en estas sierras, advertiendo que aquel beneficio de la pluuja les viene de aquellos montes: tuujeronse por obligados de yr a ujsitar aquellos lugares y hazer grās a aquella diujnjdad q̃ alli residia que embiaua el agua y lleuar sus ofrendas en agradecimjento del beneficio que de alli recebian. Y ansi los moradores de aquellas tierras que eran regadas con las nubes de aquellos montes persuadidos o amonestados del demonjo o de sus satrapas: tomaron por costumbre y devocion de venjr a ujsitar aquellos montes cada año en la fiesta que alli estaua dedicada. En mexico en la fiesta de cioacoatl que tanbien la llamã Tonantzin; en tlaxcalla en la fiesta de toçi: en tianqujzmanalco; en la fiesta de Tezcatlipuca.

Y porque esta costumbre no la perdiessen: los pueblos que gozauan della persuadieron a aquellas proujncias que venjessen como solian: porque ya tenjã tonantzin y a tocitzin y al telpuchtli que esteriormente suena o les a hecho sonar a sancta maria y a sanctana y a san Juã euangelista o baptista: y en lo ynterior de la gente popular que alli viene esta claro, que no es sino lo antiguo ya la se que la de lo antigo vienen. Y no es mj parecer que les empidan la venjda nj la ofrenda: pero es mj parecer que los desengañen del ēgaño de que padecē dandolos a ētender en aquellos dias que alli vienen la falsedad antigua y que no es aquello conforme a lo antiguo: y esto debriã de hazer predicadores bien entendidos en la lengua, y costumbres antiguos que ellos tenjan: y tanbien ē la escritura diujna

Bien creo, que ay otros muchos lugares, en estas yndias, donde paliadamente se haze reuerencia, y

idols are clandestinely practiced under the pretext of the feasts which the Church celebrates to revere God and His saints. It would be good that such be investigated, that the poor people be undeceived of the error from which they now suffer.

## EIGHTH PARAGRAPH: OF THE VARIETIES AND KINDS OF ROADS.[2]

After having gone over different kinds of mountains, valleys, marshes, gorges and roads, I consider this the proper place to deal with the roads by which the Church has come to arrive at this final abode where it now travels sowing the evangelical doctrine.

It is well known to all that the Church Militant began in the kingdom of Palestine and from there it traveled through different parts of the world: toward the east, toward the west, toward the north and toward the south. It is known that toward the region of the north there are still many provinces, there are still many unexplored lands where the Gospel has not yet been preached. And toward these southern regions, where it was thought no people lived, even now, in these times, many lands and well-populated kingdoms have been discovered where the Gospel is now preached.

The Church left Palestine and now the infidels live, reign and hold dominion in Palestine. From there it went to Asia in which there are now nothing but Turks and Moors. It went to Africa where, now, there are no Christians. It went to Germany where, now, there are none but heretics. It went to Europe where, in the greater part thereof, the Church is not obeyed. Where it now has its more tranquil seat is Italy and Spain, whence, crossing the ocean, it has arrived in these regions of the Western Indies, where there was a diversity of peoples and languages, many of which have already become extinct. And those which remain are on the road to extinction. And this New Spain has been and is the most populated and best settled of all the Western Indies. That which now predominates more and has splendor is Mexico and its territory, where the Catholic Church is established and tranquil. But, as regards the Catholic Faith, it is a sterile land and very laborious to cultivate,

## PARRAPHO OCTAUO: DE LAS DIUERSIDADES, Y CALIDADES DE LOS CAMJNOS.

Despues de aver pasados mõtes y valles y cienagas y varrancas y camjnos de diuersas maneras: pareciome lugar oportuno este para tratar de los camjnos, por donde la yglesia a venjdo hasta llegar a esta vltima mãsion donde agora peregrina sembrãdo la doctrina evãgelica.

A todos es noto que la yglesia mjllitante, començo en el reyno de Palestina: y de alli camjno por diuersas partes del mũdo, hazia el oriente, y hazia el occidente, y hazia el norte, y hazia el medio dia; sabese que hazia la parte del norte ay aũ muchas prouincias, ay aun muchas tierras ocultas, donde el euãgelio, aun no se a predicado: y hazia destas partes del medio dia, donde se pensaua que njngunas gentes abitauã, aun agora: en estos tiempos se an descubierto muchas tierras, y reynos muy poblados, donde agora se predica el euangelio.

Partiome la yglesia de palestina, y ya en palestina viuen reynan y señorean yfieles; de alli: fue a Asia, en la qual ya no ay, sino turcos, y moros, fue tanbien a Africa, donde ya no ay xp̃ianos: fue a Alemanja, donde ya no ay sino herejes: fue a Eoropa, donde en la mayor parte della, no se obedece la yglesia, donde agora tiene su silla, mas qujetamente es Italia, y españa de donde pasando el mar oceano, a venjdo a estas partes de la yndia occidental donde auja diuersidades de gentes y de lenguas: de las quales ya muchas se an acabado: y las que rrestan van en camjno de acabarse: lo mas poblado, y mas bien parado, de todas estas yndias occidentales, a sido y es esta nueua españa, y lo que mas agora preualece, y tiene lustre es mexico y su comarca, donde la yglesia catholica esta apos̃etada y pacifica. Pero en lo que toca a la fe catholica, tierra esteril, y muy trabaxosa de cultiual donde la fe catholica tiene muy flacas rayzes, y cõ muchos trabajos se haze muy poco fructo

---

2. This interpolation is found in place of a Spanish translation or text for paragraphs 8 and 9 of Chapter 12. The corresponding

Nahuatl text describes roads (§ 8) and houses (§ 9).

where the Catholic Faith has very shallow roots, and with much labor little fruit is produced, and from little cause that which is planted and cultivated withers.

It seems to me the Catholic Faith can endure little time in these parts. One thing is that the people are becoming extinct with great rapidity, not so much from the bad treatment accorded them as from the plagues God sends them. Since this land was discovered there have been three very general and extensive plagues in addition to others not so extensive nor general. The first was the year 1520 when, in warfare, they drove the Spaniards from Mexico and [the Spaniards] withdrew to Tlaxcalla. There was a plague of smallpox wherein a nearly countless number of people died. After this, the Spaniards having conquered this New Spain, and maintained it in peace, and the preaching of the Gospel being practiced very successfully, in the year 1545, there was a very great and general plague in which the major portion of the people living in all this New Spain died. And at the time of this plague I resided in this city of Mexico, in the district of Tlatilulco. And I buried more than ten thousand bodies. And at the conclusion of the plague I contracted the sickness and was near death.

After this, the matters of the Faith proceeding peacefully for more or less thirty years, the people recovered. Now, in this year of 1576, in the month of August a general and great plague began, which already continues for three months. Many people have died, die, and every day more are dying. I do not know how long it will last nor how much illness there will be. I am now in this city of Mexico, in the district of Tlatilulco, and I see that from the time it began until today, the 8th of November, the number of dead has always gone increasing: from ten [to] twenty, from thirty to forty, from fifty to sixty and to eighty. And from here on I do not know what will be. In this plague, as well as the one mentioned above, many died of hunger and from not having anyone to cure them nor provide what was necessary. It happened and happens in many homes, that all those of the house become sick without there being anyone who might offer a pitcher of water. And to give them the Sacraments, in many places there was not even anyone to carry them to the church nor anyone to say they were sick. And, this being known, the religious go from house to house confessing them and consoling them.

y cõ poca ocasion se seca, lo plantado y cultiuado:

pareceme que poco tiempo podra perseuerar la fe catholica en estas partes, lo vno es porque la gente, se va acabando con grã prissa, no tanto por los malos tratamjentos que se les hazen como por las pestilencias que dios les ẽbia. Despues que esta tierra se descubrio: a aujdo tres pestilencias muy vnjuersales: y grandes, allẽde de otras no tan grandes, nj vnjuersales. la primera fue el año de mjll, y qujnjentos y veynte: que quando hecharon de mexico, por guerra a los españoles, y ellos se rrecogieron a tlaxcalla vuo vna pestilencias de viruelas, donde morio casi infinita gente: despues desta y de auer ganado los españoles esta nueua españa, y tenjendola ya pacifica y que la predicacion del evangelio se exercitaua cõ mucha prosperidad el año de mjll y qujnjentos y quarenta y cinco, vuo vna pestilencia grandissima y vnjuersal donde en toda esta nueua españa murio la mayor parte de la gente que en ella via: y yo me alle en el tiempo desta pestilencia en esta ciudad de mexico en la parte del tlatilulco y enterre mas de diez mjll cuerpos: y al cabo de la pestilencia diome a mj la emfermedad, y estuue muy al cabo.

Despues desto procediẽdola las cosas de la fe pacificamente por espacio de treynta años poco mas o menos se torno a reformar la gente: agora este año de mjll y qujnjentos y setenta y seys: en el mes de agosto començo vna pestilencia vnjuersal y grande: la q̃l a ya tres meses que corre y a muerto mucha gente y muere y va muriẽdo cada dia mas no se que tanto durara nj que tanto mal ara: y yo stoy agora en esta ciudad de mexico en la parte del tlatilulco, y veo que desdel tiempo que començo hasta oy, que son ocho de noujembre siempre a ydo creciendo el numero de los defunctos desde diez veynte, de treỹta, a quarenta, de cincuenta, a sesẽta, y a ochenta y de aquj adelante no se lo que sera. En esta pestilencia como tanbien en la otra arriba dicha muchos murieron de hambre y de no tener qujen los curase nj los diesse lo necessario, acontecia y acontece en muchas casas cayer todos de las casas enfermos sin aver qujen los pudiesse dar vn jarro de agua: y para admjnjstrarlos los sacramẽtos en muchas partes, nj auja qujẽ los lleuase a la yglesia, nj quien dixesse que estauã enfermos y conozido: esto andan los religiosos de casa en casa, confessandolos y consolandolos.

When this present plague began, the Viceroy Don Martín Enríquez made every effort that the Indians be favored in food as well as the Sacraments. And through his persuasion many Spaniards went many days to the houses of the Indians giving them food. And the bloodletters went bleeding them and the doctors curing them. And clerics and religious, Franciscans as well as Dominicans, Augustinians, Theatins, went to their houses to confess them and console them. And this lasted as a labor for two months; then everything ceased because some tired, others became sick, others devoted themselves to their properties. Many of the said priests who helped are now finally missing; they no longer help. In this village of Tlatilulco only the religious of Saint Francis go to their houses confessing them, consoling them and giving them Castilian bread to eat, buying it with their very alms. And all [the alms] are used up, exhausted, as the bread is very expensive and unavailable. And the priests are becoming sick and tired, for which reason there is great tribulation and affliction. But with all this the Viceroy and Archbishop do not cease to do what they can. Pray to our Lord to mitigate this so great a plague, because in lasting a long time all is finished.

Our Father Commissary General Fray Rodrigo de Sequera, who has been and is in this city and never tires of working on this matter, has worked in large measure with his friars as well as with the Viceroy and the Spaniards that the Indians be helped in spiritual and temporal affairs.

Now, returning to my subject of the travels of the Church, during these years there have been discoveries in the region of the spices, where the Spaniards are already settled. And the Gospel is preached; much gold, very fine porcelain, and many spices are brought. Near there is the great Kingdom of China, and the Augustinian Fathers have already commenced to enter therein. In this year of 1576 we received precise news of how two of them entered the Kingdom of China but did not succeed in seeing the Emperor of China. After many trips [the Chinese] made them return, for, because of the event of a certain war which occurred, they brought them with much honor from the islands which are populated with Spaniards to a certain city of China. And they say that through the advice of the demon whom the Emperor of China consulted, or his agents, they sent them again therefrom to return to the island

Quando começo esta pestilencia de vgaño: el señor visorrey Don mjn enrriques, Puso mucho calor en que fuessen fauorecidos los yndios, asi de comjda: como de los sacramentos, y por su persuasion, muchos españoles anduujeron muchos dias por las casas de los yndios, dandolos comjda, y sāgradores sangrandolos, y medicos curandolos, y clerigos, y religiosos; ansi de sanct francisco, como de sancto Domjngo, como augustinos, como teatinos, andauan por sus casas, para cōfesarlos y consolarlos: y esto duro por obra de dos meses, y luego ceso todo, porque vnos se cansaron, otros enfermaron, otros se ocupan en sus haziendas: agora ya faltā muchos de los sacerdotes dichos que ayudauā ya no ayudan. En este pueblo de tlatilulco, solos los religiosos de sanct francisco andan por sus casas, confessandolos, y consolandolos, y dandolos pan de castilla que coman, comprando de las proprias limosnas y todos se ua y acabando que el pā vale muy caro, y no se puede aver; y los religiosos van enfermando y cansādo: por lo qual, ay grāde tribulacion y africion, pero con todo esto, el señor Visorrey, y el señor Arçobispo, no cesan de hazer lo que puedē. Plega a nuestro señor de remediar esta tan gran plaga porque a durar mucho todo se acaba:

Nīo padre comjssario general fray Rodrigo de Sequera, en grande manera a trabajado, ansi cō sus frayles como con el señor Visorrey, y con los españoles: para que los yndios sean ayudados, en lo spūal y tēporal: el qual a estado, y esta en esta ciudad y no se cansa de trabajar en este negocio.

Pues bolujendo a mj proposito de la peregrinacion de la yglesia: en estos años se ā descubierto por estas partes de la speceria donde ya estan poblados los españoles y se predica el euāgelio y se trae mucho oro y loza muy rica y muchas species. Cerca de alli esta el gran reyno de la China y ya ā començado a entrar en el: los padres Augustinos. En este año de mjll y qujnjentos, y setēta y seys: tuujmos nueua ciertas de como dos dellos entrarō en el reyno de la China y no llegarō a ver al ēperador de la China [despues] de muchas jornadas los hizieron boluer: porque por cierta ocasion de guerra que se ofrecio los lleuaron con mucha honrra deste las yslas donde estan poblados con los españoles hasta cierta ciudad de la China. Y de alli dizen que por consejo del demonjo a qujen consulto el emperador de la China o sus satrapas: los bolujeron a embiar para que se bolujesen a la ysla de donde aujā partido: y boluje-

whence they had departed. And they returned them in dishonor and with the many hardships in which they found themselves on the return.

I have heard that the account which these Augustinian Fathers carried is written. It will appear shortly here and in Spain. It seems to me our Lord God finally opens the way that the Catholic Faith may enter in the Kingdom of China where there are very capable people of good breeding and wisdom. When the Church enters in those kingdoms and the Catholic Faith is established in them, I believe it will endure many years in that abode because in the islands and in this New Spain and Peru, it has done no more than pass through and still be on the way in order to communicate with those peoples in the regions of China.

## MAIZE[3]

In this text the kinds of maize which exist are discussed. And since this is an obvious matter, it occurred to me to write here that in the diversity of foods there are scarcely any which resemble ours. It seems that this people had never been discovered until these times, because, of the foods which we enjoy and are enjoying in the regions whence we came, we find none here. We do not even find here the domesticated animals which those of us who came from Spain and all Europe use, from which it appears that [the people] did not come from those regions. Nor had men from those regions come to discover this land, for if they had come from there, they would have come to make them known in other times; from them we would find wheat, or barley, or rye, or chickens from there, or horses, or bulls, or donkeys, or sheep, or goats, or other domesticated animals which we utilize, whence it appears that only in these times have these lands been discovered and not before.

As to the preaching of the Gospel in these regions, there has been much doubt as to whether or not it has been preached before now. And I have always been of the opinion that the Gospel was never preached to them because I have never found anything which alludes to the Catholic Faith; rather, everything is so abhorrent and idolatrous that I cannot believe the Gospel has been preached to them at any time.

ronlos con deshõrra y con muchos trabajos en que se bierõ en la buelta.

E oydo que esta escrita la relacion que estos padres Augustinos truxeron ella parecera en breue tiempo aca y en españa. Pareceme que ya nr̃o señor dios abre camjno para que la fe catholica entre en los reynos de la china dõde ay gẽte abillissima de gran pullicia y de grã saber. Como la yglesia entre en aquellos reynos y se plante en ellos la fe catholica: creo durara por muchos años en aq̃lla mansion: porque por las yslas y por esta nueua españa y el peron, no a hecho mas de pasar de camjno y aun hazer camjno para poder conuersal con aquella gentes de las partes de la China.

## DEL MAYZ

En esta letra se trata, de las maneras que ay de mayz, y porque esto es, cosa clara: pareciome de poner, en este lugar, que en la diuersidad de los mantenjmjentos, que casi njngunos son semejantes a los nuestros: parece que esta gente, nunca a sido descubierta, hasta estos tiempos, porque de los mantenjmjentos, que nosotros vsamos, y se vsan en las partes de donde venjmos, njngunos hallamos aca, nj aun de los anjmales mansos que vsamos, los que venjmos de españa y de toda la eoropa: tanpoco los hallamos aca dõde parece que nj ellos venjeron de hazia de aquellas partes nj hombres de aquellas partes aujan venjdo a descubrir esta tierra: porque si ellos vujeran venjdo de hazia alla, vujeran venjdo a descubrirlos, en otros tiempos del allaramos aca trigo o ceuada o cẽteno o gallinas de las de halla, o cauallos o bueyes o asnos o obejas o cabras o algunos otros de los anjmales mansos de que vsamos donde parece que en estos tiempos solamente an sido deescubiertas estas tierras y no antes.

cerca de la predicacion del euãgelio en estas partes. Aujdo mucha duda si an sido predicados ante de agora o no. Y yo siempre e tenjdo opinion que nunca les fue predicado el euangelio porque nunca jamas e hallado cosa que aluda a la fe catholica sino todo tan contrario y todo tan ydolatrico, que no puedo creer que se les a sido predicado el euangelio en njngun tiempo

---

3. This interpolation is found in place of a Spanish translation or text of paragraphs 1 and 2 of Chapter 13, which deals with sustenance.

The year 70, or thereabouts, two trusted religious assured me that in Oaxaca, which is distant sixty leagues to the east of this city, they saw some very ancient paintings, painted on deerskin, which contained many things which alluded to the preaching of the Gospel. Among others was one where there were three women dressed as Indian women, and arranged like Indian women as to their hair. They were seated as Indian women sit. Two were side by side and the third was in the middle in front of them. And, according to the meaning of the painting, she had a wooden cross bound to the knot of her hair. And on the ground before them was a naked man, legs and arms stretched on a cross, arms and legs tied to the cross with cords. This seems to me to allude to Our Lady and her two sisters and to our crucified Redeemer, which they must have derived from ancient sermons.

There is also another thing which also prompts me to believe that there has been preaching of the Gospel in these parts, and it is that they had auricular confession in these parts of Mexico where the penitents related their sins to the functionary in great secrecy. And they accepted penance from them, and the functionary exhorted them to repentance with great diligence. And they made this confession once in a lifetime, near to or in old age. And they held that the penitent who reverted to sin could not be helped because they forgave no one his sins except once in a lifetime. This is recorded at great length in the second book which deals with the feasts of the gods.

Also I have heard it said that in Chanpanton or Campeche the religious who first went there to convert, found many things which allude to the Catholic Faith and to the Gospel. And if, in these two said regions, there was preaching of the Gospel, no doubt there was also in these parts of Mexico and its territory, and even in this New Spain. But I am surprised that we have not discovered more trace of that which I have mentioned in these parts of Mexico. And, although I say this, it seems to me it could well be that they were preached to for some time, but, the preachers who came to preach to them having died, they completely lost the Faith which was preached to them and reverted to their idolatries which they previously held. And I conjecture this from the great difficulty I have encountered in the implanting of the faith in this people. For in the

el año de setenta o por alli cerca: me certificaron dos religiosos dignos de fe que vieron en Quaxaca que dista desta ciudad sesenta leguas hazia el oriente que vieron vnas pinturas muy antiguas: pintadas en pellejos de venados: en las quales se contenjan muchas cosas que aludian a la predicacion del euãgelio entre otras: era vna desta, que estauã tres mugeres vestidas como yndias y tocados, los cabellos como yndias, estauã sentadas, como se sientan las mugeres yndias: y las dos, estauan a la par, y la tercera estaua delante de las dos en el medio y tenja vna cruz de palo, segun signjficaua la pitura: atada en el nodo de los cabellos: y delante dellas estaua en el suelo, vn hõbre desnudo, y tendido pies y manos sobre vna cruz y atadas las manos, y los pies a la cruz con vnos cordeles. Esto me parece que alude a nr̃a señora y sus dos hermanas, y a nr̃o redemptor crucificado: lo qual devieron tener por predicacion antiguamente.

Otra cosa ay que tanbien me ynclina a creer que aujdo predicacion del euãgelio, en estas partes: y es que tenjan confession auricular en estas partes de mexico donde los penjtentes contauã sus peccados al satrapa en gran secreto, y recebian penjtencia dellos y les exortaua el satrapa a la emjenda con gran diligencia: y esta confession hazianla vna uez en la vida ya cerca de la vez o en la vejez y tenjan que del penjtente tornaua a recayer en los peccados no tenja remedio, porque a nadie se le perdonauan los peccados sino vna uez en la vida: esta esto escrito muy a la larga en el segundo libro que trata de las fiestas de los dioses.

Tanbien e oyodo dezir que en chanpoton o cãpeche, hallaron los religiosos que fueron alli a conuertir, primeramente muchas cosas que aluden a la fe catholica, y al euãgelio: y si en estas dos partes dichas vuo predicacion del euangelio sin duda que la vuo. tanbien en estas partes de mexico y sus comarcas y aun esta nueua españa: pero yostoy admjrado como no emos hallado mas rastro de lo que tengo dicho en estas partes de mexico. Y aunque esto digo, pareceme que pudo ser muy bien, que fueron predicados por algun tiempo: pero que muertos los predicadores, que venjerõ a predicarlos: perdieron del todo la fe, que les fue predicada: y se vulvierõ a sus ydolatrias, que te de antes tenjan. Y esto conjecturo por la dificultado grande que hallado en la plãtacion de la fe, en esta gente: porque yo a mas de quarenta años, que predico por estas partes de mexico, y en lo

more than forty years that I have preached in these parts of Mexico, that in which I and many others with me have insisted most is to place them in the belief in the Holy Catholic Faith by many means and to test diverse opportunities to this end: by pictures, as well as sermons, by plays, as well as by conversations, experimenting with the adults and with the children. And I have insisted even more on this in these last five years, giving them the things necessary to believe with great brevity and clarity of words. And now, in the time of this plague, having tested the faith of those who come to confess, very few respond properly prior to the confession; thus we can be certain that, though preached to more than fifty years, if they were now left alone, if the Spanish nation were not to intercede, I am certain that in less than fifty years there would be no trace of the preaching which has been done for them.

So in conclusion I say it is possible that they were preached to and that they completely lost the Faith which was preached to them and returned to the ancient idolatries. And now it seems to me that our Lord God, having seen from experience the hardness of heart of this people and the little they have benefited from the great labors which are and have been maintained with them, has desired to give [them] the Spanish nation to be as a fountain from which flows the doctrine of the Catholic Faith; so that, although they may falter, they may always have new ministers of the Spanish nation present to return them to the principles of the Faith.

And there is another matter which has appeared in part from experience and in part from prophecy. It is the decline of this nation. And that which appears from experience is that from the Canaries to here all the native nations have failed. And here in this land we see from experience that it is likewise being confirmed. And this has also appeared in the prophecy of a holy man, a Dominican. When the Spaniards reached this land it was filled with people beyond counting. And when, by way of war, the Indians expelled the Spaniards from this city of Mexico and they went to Tlaxcalla, a great plague of smallpox struck them whereof countless Indians died. And afterwards in the war and in the labors with which they were afflicted after the war, a great number of people died in the mines and from making them slaves, taking them captive beyond their home land, exhausting them with difficult labors in

que mas he insistido, y otros muchos comjgo, es en ponerlos en la creencia de la sancta fe catholica, por muchos medios, y tentando diuersas oportunjdades: para esto ansi por pinturas, como por predicaciones, como por representaciones, como por colocotiones, prouando con los adultos y con los pequeños. Y en esto aun he insistido mas en estos cinco años pasados, tandolos las cosas necesarias de creer con gran breuedad y con gran claridad de palabras: y agora en este tiempo desta pestilencia, haziẽdo experiencia de la fe que tienen los que se viene a confessar antes de la confession qual o qual responde como conviene: de manera que pudemos tener biẽ entendido que con averlos predicado, mas de cincuenta años; si agora se quedasen ellos, a sus solas que la nacion españolla, no estuujesse de por medio: tengo entendido que a menos de cincũeta años, no abria rastro de la predicacion que se les a hecho:

ansi que digo, concluyendo que es posible, que fueron predicados, y que perdieron del todo la fe que les fue predicada: y se vulujero a los ydolatrias antiguas. Y agora pareceme que dios nõ señor, aviendo visto por experiẽcia la dureça desta gente, y lo poco que en ellos aprouechan los grãdes trabajos y con ellos se tienen y aũ tenjdo a querido dar la nacion españolla. Para que sea como vna fuente de que mana la doctrina fe catholica: para que aũnque ellos desfallezcan siempre tengã presentes mjnjstros nueuos y de nacion españolla para tornarlos a los principios de la fe.

Ay otra cosa, la qual a parecido en parte por experiencia, y em parte por profecia: y es el acabamjento desta naciõ. Y lo que parece por experiencia, es que deste las canarias hasta aca, todas las naciones naturales [han faltado], y aquj en esta tierra vemos por experiencia, que ansi va verificandose. Y tanbien esto a parecido por profecia de vn sancto varon domjnjgo, quando los españoles, llegarõ a esta tierra, estaua llena de gente, ynnumerable: y quando por via de guerra, hecharon desta ciudad de mexico los yndios a los españoles y se fuerõ A tlaxcalla diolos vna gran pestilencia de viruelas que murieron yndios sin cuenta: y despues en la guerra y en los trabajos con que fuerõ afligidos despues de la guerra murieron gran cantidad de gente en las mjnas y haziendolos esclauos lleuandolos captiuos fuera de su tierra y fatigandolos con grandes trabajos en edificios y en mjnas: y despues que estas vejaciones se reme-

buildings and mines. And, after these oppressions were corrected by the religious having complained to the Emperor Charles V, in the year 1545 a great plague came in which more than half of the people of this New Spain died, wherefore the whole land remained very depleted of people. Many large villages remained depopulated; they were never populated again. Thirty years after this plague, the plague which now, presently, prevails, occurred, wherein a great number of people have died and many villages have become depopulated and things are growing worse. If it continues for three or four months, as it now progresses, no one will remain. And the prophecy which I mentioned previously says that less than sixty years after they were conquered, not a man of them will remain. And although I do not believe this prophecy, yet the things which happen and have happened seem to go in the right direction to make it true. However, it is unbelievable that this people will end in such a brief time, as the prophecy says, because if it were so, the earth would remain wasteland, because there are few Spaniards in it and even they would come to an end, and the land would become full of wild beasts and forests so that it could not be inhabited.

What I estimate as to this matter is rather that soon this plague will cease and that many people will still remain until the Spaniards go multiplying and populating more, so that, lacking the one generation, this land will be populated by the other generation which is the Spanish. And I still think that there will always be numbers of Indians in these lands.

diaron con auer reclamado los religiosos al ēperador Carlo quinto en año de mjll y qujnjentos y quarenta y cinco vino vna gran pestilencia en que murieron en esta nueua españa mas de la mjtad de gente donde toda la tierra quedo muy menguada de gente muy grandes pueblos quedaron deespoblado: los quales nunca se tornarõ a poblar treynta años despues desta pestilencia socedio la pestilencia que agora actualmente reyna donde a muerto gran cantidad de gente y se an despoblados muchos pueblos y el negocio va muy adelante si tres o quatro meses dura como agora va no quedara nadie y la prophecia de que atras hize mencio dize que ante de sesenta años despues que fueron conqujstados no a de quedar hombre dellos. Y aunque esta prophecia yo no la doy credito: pero las cosas q̃ suceden y aun sucedido parece que van endereçadas a hacerla verdadera. No es de crerr empero que esta gente se acabe tã en breue tiempo: como la prophecia dize porque si asi fuese la tierra quedaria yerua: porq̃ ay pocos españoles en ella y aũ ellos se uendrian a acabar: y la tierra yncheria de bestias fieras y de arboles siluestres de manera que no se podria abitar.

lo que mas se me asienta en este negocio es que con breuedad esta pestilencia presente cesara y que todavia q̃dara mucha gente hasta que los españoles se va y aun mas multiplicando y poblando de manera que faltando la vna generacion quede poblada esta tierra de la otra generacion que es la españolla y aun tengo para mj que siempre abra cantidad de yndios en estas tierras.

# Book XII: The Conquest

## TO THE READER

Although many have written of the Conquest of this New Spain in Spanish, according to the account of those who conquered it, I desired to write it in the Mexican language, not so much to derive certain truths from the account of the very Indians who took part in the Conquest, as to record the language of warfare and the weapons which the natives use in it, in order that the terms and proper modes of expression for speaking on this subject in the Mexican language can be derived therefrom. To this may be added that those who were conquered knew and gave an account of many things which transpired among them during the war of which those who conquered them were unaware. For these reasons, it seems to me, to have written this history, which was written at a time when those who took part in the very Conquest were alive, has not been a superfluous task. And those who gave this account [were] principal persons of good judgment, and it is believed they told all the truth.

## AL LECTOR

Aunque muchos an escrito en romance la conquista desta nueua españa, segun la relacion de los q̃ la conquistaron: qujsela yo escreujr en lengua mexicana, no tanto por sacar algunas verdades de la relacion de los mjsmos jndios, que se hallaron en la conqujsta: quanto por poner el lenguaje de las cosas de la guerra, y de las armas que en ella vsan los naturales: para que de alli se puedan sacar vocablos y maneras de dezir proprias, para hablar en lengua mexicana cerca desta materia, allegase tambien a esto que los que fuero conquistados, supieron y dieron relacion de muchas cosas, que passaron entre ellos durante la guerra: las quales ignorarõ los que los conquistarõ, por las quales razones, me parece que no a sido trabajo superfluo, el auer escrito esta estoria. la qual se escriujo en tiempo que eran viuos, los que se hallaron en la mjsma conqujsta: y ellos dieron esta relacion personas principales, y de buen juizio y que se tiene por cierto, que dixeron toda verdad.

# INDICES

compiled by Arthur J. O. Anderson

# Subject Matter

The twelve Books of the Florentine Codex are indexed sequentially under the entries, with page references to the first edition or printing following the colon. If pagination changed in subsequent editions or printings, the references are in parentheses.

Abstinence, 1:23 (49); 2:25, 29, 35, 90, 125, 132, 139, 158, 180, 187 (25, 29, 35, 95, 135, 143, 151, 171, 193, 200); 3:11–12; 9:9

Acolhua, Acolhuaque (people), 8:11, 13, 72; 10:195, 196, 197; 11:149, 259

Adages, (1:81–84); 6:219–35

Adultery, 4:5, 6, 45, 93; 5:191–92; 6:118–19, 257, 259; 8:42–43; 10:56; punishment of, 9:39; 10:172

Agave. *See* Maguey

Age differences, in adages (1:82); terminology for, 10:11–13

Agriculture, 10:42–43

Ailments. *See* Diseases

Albinism, 10:137

Alcalde, 6:232

Alguacil, 3:53 (55)

Alum, 11:243; in coloring of feathers, 9:95; in treatment of gold, 9:75, 78; as a trade item, 9:12, 18, 22; vendors of, 10:77, 85

Amaranth, 1:2, 5, 13, 22 (7, 17, 32, 47, 48); 2:33, 43, 54, 55, 63, 69, 70, 105, 109, 118, 121–22, 123, 133, 135, 141, 155, 161, 178 (33, 44, 55, 57, 65, 71, 73, 112, 116, 127, 131–32, 133, 144, 146–47, 153, 168, 175, 192); 3:5–6, 14, 45 (5–6, 14, 47); 4:129; 6:201, 223; 7:13, 17, 19, 31, 32; 8:38-39, 44, 59, 67, 68, 85; 9:63; 10:65, 67, 70, 92, 93, 157, 188; 11:134, 194, 286–88; 12:49, 51 (51, 53)

Amber, 9:4, 21, 22, 23, 24, 30; 11:222, 225

Amethyst, 9:80, 81

Amphibians, 11:63–65, 72–73

Anatomy, bird, 11:54–56

Anatomy, human, 10:95–138

Animals. *See* Mammals

Anauaca Mixteca (people), 10:192

Ant, 5:173; 11:89–91

Antelope, 11:15

Armadillo, 11:61

Arm-wrist ornaments, 8:27

Arrows, making of, 2:25, 124–25 (25, 134–35); shooting of, 8:30

Arsenal, 2:169, 179 (183, 193)

Artisans, 4:7; 9:69–97 passim; 10:25–30, 35–36

Ash (tree), 11:108

"Ashes Are Scattered" ceremony, 2:138 (150)

Astrologers, 4:42, 101; 8:18–19

Atamalqualiztli (feast), 2:163–64, 188 (177–78, 201); 4:144; song celebrating, 2:212–13 (238–39)

Atemoztli (month), 2:29–30, 137–38, 139–42 (29–30, 149–50, 151–54); 11:28

Atlaca Chichimeca (people), 10:197

Atl caualo (month). *See* Quauitl eua

Atole, 9:42, 48; 10:93, 142, 150, 153, 155, 157, 158, 183; 11:138, 142, 148, 149, 151, 154, 155, 158, 159, 160, 161, 165, 173, 178, 180, 184, 186, 187, 234

Attorney, 10:32

Aunts, giving of, 1:12 (30); 2:152, 156 (164–65, 169–70)

Aviary, 8:45

Avocado, 11:118

Avocet, 11:34

Axin, ají (*Coccus axin*), 10:55, 77, 78, 89, 90, 139, 141, 145, 152, 158, 159

Badger, 11:8

Baldpate, 11:36

Ball game (tlachtli), 8:29, 58

Banners, 8:28, 34

Banquets, 1:14, 15, 19, 43 (33, 35, 43, 73); 2:5, 9, 16, 21, 37–38, 39, 40, 58, 89, 137, 141 (5, 9, 16, 21, 37–38, 39, 40, 60, 95, 149, 153); 4:56, 60, 87, 117–18; 6:129–30, 135, 149; 8:64–65; 9:12, 13, 28, 29, 33–43, 47–49, 51–53, 59–63, 80, 87

Baptismal ceremony, 2:39; 4:3–4, 30, 34, 38, 47, 50, 51, 53, 55–56, 70, 73, 74–75, 96, 100, 113; 6:175–77, 201–4

Barren days (Nemontemi), 2:35, 150, 157–58 (35, 162, 171–72); 4:144

Bathing, 2:138, 139 (150, 151); 3:9, 14, 42, 54 (9, 14, 44–45, 56); 6:130, 161, 167, 175–76, 201–2; 8:64; 9:9; 10:183; ceremonial, of sacrificial victims, 2:130, 155 (141, 168); 9:45, 63, 87; of priests, 2:167–68, 171, 174 (181–82, 185, 187); 3:63, 64 (65, 66); of Uitzilopochtli, 3:7, 8; on burial of flayed human skins, 2:5, 56–57 (5, 58–59)

Battle, mock, 1:4, 17 (15, 39); 2:4, 27, 31, 44, 49, 110–11, 134–35, 145–46, 190–91 (4, 27, 31, 45, 50, 118–19, 145–46, 157–58, 203–4); 6:161–62; 8:85; 9:64

Beans, 1:22 (47); 2:7, 29, 63, 149, 165 (7, 29, 65, 161, 180); 3:45

(47); 4:26, 113, 129; 6:201; 7:17, 19, 23, 72; 8:37, 44, 59, 67, 69; 9:6, 48; 10:41, 66, 69–70, 86, 87, 93, 178, 183, 188; 11:283, 284, 285

Bear, 11:5

Bedbug, 11:89

Bee, 11:93–94

Begging, by tototecti, 8:85; during Etzalqualiztli, 2:79 (84); 8:18; during Tlacaxipeualiztli, 1:17 (40)

Behavior, standards of, for children, 8:71; 10:2–3, 6, 9, 13; for lords, 10:15–22, 45–50; for maidens, 6:93–103, 216–18; 10:2–3, 4, 12–13, 46, 47; for women, 4:10, 25, 74, 79, 95, 109; 6:93–103, 132, 155–58, 172, 216–18; 8:48; 10:1–13 passim, 45–57; for youths, 6:87–92, 105–26, 213–16, 242–43, 253, 255, 256–57, 259; 10:8, 12–13

Binding of the Years, 4:143–44; 7:25

Birds, 2:185, 188 (198, 201); 11:19–57

Bissextile year, 2:33–34, 35; 4:144

Bittern, 11:33, 57

Bitumen, 10:77, 88–89, 90; 11:61

Bloodstone, 9:81; 11:222, 228

Bobcat, 11:8

Body parts. See Anatomy, human

Books, 10:5, 29, 31, 42. See also Picture writing

Boys, 2:14, 21, 32, 36, 41, 73, 108, 124, 135, 145–46, 148, 149 (14, 21, 32, 36, 41, 76–77, 115–16, 134, 146, 157–58, 160–62); 8:71–72, 75; 9:14, 15, 88; 10:2, 3, 177, 181; 12:51, 86 (54, 88); in calmecac, 6:209–11; in telpochcalli, 6:209–10

Breech clout, 8:25

Bufflehead, 11:35

Butterfly, 11:94–95

Çacachichimeca (people), 10:171–72

Cacao, 1:20 (44); 2:137, 140 (149, 152); 3:14, 31, 43 (14, 33, 45); 4:117, 123–24; 6:129, 256; 8:39–40, 43, 49, 67; 9:2, 12, 27, 28, 30, 33, 34, 35, 39, 40, 42, 51, 52; 10:65, 93, 150, 153, 154, 156, 158, 187; 11:4, 112, 119–20, 170, 176, 178, 189, 190, 192, 201, 202, 203, 206, 210; 12:41, 45, 91 (43, 47, 95); as medium of exchange, 9:48

Çacatepeca (people), 3:19 (21)

Calendar (tonalamatl), 2:35–39; 4:passim; 7:1; 10:168, 191; date of Spanish victory, 12:118 (122);

description of, 4:138–39, 145–46; Motolinía controversy, 4:139–46. See also Day signs

Calendar, civil, 2:passim; 4:137, 144–45; 10:168, 191; 12:9, 76, 79 (9, 80, 81); date of Spanish victory, 12:118 (122); fifty-two-year cycle, 2:194 (207); 4:137–38, 143–44; 7:21–32; 10:191

Calpulli, (1:22, 33, 37, 43, 45, 46); 2:7, 24, 39, 179–80, 190 (7, 24, 39, 193); 9:12, 14, 63, 64, 83, 87, 88

Cannibalism, 1:19; 2:3, 24, 47–48, 52–53, 170, 179 (3, 24, 48–49, 54, 184, 193); 4:35; 9:64, 67

Capes, 8:23–24; as medium of exchange, 9:46, 48, 87; vendors of, 10:63, 73, 75

Captives, 1:1, 13–14, 38 (1, 32, 67); 2:2, 3–4, 5, 11, 13, 17, 26, 28, 33, 35, 44–49, 57, 64, 65, 83, 89, 106–8, 113, 128–29, 136, 151, 162, 166–79 passim, 184, 203 (2, 3–4, 5, 11, 13, 17, 26, 28, 33, 35, 45–51, 59–60, 66–68, 88, 94, 113–15, 122, 139, 147–48, 163–64, 176, 180–93 passim, 197, 217); 3:41 (43); 4:5–6, 35–36, 42, 45, 91, 94; 5:185; 6:224; 7:2, 12, 25–26, 28, 31–32, 36, 62; 7:25 (26); 8:45, 53–54, 65, 83–85; 9:3, 4, 7, 66; 10:23, 24, 189; 12:18, 21, 95, 99–101 (18, 21, 99, 103–5); ceremonially bathed, 2:128, 171, 173 (139, 185, 187); 4:94; taking of, 3:53 (55); 8:53, 72–73, 75–77

Carpenters, 1:28–29 (57–58); 2:105 (112); 10:27, 81

Castor and Pollux, 7:60–62. See also Stars

Caterpillar, 11:97

Caves, 11:262, 275–77

Ceiba, 11:108, 215

Cempoalteca (people), 2:53 (55)

Centipede, 11:86

Century plant. See Maguey

Centzontotochtin singers, 2:193–94 (207)

Centzonuitznaua (sacrificial victims), 2:169, 177 (183, 191)

Ceremonial calendar. See Calendar (tonalamatl)

Chachalaca (bird), 11:53

Chachalmeca (gods), 2:200 (214)

Chachanme (captives), 2:167 (181)

Chalca (people), 9:40; 10:195, 197

Chalk, 11:243; moistening of, 2:189

(202); vendors of, 10:94

Charm against pain, 2:190 (203)

Chía, 2:7, 63, 121, 181 (7, 65, 121, 194); 4:118, 129; 7:17, 19; 8:38–39, 44, 67, 88; 9:6, 42, 48; 10:67, 75, 79, 93, 158, 188; 11:142, 151, 153, 158, 180, 181, 187, 244, 285, 286

Chichimeca (people), 4:26; 6:34, 258; 8:5, 8, 9, 13, 15; 9:83, 85; 10:67, 165; 170–75, 182, 189, 191, 195, 196–97; 11:82, 182, 256, 260; Acolhua Chichimeca, 8:13; Atlaca Chichimeca, 10:197; Çacachichimeca, 10:171–72; Cuextecachichimeca, 10:175; Chichimeca mochanecatoca, 10:175–76; Nahuachichimeca, 10:175; Otomí, 10:171; Otonchichimeca, 10:175; Tamime, 10:171; Teochichimeca, 10:171–74, 195; Toltecachichimeca, 10:170, 197; use of peyote by, 10:173

Chicle, 10:56, 77, 89–90

Childbirth, 4:111; 6:157, 159–61, 167–69; among Chichimeca, 10:174–75; ceremonies following, 6:167–77; discourses among commoners after, 6:192–94; discourses among rulers, lords, merchants, after, 6:183–92; discourses between ambassadors and ruler after, 6:189–92; discourses among midwife and relatives after, 6:179–82; dying in, 1:6, 42 (19, 71–72); 2:37; 6:161–65; midwife's discourse to newborn child, 6:167–77, 202–7; midwife's discourse to newly delivered mother, 6:179

Children, 1:6, 15 (19, 35, 82); 2:33, 34, 35, 38, 73, 91, 120, 126, 181, 199 (33, 34, 35, 38, 76, 96, 130, 136, 194, 212); 4:3–4, 34, 41, 55, 81, 107; 5:184, 185, 186, 187, 188–89, 193, 195; 6:115–16, 249; 7:8–9, 58; 8:71–72; 9:14, 15, 88, 95; 10:89, 175, 177, 178, 181; born at time of new fire ceremony, 7:31; ceremonies for recently born, 4:111, 113–15; ceremony of dedication over fire for, 2:41, 152 (41, 164–65); given pulque, 1:12 (30); 2:153, 156–57, 190, 197 (165, 169–70, 203, 210); growth ceremony for, 2:41, 153, 156, 189 (41, 165–66, 169, 202); sacrifice of, 1:39 (68); 2:1–2, 8, 42–43, 179 (1–2, 8, 42–43, 192); setting out of,

106

2:190 (203); standards of behavior of, 8:71; 10:2–3, 6, 9, 13; training of, 2:193 (206); 8:75

Chili, vendors of, 10:67–68

Chinampaneca (people), (1:79)

Chinquime (people), 10:187

Chipmunk, 11:11

Chochontin (people), 10:187

Chocolate. *See* Cacao

Cholulans, Cholulteca (people), 2:166 (180); 8:21; 12:29–30

Chontal (people), 10:75, 93; 11:256

Ciuapipiltin (goddesses), 1:6, 10, 34, 42 (19, 26, 64, 72); 2:36, 37, 38; 4:81; 6:161, 164. *See also* Ciuateteo

Ciuateteo (goddesses), 1:34, 42 (64, 72); 2:118, 175 (127, 189); 4:10, 41–42, 45, 81, 93, 107–8; 6:161. *See also* Ciuapipiltin

Clay, 11:257

Cliff, 11:261

Cloaks. *See* Clothing

Clothing, 8:23–25, 67; arm-wrist ornaments, rulers', 8:27; banners, rulers', 8:28, 34; breech clouts, rulers' and lords', 8:25; capes, rulers' and lords', 8:23–24; carried devices, 8:33–35; Chichimeca, 10:172–73; conical cap, rulers', 8:35; ear ornaments, rulers', 8:27, 35; ear ornaments, women's, 8:47; fans, rulers', 8:28; head ornament, rulers', 8:27–28, 33–35; human skins, 1:16–17 (39–40); 2:4, 19–20, 53–54, 112–15, 173, 177, 199 (4, 19–20, 54–55, 120–24, 186–87, 191, 212); 8:85; leg ornaments, rulers', 8:28; lip ornaments, rulers', 8:27–28; Michoaque, 10:188–89; neck ornaments, rulers', 8:28, 33; nose ornaments, rulers', 8:28, 35; Olmeca, 10:188; Otomí, 10:177, 178–79; sandals, rulers', 8:28; shirts, rulers', 8:33–35; skirt, rulers', 8:33; slaves', 9:45, 46; Totonaca, 10:184; war array, rulers', 8:33–35; warriors' array, 8:74, 77, 87; women's, 8:47–48. *See also* Costuming

Clouds, 7:17–18, 20, 72, 78

Cloud vessel, 2:83 (88)

Coateca (people), 2:55 (57)

Coatepeca (people), 3:19 (21)

Coati, 11:10

Cochineal, 8:48; 9:12, 18, 22; 10:55, 77, 147; 11:239–40

Cockerel, 11:53

Colors, 2:205 (219); 11:239–45, 258.

*See also* Dyes

Comets, 7:13, 64–66; 8:18; 12:2

Commerce, founding of, 9:1–8. *See also* Market place; Merchants; Vendors

Commoners, 4:9–10, 42–44, 88, 101–4; 6:57–59, 192–94, 227, 232, 241, 244–45, 246, 249, 251, 256, 257, 259; 7:29; 9:65; 10:27–28, 35–36, 41–42, 48, 51–53, 65–94; law suits, 8:41–42; protection in market place, 8:67

Communication, 11:266–69

Concubine. *See* Harlot; Paramour.

Confession, 1:8–11 (23–27); 6:29–34

Conjurers. *See* Magicians; Soothsayers; Wizards

Conquest(s), by Aztec rulers, 8:1–5; by merchants, 9:3–4, 21–23; by rulers of Tlatelolco, 8:7; of Mexico by Spaniards, 8:4, 8, 10, 18–19, 21–22; 12:passim; of Tlatelolco by Tenochtitlan, 8:2, 7; 9:2. *See also* Spaniards

Constellations. *See* Stars

Cooking, description of, 4:123

Coot, 11:26

Copal, 1:30 (59); 2:29, 39, 81, 84, 181, 182, 185, 197, 199, 215 (29, 39, 85, 89, 194, 195, 199, 210, 246); 9:4, 5, 11, 15, 37, 74, 77; 11:187; vendors of, 10:77

Copper, 9:9, 18, 76; 10:87; 11:235; knife, 9:97

Copperas, 11:243

Coppercaster, 10:26

Corn. *See* Maize

Cosmetics, women's, 8:47–48; 10:55

Costuming, 2:43, 45, 47, 48, 52, 79–80, 93–95, 98, 99, 106, 120, 151 (43–44, 45–46, 49, 54, 84–85, 98–100, 104, 105, 113–14, 129, 163–64); ceremonial, of merchant, 9:60; of ceremonially bathed slaves, 9:59–60; of dancing youths, 8:43; of newly elected ruler and assistants, 8:62–63; of singers and dancers, 8:45. *See also* Clothing

Cotinga, 11:21

Cotton, 3:14; 9:1, 8, 64, 93; vendors of, 10:75

Couixca (people), 8:68; 10:187, 197; 11:248

Courts of justice, 8:41–43, 54–55. *See also* Justice

Coyote, 5:180; 11:6–8

Cozcateca (people), 2:50, 53 (52, 55)

Craftsmen. *See* Artisans

Crag, 11:261

Crane, 11:27

Criminal court. *See* Courts of justice; Justice

Criminal(s), 11:23, 24; killing of, 2:37, 100 (37, 106); 4:42, 91; 6:242; 8:41; trials of, 8:41–42. *See also* Vicious people

Crocodile, 11:67

Crustacean, 11:59, 64

Crystal, fine, 11:229; rock, 9:8, 18, 80; 11:222, 225, 227

Cuckoo, 11:22

Cuexteca. *See* Huaxteca

Cuextecachichimeca (people), 10:175

Cypress, 11:108

Dance, 1:11, 12, 13, 15, 20, 21, 23, 45 (26, 30, 31, 35, 44, 45, 48, 75); 2:2, 13, 14, 15, 16, 17, 19, 22, 27, 28, 31, 34, 39, 41, 45, 50, 53, 54, 71–72, 79, 87–88, 93, 95–96, 98, 102–3, 106, 108, 110, 115, 120, 131–32, 144, 151–52, 153, 156, 157, 161, 163–64, 165, 173, 177, 188, 194, 197 (2, 13, 14, 15, 16, 17, 19, 22, 27, 28, 31, 34, 39, 41, 46, 51, 54, 55–56, 74–76, 84, 92, 93, 98–99, 100–2, 104, 109–10, 113, 116, 118, 123–24, 129–30, 142–43, 156, 163–65, 169, 170, 175, 177–78, 179–80, 187, 191, 201, 207); 3:7, 20, 21–22, 25, 53, 54–55 (7, 22, 23–24, 27, 55, 56–57); 4:25–27, 78, 122; 7:18, 76; 8:43, 45, 55–56, 65, 72, 76, 85; 9:38, 40, 46, 59, 63, 88, 89, 91, 92; 10:39, 183; 12:51, 53 (53, 55)

Dancers, 4:82; with dead woman's forearm, 4:101–6; 10:39

Darnel grass, 11:282

Darts, 2:25

Datura (Jimson Weed), 6:68, 70, 198, 253; 10:20; 11:147

Day signs, 2:35–40, 42, 150, 158, 170, 173, 175 (35–40, 42, 162, 171–72, 184, 187, 189); 4:passim; 6:197–98; 8:61, 64; 9:9, 10, 27, 31, 33, 56, 79; 10:31, 42, 168, 191; evil, 4:5–6, 7–8, 11–13, 20–21, 29–30, 30–31, 36–37, 41–44, 49–51, 55, 56–57, 73, 74, 82, 93–96, 99–100, 101–9; good, 4:1–4, 9–10, 19–20, 30, 31, 33–37, 53–54, 56, 57, 59–60, 73–74, 75, 77–79, 81–82, 83, 92, 97, 127; indifferent, 4:6–7, 23–25, 45–50, 71, 75, 85; readers of, 4:30, 50, 51, 54,

70, 73; 5:151, 152; 10:31, 42
Dead, disposal of, 2:121 (131); 3:39–43 (41–46); 4:102–3; 6:161–62; 9:25; 10:192; offerings to, 2:25, 125–26, 154 (25, 135–36, 167); 3:40–41 (42–43); 4:69–70
Dealers. *See* Merchants; Market place; Vendors
Debt to gods, 2:185–86 (199)
Deer, 11:15
Deer people, 2:172 (185). *See also* Quecholli
Demons, 1:40, 46 (70, 76); 7:27; 8:2
Desert, 11:262
Diseases, 1:4, 5, 6, 13, 14, 15, 16–17, 23, 41, 42, 43–44, 45 (15, 17, 19, 31, 33, 35, 39–40, 47, 71, 72, 73, 74, 79); 2:37, 38, 43, 56, 83, 158, 163, 170, 206 (37, 38, 43–44, 58, 88–89, 172, 177, 184, 220); 3:11–12, 16, 17–18, 39, 45 (11–12, 18, 19–20, 41, 47); 4:7, 21–22, 24, 34–35, 41, 70, 73, 81, 83, 107, 128; 5:161, 163, 183, 184, 185, 188–90, 192, 194; 6:29, 117–18, 232, 244, 252, 254, 258; 7:9, 12, 14, 31, 58, 62; 8:4, 5, 8, 22; 9:71; 10:13, 30, 53, 90; cures for, 10:139–63; 11:129–33, 137–39, 141–93, 201, 234; 12:81 (83). *See also* Medicine; Physicians
Divination, 1:4, 15, 32, 35, 41 (15, 35, 61, 65, 70); 2:39, 40, 42, 44 (39, 40, 42–43, 44–45); 4:passim; 9:9, 10, 27, 31, 33, 38, 39, 56, 79; 10:30, 31, 42, 53. *See also* Day signs; Calendar (tonalamatl); Omens
"Divine, sacred ear" spice, 9:27, 28, 30, 33; 10:187
Dogs, 11:15–16; as food, 9:48; breeding of, 4:19–20, 92; Spaniards', 12:19–20 (20)
Dove, 11:50
Drunkenness, 1:11, 23, 24 (26, 48, 51); 2:13, 90, 110, 141, 157, 197 (13, 95, 118, 154, 170–71, 210); 3:16 (18); 4:11–17, 47, 56, 119; 6:68–72, 130, 132, 207, 220, 230, 256–57; 9:41, 63, 87; 10:3, 4, 11, 12, 16, 20, 37, 38, 46, 47, 48, 49, 50, 55, 94, 179, 193–94
Duality, place of, 6:175, 202
Ducks, 11:26, 27, 35, 36, 37, 57
Dyes, 11:109, 112, 240, 241, 242, 245, 258; vendors of, 10:77, 91–92

Eagle, 11:40, 41; mat, 2:114 (123); men, 2:47 (48); vessel, 2:47, 52,

126, 136, 144–45, 173 (48, 53, 136, 147–48, 157, 187); 9:64
Ear, 10:113, 141; piercing of, 2:33, 34, 41, 152, 156, 192 (33, 34, 41, 164–65, 170, 205)
Ear ornaments. *See* Clothing
Earth, kissing of, 2:182, 206 (195, 220); 12:5
Education, 2:204–5 (218–19); 3:49–65 (51–67); 4:209–18, 227; 8:71–72, 76; 9:14, 95; 10:1, 4, 5, 19
Egret, 11:28, 58
Election of functionaries, 2:39
Embroiderers, 4:7, 25
Emery, 11:237, 238
Enemy's land, 2:114 (122)
Etzalqualiztli (month), 1:7 (21); 2:11–12, 74–85, 166 (11–12, 78–90, 180)
Evil people. *See* Vicious people
Exchange, of cacao, 9:48; of capes, 9:46, 48, 87
Exchange dealer, 10:61–62
Executioners, 2:100 (106); 8:43, 55

Falcons, 2:44 (45); 11:42, 43–45
Famine, 6:35–40; 7:22–24, 31; 8:1–2, 3, 5, 41; 12:100–101 (104–5)
Fans, 8:28
Farmer, 10:41
Fasting, 1:10, 11, 13, 43 (26, 31, 72); 2:27, 35–36, 41, 57, 59, 66, 67, 74, 75, 81, 124, 130, 132, 163, 165, 167, 179–80, 201, 203, 216 (27, 35–36, 41, 59, 61, 68–69, 70, 78, 79, 86, 134, 141, 143, 177, 179, 181, 193, 214, 217, 247); 3:6–9, 11, 64 (7–9, 12, 66); 4:7, 25, 78, 144; 7:1, 17, 31, 34, 74; 8:63–64; 9:65
Father of the gods, 1:9 (24)
Feasting. *See* Banquets
Featherwork, 3:13; 9:1, 2, 3, 4, 5, 6, 8, 17, 19, 21, 22, 29, 45, 47, 51, 59, 60–61, 65–66, 69, 70, 76, 80, 83–97; 10:61
Featherworkers, 8:45, 67; 9:85–97; 10:25, 61; specialists among, 9:91–92; Tolteca, 10:167
Fifty-two-year cycle, 2:194 (207); 4:137–38, 143–44; 7:21–23; 10:191
Finch 11:48
Fir, 11:107; gathering branches of, 2:78 (83); strewing branches of, 2:118–19, 186 (127–28, 199); 3:12; 5:157; 7:5
Fire, 1:11, 12, 42 (29, 30, 72, 84); 2:17–18, 33, 39, 41, 71, 106–8, 140,

176, 194, 204 (17–18, 33, 39, 41, 74, 113–15, 152, 190, 207, 218); 3:6, 8, 53, 54 (7, 8, 55, 56); 4:87; 6:239; 7:4–6, 46–50; 8:53, 58; 9:9–11; drilling new, 2:177, 178 (191, 192); 8:25–32; illumination with, 2:192 (205); laying of, 4:5; offering to, 2:154 (167); quickening of, 2:191 (204)
Firefly, 11:100–101
Fire serpent, 2:136, 171–72 (147, 185); 9:65
Firewood, 3:53, 63 (55, 65); 12:45 (47); for the gods, 2:186, 198, 204 (199, 211, 218); for Uitzilopochtli, 3:6–7, 8 (7, 8)
First fruits offering, 2:5, 16, 36, 55 (5, 16, 36, 57)
Fish, 11:58–59, 62, 63; vendors of, 10:80. *See also* Shellfish
Flaying, 1:4–5, 16–17 (16, 39–40); 2:4, 19, 46, 52, 112, 173, 177, 199 (4, 19, 47, 54, 120–21, 186–87, 191, 213); 8:85; 9:69–71
Flaying of men, pole of the, 2:57 (59–60)
Flint, 9:81–82; 11:222, 229
Flint sand, 11:238
Flooding of Mexico, 8:2, 18; 12:2
Flower of the God, 2:145 (157)
Flower Race, 2:145 (157)
Flowers, 11:197–215; offering of, 2:5, 55, 101–2, 199 (5, 57, 108–9, 212); 4:78; rulers' exclusive, 8:28; paper, 9:63
Flycatcher, 11:47
Folk beliefs, animal, 5:190, 191–92, 193; 11:2–3, 6–7, 8–9, 11–12, 16–17, 24, 33–34, 51, 52–53, 68–70, 70–71, 72–73, 77–78, 79, 80–81, 82, 84, 89; childbirth, 5:185, 186, 188–89; 6:156–57; comet, 7:13, 64–66; cooking, 5:185, 187–88, 194; creaking, snapping, 5:194; drinking, 5:185, 193; earthquakes, 5:187; eating, 5:185, 188, 193, 194; end of fifty-two-year cycle, 7:27–28; fire, 5:194; flowers, 5:183–84; hail, 5:192; hearthstones, 5:87; hunting of ocelot, 11:2–3; leaning, 5:188; lunar eclipse, 7:8–9, 58; maize, 5:184, 188–89, 194; markings on moon, 7:7, 54; merchants, 9:11, 16, 38; morning star, 7:12; precious stones, 11:221–22; pregnancy, 5:185, 186, 189–90; 6:156–57; 7:8–9, 58; rainbow, 7:18, 80;

shooting star, 7:13; sneezing, 5:193; sorcery, 5:192–93; stepping over child, 5:184; teeth, 5:194, 195; twins, 5:195; weaving, 5:192. *See also* Omens

Food, 1:2, 4, 6, 7, 12, 13, 14, 16, 20, 22 (7, 13, 19, 22, 29–30, 31, 33, 37, 44, 48); 2:7, 11, 14, 16, 21, 23, 33, 38, 44, 47–48, 53–54, 55, 59–60, 62–63, 70, 91–93, 99, 101, 122, 133, 137, 141, 154, 163–64 (7, 11, 14, 16, 21, 23, 33, 38, 45, 49, 55, 57, 61–62, 64–65, 73, 96–98, 105, 109, 132, 144, 149, 153, 167–68, 177–78); 3:9, 14, 43 (9, 14, 45); 4:25; 8:67–69; 9:27, 33–35, 48; 12:21–22, 28, 45, 71 (21–22, 28, 47, 75); cooked, 10:52–53, 69–70; lords', 8:37–40; offerings of, 2:181 (194); storage of, 8:44

Forest, 11:105–6

Four Hundred Rabbits, 4:15, 17. *See also* Pulque

Four Lords, 12:35, 104 (37, 108)

Fox, 11:9

Franciscans, 8:4, 22

Frog, 11:63; in omen, 5:173; swallowing of, 2:188 (201)

Frost, 2:113 (121); 7:119

Fruit trees, 11:116–22

Gallinule, 11:32

Gambling, 4:94; 8:29–30, 58–59

Games, striking women and girls with soft bags, 2:31–32, 145 (31–32, 157–58); patolli, 8:29–30, 59; rubber ball (tlachtli), 8:29, 58

Garden, rulers', 8:30

Gardening, 4:128

Gems. *See* Stones

Gifts, 9:8, 28, 47, 55

Girls, 2:14, 32, 41, 61, 62, 96, 99–100, 215 (14, 32, 41, 63, 64, 102, 105–6, 246); 9:88; 10:2–3, 46–47, 89, 94, 178, 179, 181; in calmecac, 6:209–11; in telpochcalli, 6:209–10

God-captive, 2:57 (60)

God of the gods, 2:9

Godparents, 2:33

Gods, 1:passim; 2:passim; 7:3–9, 42–58; arrival of, 2:21–22, 118–19 (21–22, 127–29); captive, 2:168 (182); copal figures of, 2:81, 84 (85, 89); death of, 3:1; rubber figures of, 2:80–81 (85); old, 1:9, 11–13, (24, 29–30); 2:22, 120 (22, 129)

Gold, 3:13; 8:67; 9:2, 3, 4, 5, 7, 8, 17, 18, 23, 24, 59, 73–78, 83, 85, 92; 10:25–26, 61–62, 87; 11:233–34; 12:45–46, 47, 70, 118, 121–22 (48, 49, 72, 122, 125–26)

"Gold medicine," 9:75

Goldworkers, 9:69–78; 10:25–26, 61

Goose, 11:26, 27, 57

Gopher, 11:16, 18

Gorge, 11:263

Gourd, 1:21, 22 (45, 47, 48); 10:68, 77–78; 11:134–35, 288, 289. *See also* Squash

Grackle, 11:50

Grain bin, burning of, 2:144–45 (156–57)

Grasses, 11:193–94, 196

Great Bear, 7:66. *See also* Stars

Grebe, 11:31, 37, 39

Greens, spreading of, 2:191 (204)

Green stone, 11:222, 223, 225–26

Grosbeak, 11:22

Guan, 11:46

Gull, 2:44 (45); 8:68; 11:43

Hail, 7:20

Hair, as trophy, 2:3, 46, 48, 106–7, 127, 133, 151 (3, 47, 49, 114–15, 138, 163); 9:63, 64, 67

Hairstyles, of boys and youths, 8:75–76; of women, 8:47–48; of Huaxtec, 10:185; of Otomí, 10:177, 178; of Tamime, 10:171; of Totonac, 10:184

Hare, 11:12

Harlot, 2:54, 93, 102, 110–11, 155 (56, 98, 109, 118–19, 169); 4:25, 95; 6:125–26; 10:3, 12, 13, 55, 89, 94. *See also* Paramour

Hawk, 5:153–55; 11:40, 41, 43

Head, as trophy (Huaxteca), 10:185–86

Headdress. *See* Clothing

Heavens, 6:175, 202; 10:168–69

Herbs, 9:18; 10:30, 53, 173; 11:129–88, 191–97; vendors of, 10:77, 85–86, 92

Heron, 11:27, 28, 39

Hill, 11:261

Honeycreeper, 11:21

Horticulturist, 10:42

House of the sun, 2:203 (217); 3:47–48 (49); 6:114–15, 162–63

Houses, construction of, 11:114–16, 193, 194, 254, 255, 256, 265, 270–75

Huaxteca, Cuexteca (people), 1:4

(16); 2:112–13, 195 (120–22, 208); 6:34; 8:45, 77; 9:79; 10:67, 68, 175, 184, 185–86, 193–94

Huehuetlatolli, ueuetlatolli. *See* Old people, discourses of

Human Banners, 2:179 (192)

Human skins, burial of, 2:5, 55–57 (5, 58–59); 8:86; wearing of, 1:16-17 (39–40); 2:4, 19–20, 53–54, 112–14, 173, 177, 199 (4, 19–20, 54–55, 120–122, 187, 191, 213); 8:85; 9:69–71

Hummingbird, 11:24–25

Hunting, by Chichimeca, 10:171–72; ceremony for, 2:25–26, 126–27, 167 (25–26, 137, 181); of eagles, 11:42; of monkeys, 11:14; of ocelot, 11:2–3; of turtles, 11:60

Ibis, 11:32

Idolatry, confutation of, 1:33–46 (62–76); discussion of, 1:27–46 (55–76)

Iguana, 11:61

Iiopoch (priests), 2:161 (175)

Impersonators, 1:4, 13, 15, 19, 20–21, 38, 43 (16, 31, 35, 43, 45, 68, 73); 2:9–10, 13, 14–15, 19, 26, 31, 33–34, 64–72, 83, 86–89, 97, 110–15, 122–23, 127–29, 143, 150–51, 155, 162, 167–79 passim, 195–201 passim (9–10, 13, 14–15, 19, 26, 31, 33–34, 66–75, 88, 91–95, 103, 119–24, 132–33, 137–39, 155, 162–63, 168, 176, 180–92 passim, 208–15 passim); 9:69–70, 80, 87; Tezcatlipoca's, 2:64–68 (66–70)

Incense offering, description of, 2:139, 181–82, 202 (151, 194–95, 216)

Informers, punishment of, 2:166 (180); 8:57

Insects, 11:64, 87–103, 239

Iuipapaneca temilolca (sacrificial victims), 2:177 (190)

Izcalli (month), 1:12, 42 (29, 72); 2:33–34, 147–57, 177 (33–34, 159–71, 191)

Jabiru, 11:43

Jade, 11:222, 223. *See also* Green stone

Jaguar (ocelot), 11:1–3

Jaguarundi, 11:5

Jail, 8:41, 42, 43, 44; 9:46

Jesters, 8:30

Jet, 11:222, 228

Jimson Weed (*Datura*), 6:68, 70, 198, 253, 10:20; 11:147

Judges, 8:54–55, 74; magistrate, 10:15–16. *See also* Justice
Justice, 8:41–43, 54–55, 69; 10:15–16, 32–33; among merchants, 9:23, 24. *See also* Courts of justice

Kinship, affinal, brother-in-law, 10:8; daughter-in-law, 10:8; father of parents-in-law, 10:7; father-in-law, 10:7; mother of parents-in-law, 10:7–8; mother-in-law, 10:7; sister-in-law, 10:8–9; son-in-law, 10:8; stepchild, 10:9; stepfather, 10:9; stepmother, 10:9
Kinship, consanguineous, aunt, 10:3–4; older brother, 10:9; child, 10:2, 3; daughter, 10:2–3; father, 10:1; grandchild, 10:6; grandfather, 10:4–5; grandmother, 10:5; great-grandfather, 10:5; great-grandmother, 10:5; great-great-grandparent, 10:5–6; illegitimate child, 10:2; legitimate child, 10:2; mother, 10:2; nephew, 10:4; niece, 10:4; uncle, 10:3
Kinship terms, sex of speaker in, 10:4, 8, 9

Land, sale of, 3:8 (9)
Land of the dead, 3:39–43 (41–45); 6:237; 7:21
Lapidaries, 3:13; 8:67; 9:69; 10:26, 60–61, 86–87; Chichimeca, 10:173: gods of, 9:79–80; techniques of, 9:80–82; Tolteca, 10:167–68. *See also* Stones
Law. *See* Justice
Lead, 11:234–35; pulverized, 11:237
Leap year, 4:144. *See also* Bissextile year
Leech, 1:4, 40–41 (15, 70)
Legal system. *See* Justice
Leg ornaments. *See* Clothing
Lettuce, 11:139
Libations, 2:182–83 (195–96); 4:87
Lightning, 4:10; 7:15, 72
Lime, 11:264, 265; vendors of, 10:78
Limestone, 11:244, 254, 264
Lineage. *See* Kinship, consanguineous
Linnet, 5:180
Lip, piercing of lower, 2:192 (205)
Lip ornament. *See* Clothing
Litters, 2:1, 23, 43, 122–23, 179 (1, 23, 44, 132–33, 192)
Little Bear, 7:66. *See also* Stars
Locust, 11:96–97
Lordly Dance, 2:152, 156, 177 (164,

169, 191)
Lord of the Night, 2:202 (216)
Lords, 2:14, 16, 20, 33–34, 36, 37, 39, 86, 93–96, 151–52, 156, 170, 179–80 (14, 16, 20, 33–34, 36, 37, 39, 91, 98–102, 164, 169, 184, 193); 3:67 (69); 4:9–10, 29, 33–34, 42, 88, 101–2, 121–24; 6:47–126, 213–16, 243–60 passim; 8:passim; 9:2, 19, 23, 34, 35, 53; 10:15–22, 45–50; clothing of, 8:23–35; disgrace of, 8:41; food of, 8:37–40; foreign, housing of, 8:44; houses of, 8:41–44; 11:270–71; of the sun, 8:52; standards of behavior of, 10:15–22, 45–50
Lost wax method, 9:78

Maçateca (people), 2:163–64, 188 (177–78, 201)
Maçaua, Maçauaque (people), 7:14; 10:183–84; 11:279, 282
Macaw, 11:23
Magicians, 4:43; 10:192; 12:21–22, 33–34. *See also* Wizards
Magistrates. *See* Judges
Maguey, 11:149, 162, 163, 179, 213, 216, 217, 252
Maidens, standards of behavior of, 6:92–103, 216–18; 10:2–3, 4, 12–13, 46, 47
Maize, 1:4, 6, 7, 13, 16, 17, 22 (13, 15, 19, 22, 32, 37, 40); 2:7, 21, 62–63, 116, 118, 141, 149, 164, 165, 181 (7, 21, 64–65, 124, 127, 153, 161, 178, 179–80, 194); 3:7, 14, 29, 40, 45 (7, 14, 31, 42, 47); 4:26, 49, 78, 113, 118, 123, 128–29; 5:184; 6:201, 205, 222, 226–27, 228, 231, 235, 237, 238, 240, 258; 7:8, 20, 23, 32, 72, 76; 8:37–39 passim, 44, 59, 67, 69, 85, 88; 9:6, 13, 29, 41, 48, 67, 70, 80, 97; 10:42, 65–66, 69–70, 79, 87, 93, 155, 160, 169, 171, 178, 179–80, 181, 183, 186, 188; 11:279–84; 12:21, 71 (75); gruel, 8:39; planting, 11:283–84; renewal ceremony, 2:164 (178)
Majordomo, 8:39, 44, 51
Mammals, 11:1-18, 61, 67–70
Man, possessed, 10:31–32; rich, 10:41
Mantas. *See* Capes
Manzanita, 11:109
Market place, 8:67–69; 9:24, 46. *See also* Merchants; Vendors
Marriage, 1:20 (44, 81); 2:40–41, 97, 215 (40–41, 103, 246); 3:57 (59);

6:117–18, 127–33; 10:7; Chichimeca, 10:172–73, 174–75; Otomí, 10:181
Mason, 10:28
Matlatzinca (people), 8:72; 10:66, 181–83; 11:279
Mats, 8:31; making of, 1:20, 44 (45–46, 74); vendors of, 10:86
Mature man, (1:82); 10:12
Mature woman, (1:82); 10:12
Meadowlark, 11:47
Mecateca (people), 2:53 (55)
Medicine, 1:4–5, 15, 41, 43 (1:15–16, 17, 35, 71, 73); 2:158 (172); 3:15–16 (17–18); 6:159–60, 167; 9:18; 10:30, 53, 77, 85–86, 90, 139–63, 167, 173; 11:120, 121, 129, 131, 133, 138, 141–88, 192, 193, 201, 219; charm against pain, 2:190 (203); medicine man, 10:30; medicine woman, 2:19, 110–14 (19, 118–22); "obsidian medicine," 9:63, 87. *See also* Disease; Physicians
Men, wise, 8:18–19; 10:29, 31
Merchants, 1:1, 17–20, 41, 44 (1, 41–44, 71, 74); 2:36, 37–38, 119, 120 (36, 37–38, 129); 4:45–48, 59–71; 5:153–55, 190; 9:47; 10:42–43, 59–60; as bathers of sacrificial victims, 9:7, 12, 18, 28, 32, 46, 47, 51, 55, 10:59; as burden-carriers, 9:14, 15; as warriors, 9:3, 6, 17, 18; ceremonies on death of, 4:69–70; 9:25; ceremonies on departure of, 9:9–16; discourses of old people among, 4:61–66; 9:13, 29, 55–57; disguised, 9:5, 6, 7, 12, 13, 21–23, 32, 47, 55; exploring, 9:27; justice among, 9:23, 24; foremost, 9:53; outpost, 9:5, 6, 8, 55; principal, 9:1, 2, 3, 6, 7, 12, 13, 14, 18, 22, 23, 24, 33, 38, 47, 55; 10:59–60, 63–64; reconnoitering, 9:8, 19, 24; spying, 9:6, 7, 13, 47; trading, 9:90; vanguard, 9:4, 5, 6, 7, 8, 9, 14, 16, 19, 23, 24, 27, 28, 31, 43, 48, 51, 52, 55, 88, 90; 10:60; women, 9:16, 28, 47. *See also* Vendors
Merganser, 11:35
Mesquite, 11:120
Metalsmiths, 8:45, 67, 68; 9:69, 73–78; 10:25–26, 61, 87; gods of, 9:69–71
Mexica, Mexicans (people), 2:166 (180); 8:72; 9:83; 10:165, 171,

175, 183, 189–97; 12:6, 16, 29, 47, 66, 69–70, 72, 75 (6, 16, 29, 49, 68, 71–72, 76, 79)

Mexiti. *See* Mexica, Mexicans

Mica, 11:235

Michoaca, Michoaque (people), 10:188–89, 195, 197; 11:256

Micteca (people of Mictlan), 6:163

Middle age, 10:11–12

Midwives, 1:4, 41 (15–16, 70); 2:19, 39; 4:93; 6:149–82, 201–7, 249

Military office, distinctions of, 6:110

Military rule of Tlatelolco, 9:2

Mimixcoa (gods), 7:7, 52; song of, 2:209–10 (230)

Minerals, 11:61, 237–38, 243–44, 254, 257, 264–65

Mines, 10:168; 11:222, 226

Mirror, mirror stone, 2:113 (122); 8:18, 28; 10:87, 173; 11:222, 228

Mirror stone earth, 11:237

Mixteca (people), 6:34; 10:187–88; 11:256, 260. *See also* Olmeca

Mockingbird, 11:52

Mollusk, 11:60–61, 224, 230–31

Monkey, 11:14

Moon, 7:3, 39–40; eclipse of, 7:8–9, 58; goddess of, 2:167 (181); god who became, (1:83–84); 7:3–9, 42–58.

Morning star, 7:11-12, 62; impersonator of, 2:172 (186). *See also* Stars

Mother of the gods, 1:9 (24)

Motmot, 11:21

Mountain gods. *See* Tepictoton

Mountains, 2:1, 5, 23, 29, 42, 43, 114, 121–22, 130 (1, 5, 23, 29, 42, 43, 122, 131, 132, 141); 3:35–36, 45 (37, 47); 11:258–61

Mountain lion, 11:5

Mouse, 5:173; 11:17–18

Movable feasts, 2:35–41

Mulberry, 11:121

Mushrooms, edible, 10:69; 11:132; narcotic, 9:38–39; 10:20, 37, 49, 55; 11:130

Music, 1:5, 7, 12, 13, 16, 20, 22, 45 (17, 22, 29, 31, 37, 44, 48, 74); 2:2, 6, 9, 13, 15, 16, 21, 23, 27, 28, 29, 36, 44, 45, 50, 55, 58, 63, 66, 68, 72, 77, 79, 83, 88, 93, 98, 102, 103, 109, 113–14, 115, 120, 122, 130, 132, 137, 140–41, 144, 148, 151, 152, 157, 175, 188, 193, 195, 198–99 (2, 6, 9, 13, 15, 16, 21, 23, 27, 28, 29, 36, 44, 46, 52, 57, 60, 65, 68, 75, 81, 84, 87–88, 93, 98, 104–5, 110, 117, 122,

124, 129–30, 132–33, 141, 142–43, 148–49, 152–53, 156, 161, 163, 170, 189, 201, 207, 208, 212); 3:8, 20, 21–22, 42, 53, 54–55, 65 (8, 22, 23–24, 44, 55, 56–57, 67); 4:17, 26, 81; 6:237, 239; 7:38; 8:28, 29, 35, 43, 45, 55–56, 65, 72, 76; 9:4, 9, 37, 41, 45, 46, 63, 65; 10:28–29, 39, 169

Nagual, 6:221

Nahua (people), 10:170, 171, 175–76, 195, 197

Nahuachichimeca (people), 10:175

Nahuatl, 10:171, 175, 182, 184, 186, 188, 189

Naming ceremony, 4:113; 6:203–4. *See also* Baptismal ceremony

Narcotics. *See* Jimson Weed; Mushrooms, narcotic; Medicine, "obsidian medicine"

Nations. *See* Peoples

Neck ornaments. *See* Clothing

New fire ceremony, 4:143–44; 7:25–32

Nobles. *See* Lords

Nonoalca (people), 2:53 (55); 10:170, 197; 11:256

Nopal, 11:124–26, 180, 181, 199, 217, 239, 240, 243. *See also* Tuna cactus

Nose ornaments. *See* Clothing

Oaths, 2:206 (220). *See also* Earth, kissing of

Obsidian, 11:222, 226, 227; vendors of, 10:85

Ocelot, 11:1–3

Ochpaniztli (month), 2:19–20, 110–17, 130, 173, 175–76, 177 (19–20, 118–26, 141, 187, 189, 191); 7:19

Ocuilteca (people), 10:183

Old people, 1:5, 11, 12, 16, 22–23, 44 (17, 26, 27, 37, 48–49, 74, 82); 2:3, 13, 14, 16, 21, 25, 27, 40, 41, 47, 55, 58, 63, 76, 88, 89–90, 99, 100, 103, 110–11, 115, 119, 125, 126, 137, 148, 149–50, 153, 155 (3, 13, 14, 16, 21, 25, 27, 40, 41, 48, 57, 60, 65, 81, 93, 95, 105–6, 110, 118–19, 123, 128–29, 135, 136, 148, 160–61, 162, 165, 168); 3:15–16, 27, 29, 31, 40, 42, 50 (17–18, 29, 31, 33, 42, 44, 52); 4:17, 21, 39, 47, 56, 61–64, 78–79, 97, 108, 131; 6:118; 8:61; 9:15, 16, 27, 32, 38, 41, 42, 83, 87; 10:4–6, 7, 11, 174, 189, 191, 192; discourses of (ueuetlatolli), 3:39–40, 49–51,

59–60 (41–43, 51–53, 61–63); 4:2, 61–66, 114–15; 5:154; 6:1–218; 9:13, 29, 42–43, 55–57

Olmeca (people), 6:34; 10:187–88, 192, 197. *See also* Mixteca; Tenime; Uixtotin, Uixtoti

Omacame (impersonators of Omacatl), 2:171 (185)

Omens, 2:35; 5:151–80; 7:13, 19, 62, 64–66; 8:19; 9:11, 16, 38; 11:29–30, 32; destruction of Mexico, 8:3–4, 9–10, 17–19; 12:1–3, 33–34. *See also* Folk beliefs

"One old age," 7:25

One Rabbit, 7:21–24; 8:2

One Wind, 7:14

Onion, 11:139

Opal, 9:82; 11:230

Opossum, 11:11; vendors of, 10:77

Oriole, 11:45

Osprey, 11:41

Otomí (people), 2:126 (137); 8:72; 9:21; 10:171, 176–81, 184, 186, 187, 195, 197; 12:27, 71 (27–28, 75); as warriors, 2:94, 102 (100, 109); 4:26; 6:110; 8:21, 52, 87–88; 9:32, 38, 47; 12:38, 88, 97, 106 (41, 92, 101, 110)

Otonchichimeca (people), 10:175, 197

Otter, 11:16, 67

Owl, 5:161, 163; 11:42, 46

Oyster, 11:61, 224

Painters, 2:35–36; 8:45. *See also* Scribe

Panoteca. *See* Huaxteca

Panquetzaliztli (month), 1:19 (43); 2:27–28, 129, 130–38, 161, 169, 172, 178, 196, 197 (27–28, 140, 141–50, 175, 183, 186, 192, 210); 3:5; 9:45, 67, 87

Panteca (people). *See* Huaxteca

Paper, 11:111; consecrated, 1:11, 22 (26, 47); 2:42; 9:9–12, 39–40, 51; flags, 2:37, 42, 71, 113, 122, 140 (37, 43, 74–75, 121, 132, 152); 9:69–70; flower, 9:63; garments, 1:6, 11, 12, 16, 21, 23 (19, 27, 30, 37, 46, 49); 2:23, 27, 45, 57, 69, 105, 106, 107, 113, 122–23, 133, 139, 150, 151 (23, 27, 45, 59–60, 72, 112, 113, 132–33, 144, 151, 163, 164); 3:40, 43, 45 (42, 45, 47); 4:29, 69, 87; 7:5, 46; 9:25; headdress, 1:5, 7, 12, 16, 21 (17, 22, 30, 37, 45); 2:113, 122 (121, 132);

3:4; 9:85; in featherwork, 9:94, 96, 97; on merchants' canes, 1:17 (41); 9:9–10; painted, 9:63; pendants, 9:66; pricked with thorns, 2:169 (182); rolled up, 2:134 (145); rosettes, 2:88 (93); rubber-spotted, 2:185 (199); 6:242; 9:9, 39–40; sacrificial, 2:136, 171–72 (147, 185); 9:65; streamers, 1:15 (34); 2:29, 105, 140 (27, 112, 152); 3:43 (45); 4:41; vendors of, 10:78, 91; wigs, 2:105 (112); wings, 2:43 (44); 9:60

Parakeet, 11:23

Paramour, 2:96–97 (102–3); 3:55, 57, 64 (57, 59, 66); 4:25. See also Harlot

Parrot, 11:22–24

Pass, 11:262

Paths, 11:266–69

Peak, 11:261

Pearl, 11:60, 222, 224

Pebble, 11:264–65

Peccary, 11:10

Pelican, 11:27, 29–30

Penance, 1:10–11 (26–27); 2:5, 25, 27, 29, 75, 139, 166, 167, 169, 191, 195, 206 (5, 25, 27, 29, 79, 151, 180, 181, 183, 204, 220); 3:1–2, 6–9, 14, 21, 49, 53 (1–2, 6–9, 14, 23, 52, 55); 4:2, 5–7, 25, 34, 50, 59, 63, 69–70, 85; 5:155, 157; 7:4–5; 8:57, 62–64, 72, 81; 9:13, 31; 10:177. See also Self-sacrifice

People, poor, 2:14, 91–93, 163 (14, 96–98, 177); 4:8, 113, 123; 6:225–26, 228, 229, 232; 9:14, 41, 56; vicious, 10:37–39, 55–57, 89–90, 94. See also Criminals

Peoples, 10:165–97. See also Water folk

Peru tree, 11:143

Pestilence, 8:4, 5, 8, 22; 12:81 (83)

Peyote, 11:129, 147; used by Chichimeca, 10:173

Phalarope, 11:28, 57

Physicians, 1:4, 40–41 (15, 70); 2:41; 4:81; 10:30, 53, 85. See also Diseases; Medicine

Picture writing, 1:9 (24); 3:65 (67); 6:198, 233, 258, 259; 8:42, 55; 10:29, 190, 196; burned in Itzcoatl's reign, 10:191

Pigments, 10:28, 77; 11:112, 239–45, 258. See also Dyes

Pillauanaliztli (feast), 4:144

Pine, 11:107, 242

Pinome (people), 10:187; 11:256

Pintail, 11:36

Pipes, clay, 8:35

Plague. See Pestilence

Plains, 11:261–63

Plants, 11:105–220. See also Flowers

Pleiades, 4:143; 7:60. See also Stars

Plover, 11:34

Plum, 11:119

Potters, 10:81

Pottery, 11:256–58

Prayers, 2:206 (220); 3:11–12, 39–40 (11–12, 41–42); against a bad ruler, 6:25–28; against famine, 6:35–40; against pestilence, 6:1–5; at confession, 6:29–34; for aid in war, 6:11–15; for ruler, 6:17–20, 21–24, 41–45; for riches, 6:7–10

Precipice, 11:263

Pregnancy, discourses concerning, 6:135–58; effects of lunar eclipse on, 7:8–9, 58. See also Childbirth

Priestesses, 2:98, 116, 197, 198, 215–16 (104, 124–25, 211, 246–47); 6:209–10

Priests, 1:7, 14, 22, 45 (21, 33, 48, 75); 2:13, 15, 19, 20, 21–22, 27, 29, 31, 36, 44, 46–47, 60, 68, 71, 74–85, 88, 98–99, 105, 107–8, 112–14, 119–20, 130, 133–36, 139–42, 148, 161–62, 166–77 passim, 204–5, 215 (13, 15, 19, 20, 21–22, 27, 29, 31, 36, 44, 47–48, 62, 71, 74, 78–90, 93, 105, 112, 114–15, 120–23, 128–29, 141, 145–47, 151–54, 160, 175–76, 180–91 passim, 218–19, 246); 3:5–8, 45, 59–61 (6–8, 47, 61–63); 5:157; 6:1–40, 118, 209–10, 244; 8:56–57, 71, 81–82, 84; 9:38, 63; 10:166, 169–70, 177, 187, 189, 190, 194; 12:33–34, 86 (88); costuming of, 2:82, 145 (86–87, 157); Franciscan, 8:4; choice of high, 3:67–68 (69–70); of gods, 2:193–201 (206–15); 3:6, 7 (6, 7–8); 8:61–64, 81; of tangled hair, 9:61; punishment of, 2:11, 76, 78–79, 80–81 (11, 80, 83, 85); 4:42; 7:17–18, 74–76; 8:82; Quetzalcoatl, 3:5, 67–68 (6, 69–70); 6:54, 210; robbing by, 2:74–75 (78–79)

Priests' house, 2:60, 168, 170, 176, 193, 198, 204–5 (62, 181–82, 183–84, 190, 206, 211, 218); 3:59–65 (61–67); 4:29; 8:71–72, 81–82; 9:88

Processions, 2:134–35, 161, 162, 167,

179, 188, 194 (145–46, 175, 176, 181, 192, 201, 207); 4:25

Prostitute, 10:94. See also Harlot; Paramour

Pulque (octli), 1:11, 14, 15, 16, 22–24, 44 (26, 33, 35, 37, 74); 2:16, 21, 23, 36, 50–51, 58, 90, 103, 119, 122, 133, 140, 148, 155, 194, 200 (16, 21, 23, 36, 52, 60, 95, 110, 128–29, 132, 144, 153, 161, 168, 207, 214); 3:9, 16, 34, 57–58 (9, 18, 36, 59–60); 4:11, 47, 60, 87, 108, 117, 118–19; 6:68–72, 130, 198, 230; 8:84; 10:37, 143, 144, 150, 151, 153, 154, 156, 159, 162, 180, 182, 193–94; 11:119, 154, 168, 179, 215, 217; given children, 1:12 (30); 2:153, 156–57, 197 (165, 169–70, 210); as "obsidian medicine," 9:63, 87; makers of, 1:23 (48–49); 2:149–50, 197 (162, 210); 4:78–79; origin of, 10:193; punishment for drinking, 2:99–100, 137 (106, 148); 3:57, 64 (59, 66)

Pumice stone, 11:264

Punishment, 8:52; for drinking pulque, 2:99–100, 137 (106, 148); 3:57, 64 (59, 66); in calmecac, 3:64 (66); in young men's house, 3:54 (56); 8:43–44; of adultery, 4:42, 45; 8:42–43; 9:39; 10:172; of bribery, 8:42; of careless musicians, 8:56; of concubinage, 2:95–96 (101–2); 3:64 (66); 4:42; 8:43–44, 82; of desecration of temple, 2:198 (212); of drunkenness, 8:43–44, 82; of informers, 2:166 (180); of merchants, 9:23–24; of misconduct in war, 8:53; of priests, 2:11, 76, 78–79, 80–81 (11, 80, 83, 85); 4:42; 7:17–18, 74–76; 8:82; of seduction, 2:72–73, 95 (76, 101); of theft, 4:42, 105–6; 8:44, 69; 9:39

Pyramid, 2:3, 5, 9, 10, 11, 12, 13, 15, 19, 20, 21, 26, 27, 28, 31, 36, 37, 107, 112, 116, 118, 123, 124, 127, 129, 133, 161, 165, 168, 170, 174, 175, 199 (3, 5, 9, 10, 11, 12, 13, 15, 19, 20, 21, 26, 27, 28, 31, 36, 37, 114–15, 120, 124–25, 127, 133, 134, 138, 139, 144, 175, 179, 182, 183, 184, 188, 189, 212); 4:143; 7:5, 29; 9:31, 65; 10:165, 167, 191–92; 11:269; 12:33, 56–57, 65, 99–100, 106 (58–59, 67, 103–4, 110)

Pyrite, 11:237

Quail, 2:194, 199, 215 (208, 213, 246); 8:67; 10:150, 155; 11:49; sacrifice of, 1:7, 12, 13 (22, 29, 31); 2:35, 36, 37, 38, 39, 51, 63, 70–71, 113, 162, 202–3 (35, 36, 37, 38, 39, 52, 65, 73–74, 121, 176, 216–17); 4:6, 7, 33, 46, 87; 7:31; 9:10, 37–38, 52, 69

Quaochpanme. See Michoaca

Quaquata (people), 4:26; 8:52; 10:181–83

Quauitl eua (month), 1:38 (68); 2:1–2, 8, 42–45, 48, 197 (1–2, 8, 42–46, 49, 211)

Quecholli (month), 2:25–26, 124–29, 133, 163, 167, 171, 177, 201 (25–26, 134–40, 144, 177, 181, 185, 191, 214–15)

Quecholli tlami (feast), 2:172, 201 (186, 215)

Quetzal bird, 11:19–20

Rabbit, 5:167; 11:13; in face of moon, (1:84); 7:3–4, 7, 38, 42, 54

Raccoon, 11:9

Rail, 11:25

Rain, 1:2, 3, 7, 20 (7, 9, 22); 2:1, 5, 29, 42, 44, 139 (1, 5, 29 42–43, 44–45, 151); 7:17–18, 20, 72, 78, 80

Rainbow, 7:18, 78

Rain gods. See Tepictoton; Tlalocs

Rat, 11:18

Rattlesnake, 11:75–79

Rattle boards or sticks, 1:7, 16, 17 (22, 37, 40); 2:45, 49, 55, 57, 77, 99 (46, 50, 57, 59, 81, 105); 9:69–70

Raven, 11:43

Reeds, 1:15, 20, 21, 23 (34, 45, 46, 49); 11:194–96; gathering of, 2:74–75 (78–79)

Relationship. See Kinship, affinal; Kinship, consanguineous

Reptiles, crocodile, 11:67; iguana, 11:61; rattlesnake, 11:75–79; serpents, 2:23, 163–64 (23, 177–78); 11:70–72, 75–87; turtle, 11:59

Riddles, 6:237–40

Ringtail, 11:6

Rivers, 11:247–50

Roads, 11:266–69

Rubber, 1:2, 5, 6, 11, 16, 17, 22 (7, 17, 19, 26, 37, 40, 47); 2:23, 42, 43, 45, 116, 122 (23, 43, 44, 45, 124, 132); 3:45 (47); 4:41, 107; 9:9–10, 39–40; 10:141, 145, 154, 155, 187; 11:112; figures of gods,

2:80, 81 (85); vendors of, 10:87

Ruby, 11:222, 224

Ruler, as judge, 8:42, 55; artisans of, 9:91; assistants of, 8:61–62; as war leader, 8:51–54; attributes of, 10:15; banquets by, 4:121–24; care of market place by, 8:67–69; Chichimeca, 10:192–93; clothing and adornment of, 8:23–28, 33–35, 56, 62; court life of, 8:29–30; dancing of, 8:27, 45, 56; discourses on installation of, 6:41–59, 61–65, 67–77, 79–85; discourses to daughters of, 6:93–98, 99–103; discourses to sons of, 6:87–92, 105–26; election of, 4:87–88; 8:61–65; figures of speech concerning, 6:243–59 passim; foods eaten by, 8:37–40; generosity of, 8:59; mats of, 8:31; of Azcapotzalco, 8:15; of Tenochtitlan, 8:1–5, 7, 8, 9, 10; of Texcoco, 8:9–11, 14; of Tlacopan, 8:15; of Tlatelolco, 8:7–8; of Tollan, 3:13–36 (13–38); of Uexotla, 8:13–14; palace of, 8:41–45, 58, 87; penances by, when newly elected, 8:62–64; prayers concerning, 6:17–28; proclamation of war by, on accession, 8:65; qualifications of, 8:61; seats of, 8:31; war array of, 8:33–35

Rushes, 11:194–95

"Sacred, divine ear" spice, 9:27, 28, 30, 33; 10:187

Sacrifice, 1:passim; 2:passim; 4:93; of children, 1:39 (68); 2:1–2, 8, 42–43, 179 (1–2, 8, 42–44, 192); description of, 2:2, 3, 15, 18, 19, 47, 51–52, 89, 107–8, 129, 184 (2, 3, 15, 18, 19, 48–49, 52–54, 94–95, 114–15, 139–40, 197); 9:66; fire, 2:17–18, 22, 107–8, 120, 168–69 (17–18, 22, 114–15, 129, 182–83); 3:47 (49); gladiatorial, 2:2, 4, 44–45, 49–53, 176 (2, 4, 45–46, 50–54, 190); 3:47 (49); 4:93; 8:84; 9:7; in a net (Matlatzinca), 10:183; of slaves, 3:45–46; 9:63–67, 87; origin of, 7:8, 56. See also Sacrificial victims

Sacrificial victims (amapantzitzin), 2:162, 172 (176, 185–86); 3:47–48 (49); ceremonially bathed, 2:150–51, 155–56 (162–64, 168–69); flayed, 1:16–17 (39–40); 2:4, 19, 46, 52, 112, 173, 177, 199 (4, 19,

47, 54, 120–21, 186–87, 191, 213); 8:85. See also Sacrifice

Salt, 1:7 (22); 2:86 (91); 8:44, 67, 85; 9:48; 10:69, 84, 147, 148, 149, 153, 155, 162, 178, 183; 11:254, 257

"Sand, going into the," 2:97, 127, 133, 150 (103, 138, 144, 162); 9:63

Sandals. See Clothing

Sapodilla, 11:116

Sapota, 1:17 (40); 8:33, 38; 9:70; 10:79; 12:21

Scorpion, 11:87

Scribes, 4:7, 82; 8:45; 9:93; 10:28. See also Painters

Sea, 11:247

Seamstresses, 2:35–36; 10:52

Seashells, 11:222, 230, 231

Self-sacrifice, 1:10, 13 (26, 31); 2:7, 25, 35, 59, 76, 124, 184–85, 202–3 (7, 25, 35, 61, 81, 134–35, 197–98, 216–17); 3:14, 64 (14, 66); 4:5, 6–7, 25; 5:155; 7:1–2, 4–5, 11, 28, 34, 36–38, 44–46, 62; 8:64, 81; 9:10, 11, 27. See also Penance

Serpents, 11:7, 70–72, 75–87; swallowing of, 2:163–64, 188 (177–78, 201); representations of, 2:23

Shellfish, 11:61, 224; oyster, 11:61, 224; shrimp, 11:59. See also Fish

Shoveller, 11:38

Shrike, 11:45

Shrimp, 11:59

Silver, 9:76; 10:62; 11:233–34

Singer, 4:82; 10:28–29

Skimmer, 11:31

Skin-cutting ceremony, 2:73 (76–77)

Skull rack, 2:10, 68, 107, 114, 123, 166, 169, 170, 171, 172, 175 (10, 71, 114, 122, 133, 180, 183, 184, 185, 186, 189); 12:99–100 (104)

Skunk, 5:171; 11:13

Slate, 11:264

Slaves, 1:5, 7, 41, 44 (17, 22, 45, 71, 74); 2:3, 11, 16, 25, 26, 27, 33, 37, 64, 66, 179, 184 (3, 11, 16, 25, 26, 27, 33, 37, 66, 69, 193, 197); 4:5, 33–36, 95–96; 6:241–42; 7:23; 8:41, 45; 9:7; 10:59, 189; 12:95 (99); arrayed by slave merchant, 9:46; ceremonially bathed, 1:1, 19–20, 38 (1, 43–44, 67); 2:130–36, 150–51, 155–56 (141–48, 162–64, 168–69); 4:35, 95; 6:256; 9:45–46, 59–60, 63–67, 87; confined, 9:46; costuming of, 9:45, 59–60; dealers in, 9:12, 18, 23, 32,

45–67, 51, 55; 10:59; sacrifice of, 3:43 (45–46); 9:63–67, 87
Slings, 8:30
Smallpox, 12:81 (83)
Snail, 11:60
Snakes. *See* Serpents
Snipe, 11:28
Snow, 7:19
Soap, 11:133
Soils, 11:251–58
Solicitor, 10:32–33
Song house, 8:43, 72
Songs, of Amimitl, 2:210–11 (233); of Atamalqualiztli, 2:212–13 (238–39); of Atlaua, 2:213–14 (243); of Ayopechtli, 2:211 (235); of Chicome coatl, 2:213 (241); of Chimalpanecatl, 2:209 (227); of Ciuacoatl, 2:211–12 (236–37); of Ixcoçauhqui, 2:209 (228); of of Macuilxochitl, 2:214 (244); of Mimixcoa, 2:209–10 (230); of Otontecutli, 2:211 (234); of Teteo innan, 2:208–9 (226); of Tlaloc, 2:208 (224–25); of Tezcatzoncatl, 2:213 (242); of Uitzilopochtli, 2:207 (221–22); of Uitznauac yaotl, 2:207–8 (223); of Xipe totec Youallauan, 2:213 (240); of Xochipilli, 2:210 (231); of Xochiquetzal, 2:210 (232); of Yacatecutli, 2:214 (245)
Soothsayers, 1:8–11 (23–27); 4: passim; 6:29–34, 197–99; 10:30, 31–32, 53, 175, 177, 183, 192, 194; 11:3; 12:21–22, 33–34
Southern stars, 3:1–4 (1–5)
Spaniards, 6:244; 8:3, 7–8, 10–11, 21–22; 12:5–122 passim (5–126 passim); armaments of, 12:19, 37–38, 60, 70 (19, 39–40, 62, 72); arrival of, 7:21; 12:5–6, 9, 13–17; at battle of Tonan, 12:75–76 (79–80); besieged in Tenochtitlan, 12:55–66 (57–69); capture and sacrifice of, 12:95, 99–100 (99, 103–4); capture Moctezuma, 8:22; 12:43, 45 (45, 47); capture Tenochtitlan, 8:22; 12:117–22 (121–26); Aztec description of, 12:19–20, 30, 31, 37–38 (19–20, 30, 31, 39–40); enter Tenochtitlan. 8:22; 12:37–43 (39–45); fill canals, 12:85, 96, 105 (87, 100, 109); first arrive in Mexico, 12:5–6; flee Tenochtitlan, 12:65–67 (67–69); launch brigantines, 12:83–84

(85–86); massacre Aztecs in Tenochtitlan, 8:22; 12:53–54 (55–56); massacre Cholulans, 8:21; 12:29–30; meet with Moctezuma, 12:41–43 (43–45); reappear after fleeing Tenochtitlan, 12:79 (81); received in Teocalhueyacan, 12:67–72 (69–76); return to Mexico from expedition against Pánfilo de Narváez, 12:59 (61); search for gold, 12:118, 121–22 (121, 125–26); set up catapult, 12:109 (113); take Moctezuma's gold, 12:46, 47 (48, 49); win Tlaxcallan support, 8:21; 12:27–29
Spanish moss, 11:108, 109
Sparrow, 11:47
Spider, 11:88
Spinner, 10:35
Spoonbill, 11:20
Springs, 11:250
Squash, 1:22; 2:116 (124); 3:14, 45 (14, 47); 4:118; 7:17; 8:37–38, 44, 68; 9:48; 10:151; 11:288; 12:71 (75). *See also* Gourd
Squirrel, 11:10–11
Standards of behavior. *See* Behavior, standards of
Stars, Castor and Pollux, 7:60–62; fire drill constellation, 7:11; 8:18; Great and Little Bear, 7:66; morning star, 7:11–12, 62; Pleiades, 4:143; 7:60; scorpion, 7:13, 66; shooting star, 7:13; S-shaped stars, 7:13; Venus, 7:62. *See also* Comets
Steward, 8:44. *See also* Majordomo
Stone cutter, 10:27–28
Stones, common, 11:263–66; medicinal, 10:53; 11:188–89; precious and semiprecious, 9:80–82; 10:60–61; 11:221–30. *See also* Lapidaries
Storms, 1:3, 6 (9, 21); 7:14–15, 68–70
Straw, bed of, 2:191–92 (204–5)
Striped ones, 2:44–45 (45–46)
Striping, 2:190–91 (203–4)
Sun, 2:35, 47, 48, 49, 50, 52, 59 (35, 48, 49, 51, 53, 61); 4:6; 7:1–2, 34–38; eclipse of, 7:36–38; 8:2; formation of, (1:83–84); 3:1; 7:4–8, 42–58; worship of, 2:202–3 (216–17); quickening of, 2:191 (204)
Sun god, (1:81, 83–84); 2:167 (181); 7:1–2; 8:75; adornment of, 2:203 (217)
Swallow, 11:28

Sweathouse, 1:4, 41 (15, 70); 3:14; 5:195; 6:151–52, 155–56, 167; 8:48; 10:150, 151, 162; 11:141, 149, 154, 172, 177, 178, 179, 191
Sweeping, 2:186, 204 (199, 218); 3:1–2, 53, 57, 63 (1–2, 55, 59, 65); 4:5

Tadpole, 11:63
Tailor, 10:35
Tamales, 1:12, 13, 22 (29, 32, 48); 2:14, 16, 23, 25, 33, 55, 70, 92, 99, 101, 105, 109, 122, 133, 137, 140, 141, 147–48, 154, 163–64, 188, 216 (14, 16, 23, 25, 33, 57, 73, 97–98, 105, 109, 112, 116, 132, 144, 149, 152, 159–61, 167–68, 177–78, 201, 247); 3:9; 4:26, 62, 122, 123, 132; 5:185; 6:129, 132, 201; 8:37–38, 69, 85; 9:35, 41, 59; 10:52, 69–70, 79, 80, 178, 180, 183, 184; 11:121, 134, 138, 190, 288; 12:71 (75)
Tamime (people), 10:171
Tapir, 11:3
Tarascos (people), 10:189. *See also* Michoaca
Teal, 11:34–35, 37–38
Tecuilhuitontli (month), 2:13, 86–90 (13, 91–95)
Teeth, filed, 10:185, 186; stained, 8:48; 10:55, 109, 179
Temples, 2:161–80 (175–93); 11:269–70
Tenime (people), 4:26; 10:187. *See also* Olmeca
Tenochca (people), 2:54 (55); 3:6; 11:250. *See also* Mexica, Mexicans
Teochichimeca (people), 10:171–72, 173, 195
Teotl eco (month), 2:21–22, 118–20, 168, 169 (21–22, 127–30, 182)
Tepaneca (people), 2:54 (55); 8:2, 9, 52, 72; 10:183, 191, 195, 196, 197
Tepeilhuitl (month), 2:23–24, 120, 121–23, 124, 163, 167, 173, 176, 196, 197, 199, 201 (23–24, 130, 131–33, 134, 177, 181, 187, 190, 209, 210, 213, 215)
Tepicme. *See* Tepictoton
Tepictoton (mountain gods), 1:21–24, 35, 44–45 (47–49, 64, 74–75); 2:139–41 (151–53)
Thieves, 4:93–94, 102–6; 6:162, 259; 10:38–39; punishment of, 4:42, 105–6; 8:44, 69; 9:39

Thigh bone of captive, captor's trophy, 2:57 (60)

Thigh of captive, reserved for Moctezuma, 2:47 (49)

Thrasher, 11:51

Thunderbolts, 7:72

Tin, 9:8; 11:235

Tititl (month), 2:31–32, 143–46, 167, 174 (31–32, 155–58, 181, 188); 7:19

Tlacaxipeualiztli (month), 1:16–17 (39–40); 2:3–4, 8, 45, 46–54, 155, 174, 175, 176, 178 (3–4, 8, 46, 47–56, 168, 188, 189, 190, 192); 8:87; 9:69

Tlalhuica, Tlaluica (people), 10:66, 75, 78, 186, 197; 11:279, 282

Tlalocs (gods), 1:7, 16, 20, 21–24, 38–39, 41 (22, 45, 47–49, 68, 71); 2:1, 5, 11–12, 13, 29–30, 42, 139, 165–66 (1, 5, 11–12, 13, 29–30, 42, 90, 151, 179–80); 3:45 (47); 6:35, 39, 115; 7:18, 20, 72; 11:68, 69, 70

Tlaloque (gods), 6:35, 39, 115

Tlamacazque (gods), 6:35, 36, 38, 39, 40. See also Tlalocs

Tlamatzinca (impersonators of Tlamatzincatl), 2:171–72 (185)

Tlappaneca (people), 10:187. See also Couixca; Pinome; Tenime

Tlatelolca (people), 2:53–54 (55); 3:6

Tlateputzca (people), 11:279, 282

Tlaxcallans, Tlaxcalteca (people), 2:166 (180); 8:21; 10:195, 197; 12:27–29, 39, 46, 59, 65, 66, 69, 88 (41, 48, 61, 67, 68, 71, 99)

Tlaxochimaco (month), 2:16, 101–3, 104 (16, 108–10, 111); 9:87, 88

Toad, 11:72

Tobacco, 2:48, 77, 111, 137, 198 (49, 81, 119, 149, 212); 4:78, 117, 122, 124; 6:129; 8:28, 69, 81; 9:12, 28, 33, 34, 37, 38, 40, 41, 42, 45, 55, 59, 60; 10:85, 88, 140, 149; 11:146–47

Toçoztontli (month), 2:5–6, 8, 54, 55–58 (5–6, 8, 56, 57–60); 9:71

Toloque (people), 10:181–83. See also Matlatzinca

Toltecs, Tolteca (people), 3:13–36 (13–38); 10:165–70, 175, 187, 191, 194, 195, 197; 11:227; departure from Tollan, 3:31–36 (33–38); 10:170; housing, 10:166–67; language, 10:169, 170; lapidary art, 10:167–68; mine, 10:168; Tolte-

cachichimeca, 10:170

Topographical features, 2:1, 5, 23, 29, 42, 43, 114, 121–22, 130 (1, 5, 23, 29, 42, 43, 122, 131–32, 141); 3:35–36, 45 (37–38, 47); 11:247–69, 275–77

Tortillas, 1:6, 13 (19, 31, 32); 2:44, 53, 54, 60, 62, 99, 149, 181, 190 (45, 55, 62, 64, 105, 161–62, 194, 203); 3:40 (42); 4:26, 62, 132; 5:187–88; 6:201, 226, 230, 254; 7:13; 8:37, 69, 85; 9:70; 10:52, 69–70, 79, 80, 150, 155, 158, 179, 184; 11:134, 138, 169, 181, 239, 240, 288; 12:28, 45, 56, 69 (47, 58, 71)

Totochtin (gods), 1:11 (26); song of, 2:213 (242)

Totonac, Totonaca, Totonaque (people), 10:75, 78, 184–85; 11:22, 82, 85, 117, 119, 172, 256, 279, 282

Toucanet, 11:22

Toveiome, Toueiome. See Huaxteca

Towhee, 11:47

Toxcatl (month), 1:38 (68); 2:9–10, 63, 64–73 (9–10, 65, 66–77); 12:49–54 (51–56)

Trade. See Commerce; Market place; Merchants; Vendors

Trees, 11:105–22, 164, 187, 200–205, 215–16

Tribes. See People

Tribute, 3:8–9 (9); 8:44, 53–54

Troupial, 11:20

Trumpeters, teaching of, 2:172–73 (186)

Trumpets, blowing of, 2:192 (205); 8:35, 43, 53, 57, 62, 81

Tuna cactus, 2:19; 7:17; 8:38, 68; 10:70, 79; 12:69 (71). See also Nopal

Turkey, 11:29, 30–31, 53–54; vendors of, 10:85

Turpentine, 1:5, 41 (17, 71)

Turquoise, 9:1, 2, 3, 5, 19, 38, 59, 60, 80, 82, 84, 85; 11:223–24

Turtle, 11:59

Tzonmulca (temple officials), 2:155, 177 (168, 190)

Uauhquiltamalqualiztli (feast), 2:154–57, 176 (167–70, 190)

Uei tecuilhuitl (month), 2:14–15, 91–100 (14–15, 96–107); 12:79 (81)

Uei toçoztli (month), 2:7–8, 59–63, 67, 197 (7–8, 61–65, 70, 210)

Ueuetlatolli, Huehuetlatolli. See Old people, discourses of

Uexotzinca (people), 2:166 (180); 4:77; 9:40; 10:195, 197

Uitznaua (gods), 7:70

Uitznaua (people), 2:134–36 (145–46); 7:70

Uixtociuatl (goddess), 2:13, 88 (13, 93)

Uixtoti, Uixtotin (people), 10:187–88, 192, 197. See also Olmeca

Umbilical cord, 4:3–4; 5:186; 6:169, 171–73, 175

Uncles, giving of, 1:12 (30); 2:152, 156 (165, 169)

Underworld. See Land of the dead

Valley, 11:261

Valor, terminology of, 10:23–24

Vendors, 10:59–94. See also Merchants

Venus, 7:62. See also Stars

Vigils, 2:13, 17, 29, 44, 46, 48, 52, 63, 88, 98, 106, 133, 156–57, 186 (13, 17, 29, 44, 47, 49, 54, 65, 93, 104, 113, 144, 170, 199–200); 4:123

Visions, 9:39

Vows, 1:13, 16–17, 21–22, 44, 45 (31, 39–40, 47–48, 74, 75); 2:29, 56, 72, 139, 206 (29, 58, 75, 151, 220); 3:11 49, 59 (11, 51, 61); 6:213; 9:71

Vultures, 11:42

War, 1:1, 3, 19, 38 (1, 11, 42, 67); 2:39, 115 (39, 123); 3:7, 19–20, 47, 53 (7, 21–22, 49, 55); 4:47, 59, 70, 91–92; 6:11–15, 72–74, 171, 203, 244, 256; 8:1–10, 35, 65, 72–77, 83–89; 9:3–4, 6, 17, 18, 22, 24–25; 12:27–28, 29, 53 (27–28, 29, 55); with Chichimeca, 8:5, 8; Cíbola, 8:5, 8; plans and conduct, 8:35, 43, 51–54, 56–58, 65, 69, 88; Spanish Conquest, 8:4, 10; 12:55–122 (57–126); spies, 2:166 (180); 8:57; Tenochtitlan vs. Tlatelolco, 8:2, 7; Texcoco vs. Tepaneca, 8:9. See also Battle, mock; Merchants, disguised, exploring, reconnoitering, spying

Warbler, 11:48

Warriors, 1:4, 17, 19 (14–15, 39, 42); 2:4, 15, 20, 49–52, 66, 70, 75, 93–96, 102, 103, 108, 114–15, 124–25, 134–36, 152 (4, 15, 20, 50–53, 69, 72, 79, 98–102, 109, 110, 115, 122–23, 134–35, 146–47,

164); 3:7, 47–48, 49, 53–54, 57–58 (7, 49, 51–52, 55–56, 59–60); 4:9, 17, 26, 33, 38–39, 47, 59, 70, 91, 94, 108; 6:11–15, 110, 114–15, 162, 171, 203–4, 224, 256; 8:42, 43, 51–54, 57, 61, 65, 72–77, 83–89; 9:2, 3, 32, 34, 47, 52, 53, 64; 10:23–24; 12:21, 41, 65–122 passim (21, 44, 67–126 passim). *See also* Merchants as warriors

Water folk, 1:16, 41, 43 (37, 71, 73); 2:39; 4:99; 7:14–15, 20, 68–70; 10:80

Waterfowl, 11:26–39, 57, 58

Waters, 11:247–51

Weapons, arrows, 2:25, 124–25 (25, 134–36); bird nets, 8:30; bow and arrow, 8:30; bow and arrow, Chichimeca, 10:171–72, 175; shield, rulers', 8:33–34; sling, 8:30; sling, Matlatzinca, Quaquata, Toloque, 10:182–83; sword, rulers', 8:35

Weasel, 5:165; 11:13

Weaver, 10:35, 51–52

Weaving implements, 2:128, 141 (138, 153); 6:201, 239, 240; 8:49; Otomí, 10:180–81

Wells, 11:250–51

Whip-poor-will, 11:46

Whore. *See* Harlot; Paramour

Willow, 11:110

Wind, 7:14–15, 68–70

Wine, 12:16. *See also* Pulque

Wisdom, Book of, 1:27–33 (55–62)

Wise men, 8:18–19; 10:29, 31, 190

Wizards, 4:101–5; 12:21. *See also* Magicians; Soothsayers

Wolf man, 2:176 (190)

Women, chewing of chicle by, 10:89; commoners, 10:51–54; dying in childbirth, 1:6, 42 (71–72); 2:37; 6:161–65; merchants, 9:16, 28, 47; noblewoman, 10:45–50; standards of behavior, 4:10, 25, 74, 79, 95, 109; 6:93–103, 132, 155–58, 172, 216–18; 8:48; 10:1–13 passim, 45–57; training, 1:20 (44); 6:216–18; 8:49; harlot, 10:55–56; hermaphrodite, 10:56; procuress, 10:57; scandalous woman, 10:56; visited when recently delivered, 4:111. *See also* Childbirth

Wood carvers, 8:45

Woodpecker, 11:46, 52

Worms, 11:98–100, 161, 190

Wren, 11:46–47

Wrist ornaments. *See* Clothing

Xilomanaliztli (month), 2:173 (187). *See also* Quauitl eua

Xocotl uetzi (month), 2:17–18, 104–9, 175 (17–18, 111–17, 189)

Xoxouhque (gods), 6:40. *See also* Tlalocs

Year, count, 10:168, 191; signs, 7:21–22. *See also* Calendar, civil

Yopime (people), 10:187. *See also* Tenime

Young men's house, 2:16, 40, 60 (16, 40, 62); 3:49–58 (51–60); 8:43, 76

Youth, (1:82); 2:9–10, 16, 20, 21, 22, 40–41, 70, 73, 93–97, 99–100, 108, 118, 124, 137–38, 141, 148, 149, 198 (9–10, 16, 20, 21, 22, 40–41, 72, 76, 98–103, 106, 115–16, 127, 134, 148–50, 153, 160, 161–62, 211); 3:7, 49–58 (7, 51–60); 4:108; 6:115, 127–33, 161–62; 8:43, 57–58, 72–73, 75–76; 9:13, 14; 10:8, 12–13, 37; 12:51 (54); leaders of, 8:61; 9:14; masters of, 3:7; 6:127–28; 8:43, 51, 57, 76; rulers of, 8:43; standards of behavior of, 6:87–92, 105–26, 213–16, 242–43, 247, 253, 255, 256–57, 259; 10:8, 12–13

Zapote. *See* Sapota

Zapotecs (people), 1:16 (39)

Zoo, 8:45

# Persons and Deities

Acalua, 2:196 (209)

Acamapichtli (ruler of Tenochtitlan), 6:22; 8:1, 7, 15

Acatl iacapanecatl, 8:55

Acolhua, 1:24 (51)

Acolmiztli, 2:190, 201 (203, 214)

Acolnauacatl, 2:201 (203); 3:39 (41). *See also* Mictlan tecutli

Acxomocuil, 1:19, 35 (43, 64)

Alvarado, Pedro de, 8:22; 12:41, 49, 81, 87 (43, 51, 84, 91)

Amapan, 2:134, 162, 172 (145, 176, 186)

Amimitl, (1:79); 10:195; song of, 2:210–11 (233)

Anauatl itecu, 7:7, 62. *See also* Xipe totec; Red Tezcatlipoca; Tlatlauic Tezcatlipoca

Atempanecatl, 2:100 (106); 8:43, 77

Atetein, 10:181

Aticpac calqui ciuatl, 2:199 (212)

Atlatonan, 2:67, 177 (70, 191)

Atlaua (1:79); song of, 2:213–14 (234)

Atlauhcatl, 8:55

Atlixcatzin, 12:43 (45)

Aua, 2:111 (119)

Auelitoctzin, 12:112, 116, 119, 122 (117, 120, 123, 126)

Auelittoc, don Juan (ruler of Tlatelolco), 8:8; 11:34

Auitzotl, Auitzotzin (ruler of Tenochtitlan), 6:22; 8:2; 9:3–8, 17, 18, 19, 22–23, 90; 11:50; 12:42, 113 (44, 117)

Axayacatl (ruler of Tenochtitlan), 6:22; 8:2

Axoquentzin, 12:104 (108)

Ayopechtli, song of, 2:211 (235)

Ayotzin tecutli (ruler of Uexotla), 8:13

Aztatzon, 6:71

Aztauatzin, 12:115 (119)

Blue Xiuhtecutli, 2:177 (190)

Cacamatzin (ruler of Texcoco), 8:10; 12:43 (45)

Çacancatl, 2:105 (112)

Çacatzontli, 9:10, 11

Camaxtli, 2:38; 4:77

Çanatzin, 9:3, 24, 55

Captor of Xiuhtlamin, 7:32

Castañeda, Rodrigo de (Xicotencatl), 12:95–96 (99–100)

Cecepatic, don Cristóbal (ruler of Tenochtitlan), 8:5

Cenyaotl. 4:34 (*see also* Tezcatlipoca); 12:116 (120)

Ceres, 6:35

Chahuacuetzin, 6:13

Chalchiuhciuatl, 6:176. *See also* Chalchiuhtli icue

Chalchiuhtepeua, 2:176 (190); 12:110 (114)

Chalchiuhtlatonac, 6:175–76, 202. *See also* Chalchiuhtli icue

Chalchiuhtli icue, 1:6–7, 22, 34, 41 (21–22, 47, 64, 71); 2:1, 39, 140, 200–201 (1, 39, 152, 214); 4:99; 6:175–76, 202, 205–6; 11:247; adornment of, 1:7 (22)

Chalmecaciuatl, 1:19, 35 (43, 64)

Chamotzin, 6:164; 10:192

Chicome coatl, 1:4, 7, 34, 40 (13, 22, 63, 70); 2:7, 60, 103, 111, 116, 140, 173 (7, 64, 110, 119, 124–25, 152, 186–87); 4:50, 57, 73; 6:35, 38; adornment of, 1:4 (13); song of, 2:213 (241); temple of, 2:60, 62 (62–63, 64)

Chicome xochitl, 2:36

Chiconauecatl, 2:194 (207)

Chiconaui itzcuintli, 9:79

Chiconquiauitl, 1:19, 35 (43, 64); 2:200 (213)

Chicoyaotl, 4:34. *See also* Tezcatlipoca

Chimalpanecatl, 1:24 (51); song of, 2:209 (227)

Chimalpopoca (ruler of Tenochtitlan), 8:1; (ruler of Tlacopan), 8:15; (son of Moctezuma II), 12:66 (68)

Chinquitl, 10:187

Chochon, 10:187

Chonchayotl, 2:137 (149)

Cinteotl, 2:7, 60–61, 112–14, 210 (7, 62–63, 120–22, 230–31); 6:38; 9:79, 80; adornment of, 2:63 (65); temple of, 2:99, 173 (105, 187)

Cipac, 4:3

Cipactonal, 2:210 (231); 4:4; 6:153; 10:167, 191

Citlallatonac, 6:203

Citlalli icue, Citlalicue, 4:54; 6:203

Citli, 10:189

Ciuacoatl, 1:3–4, 34, 40 (11, 63, 69); 2:168 (182); 6:160, 164, 179–80, 185, 194; 8:3, 8; adornment of, 1:3–4 (11); song of, 2:211–12 (236–37); (judge), 8:55

Ciuapilli, 6:155, 164. *See also* Ciuacoatl

Ciuatecpancatl tequiua, 8:77

Ciuatecpanecatl, 8:55

Ciuateotl, 2:175–76 (189)

Ciuatontli, 2:177 (190)

Coanacochtli, Coanacochtzin, Coanacotzin (ruler of Texcoco), 8:10; 12:119 (123)

Coatlan tonan, 2:5, 55 (5, 57). *See also* Coatl icue

Coatl icue, 2:5, 55, 127 (5, 57, 137); 3:1–2

Coatl xoxouhqui, 2:103 (110)

Coatzin, 12:119 (123)

Cochimetl, Cocochimetl, 1:19, 35 (43, 64); 9:9. *See also* Yacatecutli

Cocotl, 2:43, 140 (43, 152)

Colhuatzincatl, Colhuatzintecatl, 1:24 (51)

Coltzin, 10:183
Cortés, don Hernando, 8:10, 21–22;
    12:11, 15–18, 81–82, 115, 117, 119
    (11, 15–18, 84, 119, 121, 123);
    entry into Mexico, 8:21–22; first
    meeting with Moctezuma II, 12:42
    (44); imprisonment of Moctezuma
    II, 8:22; interview with Quauhtemoc
    after Spanish victory, 12:121–22
    (125–26); return from expedition
    against Pánfilo de Narváez, 12:59
    (61)
Couixcatl, 10:187
Coyolxauhqui, 3:1–4
Coyotl inaual, 9:83, 84, 87, 88
Coyoua, 2:105 (112)
Coyoueuetzin, 12:106, 112, 114, 116,
    117, 119 (110, 117, 118, 119, 121,
    123)
Cozcamiauh, 2:31. See also Ilama
    tecutli
Cozcaquauh, 4:97
Cozmatzin, 9:1
Cruz, Francisco de la, 10:163
Cueçalli, 6:4, 21. See also Mictlan
    tecutli
Cueçaltzin, 1:42 (29, 72); 2:155
    (168). See also Xiuhtecutli
Cuecuextzin, 10:192
Cuetlaciuatl, 2:172 (186)
Cuexcochtzin, 3:25 (27)
Cuextecatl, 10:185, 186, 193–94
Cuitlalpitoc, 12:5
Cuitlauac, Cuitlauatzin (ruler of
    Tenochtitlan), 8:4; (rulers of
    Uexotla), 8:14

Daniel, Pedro, 11:34

Ecatenpatiltzin, 12:9, 43 (9, 45)
Ecatl, Ehecatl, 2:103, 140 (110, 152);
    6:34; 7:7–8, 52; don Martín (ruler
    of Tlatelolco), 8:8
Epcoaquacuilli Tepictoton, 2:198
    (212)
Epcoatl, 2:43; temple of, 2:165 (179)
Ezuauacatl, 2:100 (106); 8:55

García, Miguel, 10:163
Guzmán, Nuño de, 8:4

Hernández, José, 10:163
Hernández, Pedro, 10:163
Huitzilopochtli. See Uitzilopochtli

Ihuitl temoc, 6:13
Ilama tecutli, 2:31, 143–44 (31,
    155–56)

Ilhuicamina. See Moctezuma
Ilhuicatl xoxouhqui, 2:165 (179).
    See also Uitzilopochtli
Iocippa, 10:177, 181
Iopitli, temple of, 2:49, 56 (51, 58)
Ipalnemoani, 6:34
Itlacauhtzin (ruler of Uexotla), 8:13
Itzcaque, 6:34
Itzcoatl, Itzcoatzin (ruler of Tenochti-
    tlan), 8:1, 7, 9; 10:191; 12:42
    (44); merchant, 9:1
Itzcuin, Itzcuintzin, 7:32; 12:105
    (109)
Itzpapalotl, Itzpapalotzin, 2:209
    (226); 6:14; 12:106 (110)
Itzquauhtzin, 9:2; 12:43, 45, 55–56,
    63–64 (45, 47, 57–58, 65–66)
Itztlacoliuhqui, 2:113 (121–22); 7:19
Ixcoçauhqui, 1:12, 42 (29, 30, 72);
    2:17, 33, 120, 150, 151, 154, 155,
    198 (17, 33, 129, 163, 164, 167,
    168, 211); song of, 2:209 (228–
    29)
Ixcuina, 1:8, 10 (23, 26). See also
    Tlaçolteotl
Ixteucale, 2:73 (76)
Ixtlilcuechauac, 6:13
Ixtlilton, 1:35, 43 (64, 73); adorn-
    ment of, 1:15–16 (35–36); temple
    of, 2:199 (212)
Ixtlilxochitl the Elder, Ixtlilxochitzin,
    (I, ruler of Texcoco), 8:9; (II, ruler
    of Texcoco), 8:10
Izquitecatl, 1:24 (51); 2:36, 127, 134
    (36, 137, 145); 4:17
Iztac ciuatl Ciuaquacuilli, 2:198 (211)
Iztaca mixcoatlailotlac, 8:42

Juárez, Baltasar, 10:163

Lord of the Night, 2:202 (216)

Maçatecatl, 2:100 (106)
Maçatl tecutli (leader of Maçaua),
    10:184
Maçatzin tecutli (ruler of Uexotla),
    8:13
Maceuhcatzin, 6:13
Macuilcalli, 9:79, 80
Macuilmalinalli, temple of, 2:175
    (189)
Macuilocelotl, 9:84
Macuiltochtli, 9:84
Macuiltotec, 2:178 (192)
Macuilxochitl, 1:13–14, 35 (31–32,
    64); 4:49; adornment of, 1:14
    (32); song of, 2:214 (244)

Marina, 12:25, 42, 47, 69, 72, 119,
    121–22 (25, 45, 49, 71, 76, 123,
    125–26)
Martínez, Antonio, 10:163
Matlalcueye, 2:23, 122 (23, 132)
Mayauel, 2:23, 122, 174 (23, 132,
    188); 10:193
Mayeuatzin (ruler of Cuitlauac),
    12:92, 106–7 (96, 110–11)
Mecitli, 10:189
Mendoza, don Antonio de (Viceroy),
    8:8
Mexicatl, 10:189; tequiua, 8:77;
    tezcacoacatl, 8:55
Michoacatl, 10:189
Mictecaciuatl, 3:39 (41); 5:163
Mictlan tecutli, 2:167 (180); 3:39,
    41–42 (41, 43–44); 4:38, 49;
    5:163; 6:4, 21, 27, 31, 38, 48, 58,
    152, 190
Micxochtziyautzin, 9:2
Milintoc, 2:148–49 (161); adornment
    of, 2:149 (161–62). See also
    Xiuhtecutli
Milnauatl, 2:23, 122 (23, 132); 8:55
Miquiz, 4:34. See also Tezcatlipoca
Mixcoatl, 2:25, 26, 126–29, 172 (25,
    26, 136–40, 186); 6:34; temple of,
    2:126, 168, 172 (136, 181, 185);
    warrior, 6:114–15
Mixcoatlailotlac, 8:42
Moctezuma, Motecuçoma, Ilhuicamina,
    the Elder (I, ruler of Tenochtitlan),
    6:22, 71; 8:1–2, 7; 12:42 (44–45);
    the Younger (II, ruler of Tenoch-
    titlan), 1:7, 12, 19 (22, 30, 42);
    2:11, 47, 53, 54, 66, 68, 71, 75, 95,
    111, 114–15, 117, 127, 134, 151,
    166, 167, 176, 177, 197, 201 (11,
    49, 55, 69, 70, 74, 79, 101, 119, 123,
    125, 137, 146, 164, 180, 181, 190,
    191, 210, 214); 3:6; 4:6, 25–26, 42,
    45, 78; 7:31; 8:2–4, 18, 19, 21–22,
    41–43, 72–74, 76–77, 83–84,
    87–88; 9:6, 23, 24, 32, 65, 91;
    11:209; 12:3, 5, 6, 7, 9–10, 13, 15,
    16, 17–18, 21–27, 30–32, 33–34,
    71–72 (3, 5, 6, 9, 13, 15, 16, 17–18,
    21–27, 30–32, 33–34, 75); attempts
    to deflect Spaniards, 12:22, 31–35
    (22, 31–37); captured by Spaniards,
    12:43, 45 (45, 48); death of, 8:22;
    12:63 (65–66); first meets with
    Cortés 12:41–43 (43–45); gives
    Cortés gifts, 12:11–13; imprison-
    ment of, 8:22; 12:43–49, 55–56
    (45–51, 57–59); plans flight,

12:26; strengthening ceremony for, 4:42, 45

Molpilli, 7:31

Monenequi, 6:11. *See also* Tezcatlipoca

Moquequeloa, 6:14, 21, 22, 27, 34, 91. *See also* Tezcatlipoca

Moquiuixtli, Moquiuixtzin (ruler of Tlatelolco), 8:2, 7; 9:2

Motecuçoma. *See* Moctezuma

Motelchiuh, Motelchiuhtzin, don Andrés (ruler of Tenochtitlan), 8:4; 12:114, 115, 119 (118, 119, 123)

Moyocoya, Moiocoian, Moyocoyatzin, 1:38 (67); 3:12; 6:2, 4, 11, 14, 22, 27, 33, 34, 91, 210. *See also* Tezcatlipoca

Nacxitl, 1:19, 35 (43, 64)

Nanauatl, Nanauatzin, (1:83); 2:172 (186), 7:4–6, 44–52; 11:234

Nancotlaceuhqui, 2:177 (191)

Napa tecutli, 1:20–21, 35, 44 (45–46, 64, 74); 2:176, 197 (190, 210); adornment of, 1:21 (46); temple of, 2:176 (190)

Narváez, Pánfilo de, 12:49 (51)

Naualpilli, 9:79

Nauhyoueue, 2:155 (168). *See also* Xiuhtecutli

Neçaualcoyotzin (ruler of Texcoco), 6:118; 8:9, 14

Neçaualpilli (ruler of Texcoco), 2:54 (55); 8:9–10; alternative name for Tezcatlipoca, 1:38 (67); 3:12

Necoctene, 6:14

Necoc yaotl, 1:38 (67); 3:12; 4:34; 6:11, 14. *See also* Tezcatlipoca

Nemo, 2:35, 150, 158 (35, 162, 171)

Nemoquich, 2:35

Nenciuatl, 2:35, 158 (35, 171)

Nenquizqui, 2:158 (171)

Nentlacatl, 2:158 (171)

Nentlamatitzin, 9:3, 24

Old Wolf (Old Bear), 2:51, 53 (52, 54); 8:84, 85

Olmecatl Uixtotli, 10:192

Omacatl, 1:14–15, 35, 43 (33–34, 64, 73); 2:38, 103, 170, 171 (38, 110, 184, 185); 4:56; adornment of, 1:14–15 (34)

Ome ciuatl, Ome cihuatl, 6:141, 168, 175, 176, 183, 202, 206; 10:169

Ome tecutli, 6:141, 168, 175, 176, 183, 202, 206; 10:169

Ome tochtli, 1:24 (51); 2:167 (181); Acalua, 2:196 (209); Napatecutli,

2:197 (210); Papaztac, 2:197 (210–11); Pâtecatl, 2:197 (210); Quatlapanqui, 2:196 (210); Tezcatzoncatl, 2:196 (209); Tlilhua, 2:197 (210); Tomiauh, 2:196 (209–10); Yiauhqueme, 2:196 (209)

One Serpent, 9:10–11, 13

Opoche, 6:34

Opochtli, 1:16, 35, 43 (37, 64, 73); 2:51, 199 (53, 213); adornment of, 1:16 (37)

Otoncoatl, 12:69 (71)

Otontecutli, 10:181; song of, 2:211 (234)

Otomitl, 10:176

Oton, 10:176, 177

Oxomoco, 4:4; 6:153; 10:167, 191

Painal. *See* Paynal

Painalton. *See* Paynal

Pantecatl, 1:24 (51)

Papaloxaual, 9:79

Papaztac, Papaiztac, 1:24 (51); 2:173 (187); 10:193

Patecatl, 2:194 (207)

Paynal, Painal, Painalton, 1:1–2 (3); 2:27, 107, 108, 133–36 (27, 114–15, 145–58); 9:64, 65–66; adornment of, 1:2 (3); 2:161–62 (175–76); impersonator of, 2:151 (163); procession for, 2:134–35, 162 (145–46, 176)

Pérez, Juan, 10:163

Pérez, Pedro, 10:163

Petlauhtzin, 12:112, 115, 119 (117, 119, 123)

Piltzintecutli, 2:210 (232)

Piltzintli, 3:50 (52). *See also* Tezcatlipoca

Pimentel, don Hernando (ruler of Texcoco), 8:10–11

Pinotl, 10:187; 12:5, 9

Pochtecatlailotlac, 8:55, 61–62

Popoyotzin, 9:2

Poyauhtecatl, 1:22 (47); 2:43

Quappiaztzin, Quappiatzin, 12:9, 43 (9, 45)

Quappoyaualtzin, 9:24, 55

Quaquapitzauac, Quaquauhpitzauac (ruler of Tlatelolco), 8:7; 9:1

Quatatl, 10:182

Quatlapanqui, 2:196 (210); 10:193

Quatlauice tecutli (ruler of Uexotla), 8:13

Quauhciuatl, 6:164

Quauhnochtli, 2:100 (106); don Alonso (ruler of Tlatelolco), 8:8

Quauhpoyaualtzin, 9:3

Quauhtemoc (ruler of Tenochtitlan), 8:4, 10; 12:91–92, 112–13, 115–22 (95–96, 117, 119–25)

Quauhtlatoa, Quauhtlatoatzin (ruler of Tlatelolco), 8:7; 9:2

Quauhtleuanitl, 6:4, 38, 74. *See also* Tonatiuh

Quauic onoc, don Juan (ruler of Tlatelolco), 8:8

Quauitl icac, 2:134 (145); 3:2–3 (2–4)

Quaxolotl Chantico, 2:170–71 (184)

Quetzalaztatzin, 12:9

Quetzalcoatl, 1:2–3, 22, 34, 39–40 (9, 47, 63, 69); 2:1, 36–37; 3:13–16, 23, 31–36, 59–60 (13–18, 25, 33–38, 62); 4:29, 101–2; 6:31, 54, 141, 181, 210, 219; 7:7, 14, 27, 52, 68; 8:21; 10:100–101, 169, 188; adornment of, 1:3 (9); 12:11–12; Topiltzin, 12:5; temple of, 3:13; priest, 3:5, 67–68 (6, 69–70); 6:54, 210; priest, ruler of Tula, Tollan, 10:166, 169–70

Quetzalxiuh, 8:31

Quetzalxoch, 2:43

Quilaztli, 6:155, 160, 164, 179–80, 185, 194. *See also* Ciuacoatl

Quitzicquaquatzin, 6:13

Red Cinteotl, 2:177, 210 (191, 231)

Red Tezcatlipoca, 7:7; 10:187

Red Xiuhtecutli, 2:177 (190)

Tamin, 10:171

Taras, 10:189

Teccizquacuilli, 2:112 (120)

Techichiuani, 6:14, 20, 25–26, 42–44, 62

Techotlalatzin (ruler of Texcoco), 8:9

Teci, 6:153, 155

Tecocoltzin (ruler of Texcoco), 8:10

Teçoçomoctli (ruler of Azcapotzalco), 8:15

Tecuciztecatl, 7:3–8, 42–58

Tecutlatoa, 10:177

Teicautzin, 2:73 (76). *See also* Ixteucale

Teicnotlamachti, 8:42

Teicu, 1:8, 41–42 (23, 71); 7:7, 52. *See also* Tlaçolteotl

Teimatini, 6:14, 18, 20, 25, 42–44, 62. *See also* Tezcatlipoca

Telpochtli, 2:118 (127). *See also* Tezcatlipoca

Temilo, don Pedro (ruler of Tlatelolco), 8:7–8

Temilotzin, 12:106, 111–12, 116 (110, 115–17, 120)

Temoctzin, 12:88 (93)

Teuoa, 12:10

Tentlil, 12:5

Teociniacatl, 12:5

Tepanecatl Quaquatzin, 12:105 (109)

Tepepetzton, 6:101

Tepeuatzin, 12:43 (45)

Tepexoch, 2:23, 122 (23, 132)

Tepoztecatl, Tepuztecatl, 1:24 (51); 2:173 (187); 9:84; 10:193

Teputzitoloc, 12:116 (120)

Tepuztecatl, 10:193

Tequitzin, 2:174, 199 (188, 213)

Tequixquinaoacatl, 8:55

Teteo innan, 1:4–5, 34, 40–41 (15–16, 63, 70); 2:19, 110–11 (19, 119); adornment of, 1:5 (16); song of, 2:208–9 (226)

Tetlaueuetzquititzin (ruler of Texcoco), 8:10

Tetlepanquetzatzin (ruler of Tlacopan), 12:45, 119 (45, 123)

Teuetzquiti, don Diego (ruler of Tenochtitlan), 8:5

Texiuh, 7:31

Teyocoyani, 6:18, 26, 42–44, 62. *See also* Tezcatlipoca

Tezcacoacatl, 2:100 (106); Xiuhcozcatzin, 12:105 (109)

Tezcatlipoca, 1:2, 9, 34, 38 (5, 63, 67–68); 2:9, 37–38, 64, 118–19 (9, 37–38, 66, 127–28); 3:11–12, 49 (11–12, 51); 4:33–35, 56, 74; 5:157, 171, 175, 177, 180; 6:1–28, 41–45, 210, 254; 12:34; adornment of, 12:12 (11–12); costuming of impersonator of, 2:64–65 (66–68)

Tezcatzin, 9:2

Tezcatzoncatl, 1:24, 44 (51, 74); 2:196 (209); adornment of, 1:24 (51); song of, 2:213 (242)

Tiacapan, 1:8, 41–42 (23, 71); 7:7, 52. *See also* Tlaçolteotl

Tiçaua, 9:84; adornment of, 9:84

Ticitl, 6:153. *See also* Teteo innan

Tiçoc, Tiçocicatzin (ruler of Tenochtitlan), 6:22; 8:2; 12:42 (44)

Tiçociauacatl, 2:100 (106); 8:55, 61–62, 77

Tinemachxoch, 6:101

Titlacauan, 1:38 (67–68); 2:9, 21, 66, 73, 168 (9, 21, 68, 76, 182); 3:11–12, 15–29, 49 (11–12, 17–31, 51); 4:33, 35, 56; 5:184; 6:1–2, 4, 7, 12–13, 21, 33. *See also* Tezcatlipoca

Tlacateccatl, 8:77; don Martín (ruler of Tlatelolco), 8:8

Tlacatecutli, 12:5 (*see also* Moctezuma II); of Teocalhueyacan, 12:69 (71)

Tlacateotl (ruler of Tlatelolco), 8:7; 9:1

Tlacatzin, 12:107 (111)

Tlacauepan, 2:73 (76); 3:15, 25–26 (17, 27–28) (*see also* Ixteucale); Cuexcochtzin, 2:161, 165, 178 (175, 179, 192)

Tlacauepantzin, 6:13

Tlachinoltzin, 6:71

Tlaciuhqui, 10:177

Tlaco, 1:8, 41–42 (23, 71). *See also* Tlaçolteotl

Tlacochcalcatl, 8:42, 55, 61–62, 77; 12:27

Tlacochintzin, 9:2

Tlaçolteotl, 1:8–11, 34, 41–42 (23–27, 64, 71); 4:74; 6:34

Tlaçolyaotl, 12:119 (123)

Tlaçolyaotzin (ruler of Uexotla), 8:13–14

Tlacotzin, 12:111–13, 115, 119, 121–22 (115–17, 119, 123, 125–26)

Tlacotzontli, 9:10–11

Tlacoyehua, 7:7, 52. *See also* Tlaçolteotl

Tlaelquani, 1:8 (23). *See also* Tlaçolteotl

Tlalhuicatl, 10:186

Tlalli iyollo, 1:4, 40 (15, 70). *See also* Teteo innan

Tlaloc, 1:2, 22, 34, 38–39 (7, 47, 63, 68); 2:5, 29, 75, 85, 139, 163–64, 165, 191, 201 (5, 29, 79, 90, 151, 177–78, 179, 204, 214); 3:67 (69); 6:35–40; 7:14, 17, 27; adornment of, 1:2 (7); 12:12; feast of, 2:189 (202); pyramid of, 2:13; song of, 2:208 (224–25); temple of, 2:82–83, 89, 123, 139, 165 (87–88, 94, 133, 151, 179); tlamacazqui (priest), 3:67 (69); 6:54; Tlalocan tecutli, 1:34 (63)

Tlaltecatzin (ruler of Texcoco), 8:9; (lord of the Tepaneca), 12:66 (68)

Tlaltecauananotl, 2:209 (227)

Tlaltecavoua, 1:24 (51)

Tlaltecutli, 1:35 (64); 2:209; 3:49 (51); 6:11, 15, 36, 39, 106, 172,

198, 203–4; 9:9, 10. *See also* Tonatiuh

Tlaltetecui, 10:167, 189

Tlaltetecuini, 1:15, 35, 43 (35, 64, 73). *See also* Ixtlilton

Tlalxictentica, 2:155 (168); 4:87; 5:152; 9:9, 11. *See also* Xiuhtecutli

Tlamacazqui, 6:35–36, 40, 115. *See also* Tlaloc

Tlamatzincatl, 2:21, 118, 127–29, 171 (21, 127, 137–40, 185). *See also* Tezcatlipoca

Tlamayocatl, 12:107 (111)

Tlapaltecatl opochtzin, 12:113 (117)

Tlapaneca Ecatzin, 12:97 (101)

Tlapanecatl, 12:107 (111)

Tlappapalo, 9:79

Tlatlauic Tezcatlipoca, 7:52. *See also* Red Tezcatlipoca

Tlauitecqui, 2:111 (119)

Tlauitoltzin, don Antonio (ruler of Texcoco), 8:10

Tlilhoa, 1:24 (51); 10:193

Tlilpotonqui, 12:9

Tloque nauaque, 6:34

Tochancalqui, 3:4

Tochin tecutli (ruler of Uexotla), 8:13

Toci, 1:4–5, 40 (15, 70); 2:19, 111–17, 195, 197 (19, 119–26, 208, 211). *See also* Teteo innan

Tollamimichtzin, 9:2

Tolnauacatl tequiua, 8:77

Tolo, 10:182

Toltecatl, 1:24 (51)

Tonacatecutli, 4:54; 6:115

Tonan, 2:31; 6:153. *See also* Ilama tecutli; Teteo innan

Tonatiuh, 3:49 (51); 4:54; 6:172, 203

Topantemoctzin, 12:43, 111–12, 116 (45, 115–17, 120)

Topantlacaqui, 2:175 (189)

Topiltzin, 1:39 (69); 3:59–60 (62); Quetzalcoatl, 6:83, 183, 185, 202, 213; 10:170, 176; 12:9; priest, 2:161 (175)

Toqual, 8:42

Tota, 1:42 (29, 72). *See also* Xiuhtecutli

Totec, 2:3, 50, 52 (3, 51, 53); 7:7, 52; 9:69–71; 10:187 (*see also* Xipe totec; Red Tezcatlipoca); tlamacazqui, 3:67 (69); 6:54

Totocacatzin (governor of Tlatelolco), 9:2

Totoltecatl, 2:173, 201 (187, 214–15)

Totomochtzin (ruler of Uexotla), 8:13
Totomotzin, 12:43 (45)
Totonametl in manic, 6:38, 171. *See also* Tonatiuh
Totoquiuaztli, 2:54 (55)
Toueio, 10:185–86
Tzapocuetzin (ruler of Uexotla), 8:14
Tzapotlan tenan; Tzapotla tenan, 1:5, 34, 41 (17, 63, 71); 2:195 (208–9); adornment of, 1:5 (17)
Tzayectzin, 12:88 (93)
Tzilacatecutli Temilotzin, 12:114 (118)
Tzilacatzin, 12:87–88, 95 (91–93, 99)
Tziuacpopocatzin, 9:2; 12:31, 34
Tziuhtecatzin, 9:1
Tzocaca, 10:193
Tzompantzin, 9:1
Tzontemoc, 3:39 (41); 6:4, 21. *See also* Mictlan tecutli
Tzontemoctzin (ruler of Uexotla), 8:14

Uanitl, don Diego (ruler of Tenochtitlan), 8:5
Uapatzan, 2:134 (145)
Ueicamecatl, 2:105 (112)
Uei oçomatzin, 9:24
Uemac, 3:17–20 (19–22)
Uetzcatocatzin, Vetzcatocatzin, 9:3, 24, 25
Ueue Motecuçoma, 6:22. *See also* Moctezuma I
Ueueteotl, 1:42 (29, 27); 6:19, 41, 89. *See* Xiuhtecutli
Uictolinqui, 8:42
Uitzilinquatec, 2:174 (188)
Uitziliuitl (ruler of Tenochtitlan), 8:1, 7
Uitziliuitzin, 12:116 (120)
Uitzilopochtli, 1:1, 19, 34, 38 (1–2, 43, 63, 67); 2:16, 20, 27–28, 38, 47, 101–2, 107, 130, 131, 134, 135, 136 (16, 20, 27–28, 38, 48, 109, 114, 141, 142, 145, 146, 147); 3:1–9, 15, 25, 67 (1–9, 17, 27, 69); 4:77–79; 6:254; 7:29; 8:17, 22, 53, 61–65, 72–73; 9:4–6, 23, 37, 52, 55, 63, 65, 67, 91; 12:2; adornment of, 1:1 (2); 3:3–4 (3–5); bathing of, 3:7–8 (8); banquet table of, 2:116 (124); birth of, 3:1–3 (1–4); costuming of, 2:69 (71–72); eating of, 3:6 (6–7); feast of, 2:178 (191); 12:49–51, 53–54 (51–53, 55–56);

forming figure of, 2:68–69, 179 (71, 192); 3:5–6; 12:49–50 (51–52); pyramid of, 2:28; song of, 2:130, 207 (141, 221–22); temple of, 2:102, 112, 124–25, 131, 135–36, 161–62, 165 (109, 134–35, 142, 146–47, 175–76, 179); 4:77; 8:61–64; 12:86 (88)
Uitziluatzin, 12:112 (116)
Uitzitzin (ruler of Tlacopan), 12:105, 116 (109, 120)
Uitznauatl, 2:171 (185); song of, 2:207–8 (223)
Uitznauatlailotlac, don Diego (ruler of Tlatelolco), 8:8; (judge), 8:55, 61–62
Uitznauatl ecamalacotl, 8:42–43
Uixtociuatl, 1:7, 34 (22, 64); 2:13, 67, 82, 86 (13, 70, 87, 91); adornment of, 2:86–87 (91–92)
Umaca, 8:42

Vanitl. *See* Uanitl
Vei oçomatzin, 9:3. *See also* Uei oçomatzin
Vetzcatocatzin. *See* Uetzcatocatzin

White Cinteotl, 2:177 (191); temple of, 2:170 (184)
White Xiuhtecutli, 2:177 (190)

Xicotencatl (Rodrigo de Castañeda), 12:95–96 (99–100)
Xilo, 9:88; adornment of, 9:84–85
Xilonen, 2:14–15, 67, 97–99, 195 (14–15, 70, 103–5, 208); costuming of impersonator of, 2:97 (103)
Xilotzin tecutli (ruler of Uexotla), 8:13
Xipe totec, 1:16–17, 35, 43–44 (39–40, 64, 73); 2:3, 44, 49, 57, 199–200 (3, 45, 50, 59, 213); adornment of, 1:17 (40); song of, 2:213 (240)
Xippilli, 6:38. *See also* Tonatiuh
Xiuhcoçol, 8:31
Xiuhcue, 7:31
Xiuhnenetl, 7:31
Xiuhquen, 7:31
Xiuhtecutli, 1:11–13, 35, 42 (29–30, 64, 72); 2:17–18, 33–34, 39, 108, 120, 155, 176, 195, 198 (17–18, 33–34, 39, 115, 129, 168, 190, 209, 211); 4:87; 6:41, 89; 8:18; 9:9, 28; adornment of, 1:12–13 (30); 2:147 (159); temple of, 2:148 (161); 12:2

Xiuhtlalpil, 7:31
Xiuhtlati, 9:84, 88; adornment of, 9:84–85
Xiuhtlatlac, 7:31
Xiuhtlamin, 7:31–32
Xiuhtli, 7:31
Xiuhtzitzqui, 7:31
Xochicaua, Xochicauaca, 10:167, 191
Xochipilli, 1:13, 43 (31, 72); 2:199 (212); song of, 2:210 (231). *See also* Macuilxochitl
Xochiquen, don Pablo (ruler of Tenochtitlan), 8:4, 8
Xochiquetzal, 2:36, 67 (36, 70); 4:7; song of, 2:210 (232)
Xochquaye, 2:172 (186)
Xochtecatl, 2:23, 122 (23, 132)
Xocotzin, 1:8, 41–42 (23, 71). *See also* Tlaçolteotl
Xocoyotl, 7:7, 52
Xolotl, 7:8, 54; 9:89
Xoquauhtli, 2:111 (119)
Xoxouhqui, 6:35, 39, 115. *See also* Tlaloc

Yacacoliuhqui, 1:44 (74). *See also* Yacatecutli
Yacapitzauac, 1:19, 35 (43, 64); 2:119 (129); 9:9. *See also* Yacatecutli
Yacatecutli, Yiacatecutli, 1:17–20, 35, 44 (41–44, 64, 74); 2:119, 200 (129, 213); 5:155; 9:9–10, 27–28, 51, 88; adornment of, 1:20 (44); song of, 2:214 (245); temple of, 2:174–75 (188–89)
Yacauitztli, 6:206; 7:11, 60; 8:52
Yamanyaliztli, 6:206
Yaomauitl, 4:34. *See also* Tezcatlipoca
Yaomiqui, 6:74. *See also* Tonatiuh
Yaotl, Iaotl, 1:38 (67–68); 4:34; 6:1, 11–12, 210 (*see also* Tezcatlipoca); (person's name), 6:204
Yaotzin, Iaotzin, 3:12, 49–50 (12, 51–52); 6:7 (*see also* Tezcatlipoca); (steward), 12:5; tecutli (ruler of Uexotla), 8:13
Yauhtecatl, Ijouhtecatl, 1:24 (51)
Yaztachimal, 12:116 (120)
Yellow Xiuhtecutli, 2:177 (190)
Yeuatl icue, 2:127 (137)
Yiacatecutli. *See* Yacatecutli
Yiauhqueme, 2:43, 196 (44, 209)
Yiopoch, 2:168 (182)
Yoalli (god), 6:34; ichan (lord), 12:10
Yoaltecatl, 2:43, 140 (43, 152)

Yoaltecutli, 6:171–72, 206; 7:11, 60
Yoalticitl, 6:151, 153, 155, 160,
    171–72, 206

Yopicatl Popocatzin, 12:119 (123)
Yopitli, 2:56 (58); temple of, (2:51)
Yopoch, 3:7

Youallauan, 2:49–50, 52, 175–76
    (50–51, 53, 188–90)
Yoyontzin (ruler of Texcoco), 8:10

# Places

Acachinanco, 2:134, 162 (145, 176);
9:4; 12:82, 83, 86, 118 (84, 85, 89,
122)
Acaquilpan, 2:68 (70–71)
Acatl yiacapan, 12:53, 104 (55, 108);
Uei Calpulli, 2:179 (193)
Achcauhcalli, 8:43, 58
Acolhuacan, 5:179; 8:2, 7, 9, 52;
10:66, 78; 11:260; 12:96, 99 (100,
103)
Acontepetl, 11:260
Acuecuexatl, 8:2; 11:250
Acueco, 11:67, 70
Acxotla, Acxotlan, 9:12, 63
Amacozatl, 11:248
Amanalco, 12:106 (110)
Amantlan, 2:207 (222); 4:87; 9:83;
10:168
Amaquemecan, 12:35 (37)
Amaxac, 12:105, 109, 110, 111, 115,
117 (110, 113, 114, 116, 119, 121)
Amaxtlan, 8:2; 9:3
Anauac, 2:177 (191); 3:31 (33);
4:25; 8:45, 65; 9:3, 4, 6–8, 17–25,
30, 31, 39, 41, 49, 90; 10:65, 67, 78,
188; 11:14, 20, 21, 26, 28, 233, 273,
279, 282
Anauacatlalli, 11:256
Anauac Ayotlan, 9:17
Anauac Xicalanco, 9:17, 18
Apauazcan, 12:105 (109)
Apetlac, 3:3; 9:66
Atactzinco, 12:119 (123)
Atecocolecan, 12:103, 109 (107, 113)
Atempan, 2:114, 179, 195 (122, 192,
208)
Atenchicalcan, 2:97, 197–98 (103,
211)
Atenchicalco, 12:65 (67)
Atepec, 8:3
Atetemollan, 12:107 (111)
Atezcapan, 12:105, 107 (109, 111)
Aticpac, 2:175, 199 (189, 212)

Atlacuiuayan, 11:260
Atlan, 9:3
Atlauhco, 2:174, 175–76 (188, 189);
9:12
Atliceuhyan, 12:105, 106 (109, 110)
Atlixco, 8:73, 77, 88
Atlixeliuhqui, 2:199 (213)
Atocpan, 8:51
Atotonilco, 8:51
Atzaccan, 11:4
Atzitziuacan, 8:68; 10:67
Auachtlan, 9:12
Auilizapan, 11:258
Axocopan, 8:51
Ayacac, 12:105, 106 (109, 110)
Ayamictlan, 6:89
Ayauhcalco, Aiauhcalco, 2:30; 11:68
Ayauhcaltitlan, 12:88 (92)
Ayotlan, 8:2; 9:3, 4, 6
Ayotzintepec, 8:51; 12:56 (58)
Azcapotzalco, 1:19 (43); 4:95; 8:1, 7,
8, 15; 9:13, 17, 24, 45, 49; 10:196
Aztacalco, 8:51
Aztaquemecan (mountain, town),
12:74 (78)

Babylon, 10:165

Çacamulco, 12:74 (78)
Çacatepec, 2:25, 126–27, 167 (25,
136–37, 181); 3:19 (21); 8:3
Çacatepetl, 2:127 (137); 3:27 (29)
Çacatollan, 10:65
Calacoayan, 12:70 (73)
Callimaya, 8:2
Callixtlauacan, 8:2
Calpixcalli, 8:44
Caseapan, 11:4
Castille, Castilian, 6:232; 8:10; 10:71,
78, 85, 87; 11:10, 160, 165, 171,
185; 12:6, 16
Catemahco, 11:25

Caualtepec, 2:68 (71)
Cempoalla, 12:27, 29, 31, 59, 69 (27,
29, 31, 61, 71)
Centzontotochtin, Temple of, 2:173
(187)
Chacallan, 2:212 (239)
Chalchiuapan, 10:167
Chalco, 8:1; 9:24, 49; 10:66; 11:148,
179, 258, 279, 282; 12:33, 35, 81,
96, 99 (33, 37, 83, 100, 103)
Chalman, 2:213 (243)
Chapoltepecuitlapilco, 3:27 (29)
Chapultepec, 2:162 (176); 4:91;
6:232; 9:64; 10:196; 11:250
Chapultepetl, Chapoltepetl, 2:134
(145); 11:250, 260
Chiapan, 8:2; 9:18
Chichimecatlalli, 11:256
Chichinauhia (mountain), 10:193
Chichiualtatacalan, 8:3
Chicomecatl, Temple of, 2:171 (184)
Chicomecoatl, Temple of, 2:60
(62–63)
Chiconauhtlan, 7:42
Chicomoztoc, 2:209 (230); 10:195–
96, 197
Chiconauhtla, 11:178
Chicunauatl, 11:248
Chicunauhtecatl, 11:260
Chilapan, 10:187
Chililico, 2:173 (187)
Chillocan, 11:144, 145
Chinampas, 11:279, 282
Chinantla, 12:56 (58)
Chiquiuhtepetitlan, 10:196
Cholollan, Cholula, 2:212 (239);
8:21, 64; 10:192; 12:29–30
Chontal (land), 9:21
Cíbola, 8:5, 8
Cimatlan, 9:18, 21
Cincalco, 12:26
Cinteopan, 2:60 (62–63)
Cinteotl, Temple of, 2:173 (187)

Citlaltepec, 2:11, 74 (11, 78); 12:73 (77)
Ciuatlampa, 7:14, 21
Coaapan, 2:174, 192 (187, 205); 3:33 (35)
Coaatl (spring,) 8:2
Coacalco, 2:168, 177 (182, 191); 8:7
Coacalli, 8:44, 58; 12:18, 86 (18, 88)
Coaixtlauacan, 8:7
Coapan, 2:192, 213 (205, 240)
Coatepec, 3:1, 5, 19 (1, 5, 21); 8:2; 10:195
Coatepetl, 2:209 (227); 3:2, 4; 11:260; Temple of Uitzilopochtli, 2:161, 162 (175, 176)
Coatitlan, 10:156, 158
Coatlan, 2:55, 129, 176, 177 (57, 140, 189, 191); 9:28, 64; 12:113 (117)
Coatl ichan, 9:24, 48; 10:196
Coatlixtlauacan, 8:51
Coatolco, 10:65
Coatzaqualco, 9:18
Coaxalpan, 3:3
Cochtocan, 3:34 (36)
Çocollan, 8:3
Cocotl (mountain), 2:43, 140 (43, 152)
Colhuacan, 2:211–12 (236–37); 8:1, 4; 10:196; 12:35, 91 (37, 95)
Colhuacatonco, 12:99 (103)
Copalnamacoyan, 12:103, 107, 109, 110 (107, 111, 113, 114)
Copulco, 7:26, 27; 12:63 (65)
Çoquipan, 12:83–84 (85–86)
Corpus Christi, 11:259
Coyoacan, 2:134 (145); 8:2; 11:250, 259; 12:82 (84)
Coyonacazco, 6:234; 12:95, 115 (99, 119)
Coyotepec, 11:144
Cozcaapan, 3:34 (36)
Cozcaquauhtenanco, 8:2
Cozcatlan, 4:25
Cuepopan, 12:105 (109)
Cuetlaxtlan, 8:7, 51; 12:5, 9, 17
Cuextlan, 4:25; 8:3, 4, 8, 64; 10:185; 11:21, 22, 23, 50, 248
Cuezcomaixtlauacan, 8:3
Cuicacalli, 2:6; 8:43, 58
Cuitlapilco, 8:2
Cuitlauac, (1:79); 11:259; 12:35, 91–92 (37, 95–97)

Duality, place of, 6:175, 202

Eagle Gate, 8:87, 88; 12:85 (87–88). See also Quauhquiauac

Ecatepec, 8:2; 10:196
Epcoatl, Temple of, 2:165–66 (179–80)
Euacalco, 2:177 (191)

Guatemala, 6:232; 8:7; 10:65, 78. See also Quauhtemallan

Heavens, 6:175, 202, 237; 10:168–69
Hecatepec, 11:177
Home of Tonacatecutli, 6:115–16
Honduras, 8:4, 8
House of the sun, 2:203 (217); 3:47–48 (49); 6:114–15, 162–65
Huaxtepec, 10:67; 11:177
Huexotzinco. See Uexotzinco

Ichpuchco, 10:196
Icpatepec, 8:3
Ilhuicatitlan, 2:172 (186)
Iliacac, 12:82, 87 (84, 91)
Iolloxonecuillan, 8:3
Iopico. See Yopico
Iopitli, Temple of, 2:49, 56 (51, 58)
Itepeyoc, 1:38 (67); 2:161, 178 (175, 192); 3:8; 12:2
Itualco, 8:21
Itzcoatlan, 2:207 (223)
Itzcuincuitlapilco, 8:51
Itziocan, 9:31; 10:75
Itztapalapan, 4:143; 12:35, 37, 91 (37, 39, 95)
Itztepec, 11:188
Itzteyocan, 10:78
Itztolco, 9:12
Ixcoçauhqui, Temple of, 1:12 (30)
Ixillan, tonan, 2:126 (136)
Ixtlilton, Temple of, 2:199 (212)
Izoatlan, 8:2
Izquitlan, 2:134, 200 (145, 214)
Iztacalla, 12:80 (82)
Iztac ciuatl (mountain), 2:140 (152); 8:21; 11:258. See also Iztac tepetl
Iztac tepetl, 1:22 (47); 2:114, 140 (122, 152); 3:35 (37); 11:258; 12:31. See also Iztac ciuatl
Iztapalapan, 11:259
Iztec tlalocan, 8:3
Izuatlan, 9:3

Lake of Mexico, 2:12; 8:18; 12:2

Maçatlan, 2:134 (145); 8:2; 9:64
Maçatzintamalco, 9:64; 12:64, 117 (66, 121)
Maçauacan, 7:14; 8:1
Macuilcalli, 2:166 (180)

Macuilcipactli, Temple of 2:170 (184)
Macuilmalinalli, Temple of, 2:175 (189)
Macuilquiauitl, 2:166 (180)
Malcalli, 8:45
Malinalco, 11:146, 189
Malinaltenanco, 8:2
Mapachtepec, 8:2; 9:3
Matlalcueye, 11:259
Matlatzinco, 8:51; 9:81; 10:182; 11:282
Mecatlan, 2:172–73, 198, 209 (186, 211–12, 228)
Metepec, 8:2
Metztitlan, 4:26; 8:64
Mexicatzinco, 12:35, 91 (37, 95)
Mexico, 1:13 (32); 2:11, 68, 166, 167 (11, 71, 180, 181); 3:14 (15); 4:29, 61, 143; 6:244; 7:27, 29; 8:1, 2, 4, 15–16, 57, 65, 73, 81, 89; 9:1, 4, 5, 6–7, 9, 19, 22, 23, 53; 10:78, 170, 185, 189, 191, 196; 11:50, 250, 260; 12:2, 6, 13, 15, 17, 29, 34, 35, 37, 42, 43, 59, 65, 75, 79, 83 (2, 5–6, 13, 15, 17, 29, 34–35, 37–38, 44, 45, 61, 67, 79, 81, 85); calmecac, 2:168 (182); City of, 8:56; 11:256; 12:1
Michoacan, 6:34; 8:64; 10:66, 67, 78; 11:21, 244, 256, 260, 279, 282
Michoacatlalli, 11:256
Mictlampa, 7:14
Mictlan, 3:35 (37); 6:163; 8:3; 11:129; 12:26
Mictlanquauhtla, 12:5, 9
Mictlantonco Macuilcuitlapilco, 12:65, 69 (67, 71)
Mist House (ayauhcalco), 2:44, 121, 123, 141 (44, 131, 133, 153); 3:7
Mixcoac, 9:24, 49
Mixcoacalli, 8:45
Mixcoapan, 2:166 (180)
Mixcoatechialtitlan, 12:65 (67)
Mixcoateopan, 2:26
Mixcoatl, Temple of, 2:172 (185–86)
Mixtecatlalli, 11:256
Mixtlan, 2:207 (221); 11:260
Mizquic, 12:35, 91 (37, 95)
Mollonco, Molonco, 2:194 (207); 8:2
Motlauhxauhcan, 11:148, 259

Nappa tecutli, Temple of, 2:176 (190)
Nauhtlan, 12:9
Necoquixecan, 2:97 (103)
Netlatiloyan, 2:172, 175 (186, 189)
Netotiloyan, 2:173 (187)

124

New Spain, 11:235
Nextlatilco, 12:82 (84)
Nochtlan, 8:8
Nonoalco, 2:134, 211 (145, 234);
4:25; 9:64; 12:65, 82, 87, 88, 92,
117 (68, 84, 91, 92, 96, 121)
Nopalan, 8:3

Ocuillan, 8:2, 51; 12:119 (123)
Oholpan, 2:207 (223)
Omitlan, 9:3
Otoncalpulco, 12:67 (69)
Otompan, Otumba, 7:42; 9:24, 49
Oztoman, 10:75

Panotla, Pantla, 10:185, 190, 193
Pantitlan, 1:24 (49); 2:42, 43, 84
(42, 43, 89)
Pantla. See Panotla
Petlacalco, 8:44, 51; 12:66, 69 (68,
71)
Petlacaltepetl, 11:260
Pichauaztlan, 2:207 (221)
Pinauizatl, 11:249
Pochtlan, 2:112, 174, 200 (120,
187–88, 213); 4:87, 121; 9:12, 37,
63
Poçonaltepec, 10:194
Poçonaltepetl, 10:193
Popocatepetl (mountain), 1:22 (47);
2:140 (152); 3:35 (37); 8:21;
11:258, 12:31
Popotlan, 2:134, 162 (145, 176);
9:64; 12:66 (68)
Popotl temi, 2:114 (122)
Poyauhtecatl, 1:22 (47); 3:35 (37);
11:258
Poyauhtlan, 2:43, 166, 208 (43, 180,
224–25)

Quauecatitlan, 12:96 (100)
Quauhcalli, 8:43, 58; 9:23. See also
Tequiuacacalli
Quauhnauac, 8:1, 7, 51; 11:146, 148
Quauhquechollan, 12:103–4 (107–8)
Quauhquiauac, 12:53, 85 (55, 87, 88).
See also Eagle Gate
Quauhtechcac, 12:31
Quauhtemallan, Quauhtemalla, 10:190;
11:189. See also Guatemala
Quauhtenanco, 9:3
Quauhtepec, 2:43, 179 (43, 192);
10:159
Quauhtepetl, 2:43, 140 (43, 152);
11:259
Quauhtitlan, 2:31; 4:143; 6:71; 9:13,
17, 24, 49; 12:79, 80, 81 (81, 84)

Quauhtlaxcalla, 12:28
Quauhtlinchan, 8:7
Quauhtzontlan, 9:3
Quauhxicalco, 2:168, 170, 171–72
(182, 184, 185); 12:55, 64, (57,
66)
Quauhxicalli, 2:203 (217)
Quetzalatl, 11:248
Quetzaltepec, 8:3
Quetzaltepetl, 11:259
Quetzalxoch (mountain), 2:43. See
also Tepetzinco, Tepetzintli

San Juan (Teotihuacan), 7:42, 46;
10:163
San Lorenzo, 11:259
San Martín, Church of, 12:99 (103)
San Miguel, 11:260
San Pablo, 10:163
San Pedro, 11:260
San Sebastián, 10:163
Santa Ana, Church of, 12:92 (96)
Santa Clara, 11:260; Coatitlan, 11:259
Santa Cruz Quauhacalco, 11:33
Santiago Tlatelolco, 11:33

Tamoanchan, 2:208–9 (226); 10:190,
191, 192, 194
Tecanman, 2:48, 68, 117, 195 (49, 70,
125, 209)
Teccalco, 2:168–69 (182); 8:42. See
also Teccalli
Teccalli, 8:42, 54, 55, 58. See also
Teccalco
Teccizcalco, 2:169 (183)
Teccizcalli, 2:166 (180)
Techielli, 2:179 (193)
Tecoac, 12:27
Tecolotlan, 11:20
Tecomaixtlauacan, 8:3
Tecomic, 11:152
Tecpancaltitlan, 12:109 (113)
Tecpan tlayacac, 12:17
Tecpantzinco, 2:198 (212); 12:53, 65
(55, 67)
Tecpilcalli, 8:42–43, 58
Tehuantepec. See Tequantepec.
Temacpalco, 3:33 (35)
Temalacatl, 2:176 (190)
Temetztla, 11:187
Temilco, 2:11, 74 (11, 78)
Temitztla, 11:273
Temple Courtyard, Tenochtitlan,
12:53, 56, 64 (55, 58, 66)
Tenayocan, Tenayuca, 8:7; 11:259, 263
Tenexnamacoyan, 12:103 (107)

Tenochtitlan, 2:48, 95, 124 (49, 101,
134); 4:61; 8:1–5, 21–22, 45, 52,
57, 72, 73; 9:3, 8, 13, 17, 23, 24, 48,
49, 64, 91; 10:196; 11:260; 12:43,
55, 56, 65, 82–83, 87 (45, 57, 58,
67, 84–85, 91)
Teoayoc, 12:63 (65)
Teocalco, 12:46 (48)
Teocalhueyacan, Teucalhuiyacan,
11:259; 12:67–72 (69–76)
Teociniocan, 12:5
Teotenanco, 8:2
Teotihuacan, Teotiuacan, 3:1; 7:4, 42,
46; 10:191–92, 194
Teotlachco, 2:162, 172 (176, 186)
Teotlachtli, 2:27
Teotlalpan, 2:167 (181)
Teoxaualco, 8:2
Teotlixco, 11:25
Tepanoayan, 3:33 (35); 8:13
Tepçolatl, 12:66 (69)
Tepçolco, 11:142
Tepepan, 10:160
Tepepolli (mountain), 2:140 (152)
Tepepul, 11:260
Tepepulco, 2:68 (70); 10:160;
11:178, 260
Tepequacuilco, 8:51; 10:187
Tepetitlan, 9:12
Tepetlan, 4:26
Tepetocan, 2:134, 162 (145, 176);
9:64
Tepetzinco, 1:24 (49); 2:42, 43, 68,
179 (42, 43, 70, 192); 12:96 (100)
Tepetzintli (mountain), 2:43, 140
(43, 152)
Tepexicoztoc, 2:74 (78)
Tepeyacac, 12:59, 110, 111, 117 (61,
115, 116, 121)
Tepotzotlan, 10:168; 11:4; 12:72–73
(76–77)
Tepoztlan, 10:159; 12:10
Tequaloyan, 8:2
Tequanatl, 11:248
Tequantepec, 8:65; 9:3, 18
Tequiuacacalli, 8:43. See also Quauh-
calli
Tequixquiac, 11:182
Tetamaçolco, 2:84, 97 (90, 103);
12:86 (89)
Tetenanteputzco, 12:96 (100)
Tetepetzinco, 11:34
Teteutitlan, 12:110, 111 (115)
Teticpac, 12:25
Tetlanman, 2:170 (184); priest's
house, 2:170 (184)
Tetzauatl, 11:249

125

Teuantepec. *See* Tequantepec
Teucalhuiyac (mountain), 11:259
Teucalhuiyacan. *See* Teocalhueyacan
Teuhtlalpan, 11:144
Teutlixco, 11:26
Texancalli, 8:44
Texcalla, 12:28, 29
Texcalpan, 3:21–22 (23–24)
Texcoco (Tetzcuco, Tezcuco), 2:54
    (55); 4:143; 8:9–11, 14, 15, 22, 52,
    65; 9:24, 48; 11:259; 12:35, 43, 81,
    83, 99, 119 (37, 45, 84, 85, 103,
    123)
Texopan, 12:121 (125)
Tezcaapan, 2:171 (185)
Tezcacalco, 2:169 (183)
Tezcacoac, 2:156 (169); 12:53 (55);
    Tlacochcalco, 2:179 (193)
Tezcatepec, 11:144
Tezcatlachco 2:171 (185)
Tezcatzonco, 2:214 (244)
Tiçapan, 12:70 (73)
Tiçatlan, 12:10
Tiliuhcan, 12:66 (68)
Tilocan, 2:178 (192)
Tlacateccan, 8:17; 12:2. *See also*
    Tlacatecco
Tlacatecco, 2:38; 4:77; 8:63. *See also*
    Tlacochcalco
Tlachco, 8:51
Tlachmalacac, 10:187
Tlachquiauhco, 8:3
Tlacochcalco, 2:10, 68, 207 (10, 71);
    8:63; 12:95 (99); Acatl yiacapan,
    2:169 (183); Quauhquiauac, 2:178
    (192)
Tlacopan, 8:15, 52, 65; 12:43, 65, 66,
    79, 81, 87, 119 (45, 68, 81, 84, 91,
    123)
Tlacotepec, 8:2
Tlacuilocan, 1:15 (35)
Tlacxitlan, 8:41–42, 55, 58
Tlaixcuipan, 12:110 (115)
Tlalhuacan, 12:96 (100)
Tlaliztacapan, 12:80 (82)
Tlaloc (mountain), 2:140 (152);
    Temple of, 1:7 (22); 2:82–83, 89,
    123, 165 (87–88, 94, 133, 179)
Tlalocan, 1:7 (22); 2:165–66, 208–9
    (179–80, 224–25); 3:45, 67 (47,
    69); 6:35–36, 39, 115; 7:14, 17,
    68; 10:188; 11:68–69, 247; 12:12,
    26; Temple of, 2:168 (182)
Tlaltecayoacan. 12:66 (68)
Tlalxicco. 2:167 (180–81)
Tlamatzinco, 2:26 171 (26, 185);
    9:37; priest's house, 2:171 (185)

Tlanquilapan, 11:4
Tlapallan, 1:40 (69); 3:31, 34, 36
    (33, 36, 38); 10:170
Tlapan, 8:2
Tlapitzauayan, 2:10, 68 (10, 71)
Tlapitzauhcan, 2:68 (71). *See also*
    Tlapitzauayan
Tlappan, 8:51
Tlatelolco, Tlatilolco, Tlatilulco, 2:95,
    124, 134, 162 (101, 134, 145, 176);
    4:61; 7:32; 8:2, 7–8, 42, 45, 52,
    72–73; 9:1–2, 6, 8, 17, 23–24,
    48–49, 51, 64, 91; 11:33–34; 12:43,
    55, 63–64, 65, 75, 81, 103–22
    (45, 57, 65–66, 67, 79, 84, 107–26)
Tlatlauhquitepec, 11:188
Tlauapan, 8:3
Tlaxcala, Tlaxcalla, 8:9, 21–22, 64;
    10:66, 78; 11:259; 12:27–29, 31,
    39, 46, 59, 65–66, 96, 99 (27–30,
    31, 41, 48, 61, 67–68, 100, 103)
Tlaxotlan, 2:134, 207 (145, 222)
Tlilapan, 2:167–68, 192 (181, 205)
Tlilhuacan, 12:105 (109)
Tliliuhquitepec, 8:77; 12:66, 71, 107
    (68, 75, 111)
Tliliuhquitepetl, 12:39 (41)
Tlillan, 2:167 (181); calmecac, calme-
    catl, 2:168 (182); 8:18–19; 12:3
Tlillatl (spring), 8:2
Tochinco, 2:167 (181)
Tocimilco, 10:67
Tochpan, 8:51
Tochtepec, 9:17, 22, 31, 48–49, 51;
    10:65
Toci, Temple of, 1:5
Tocititlan, (1:16); 2:117 (125)
Tocuillan, 2:207–8 (223)
Tollan, Tula, 1:39 (69); 2:201
    (214); 3:1, 13, 15, 21, 27, 29 (1,
    13, 17, 23, 29, 31); 6:219; 8:15;
    10:27, 165–70, 195–96; 11:249; atl,
    11:249; Tlapallan, 3:16 (18)
Tollantzinco, 10:165, 195; 11:183
Tolmayecan, 12:116, 18 (120, 122)
Tolnauac. 2:178 (192)
Tolocan, 10:182–83; 11:248, 260
Tolotepetl (mountain), 10:182
Tolotzin (mountain), 10:182
Tonan (mountain). 12:75 (79)
Tonatiuh ichan. 12:26
Tolteca canal, 12:66, 69, 79, 121 (68,
    71, 81, 125)
Totec. Temple of, 9:71
Totecco. 1:17 (39); 2:81 (85); 9:70;
    12:96. 105, 106 (100, 109, 110)
Totectzontecontitlan, 8:85

Totocalli, Totocalco, 8:45; 12:47 (49)
Totolatl, 11:249
Totonacapan, 11:50, 222, 230, 262
Totonacatlalli, 11:256. *See also*
    Totonac country
Totonac country, 8:64; 11:22, 82, 85.
    *See also* Totonacatlalli
Toxpalatl, 2:178 (191)
Toztlan, 11:4, 25–26; 12:9
Tula. *See* Tollan
Tzapotlan, 8:65; 9:6, 18; 12:65 (67)
Tzatzitepetl, 3:14, 18, 21 (14, 20, 23)
Tzinacantepec, 8:2
Tzinacantlan, 9:21, 23
Tziuhcoac, 8:2, 51
Tzompantitlan, 3:3
Tzonmolco, 1:12 (30); 2:150, 177,
    198, 209 (163, 190, 211, 228);
    8:18; 9:12; 12:2; priest's house
    (calmecac), 2:176 (190)


Uapan, 8:51
Uaxtepec, 8:51; 11:244
Ueicamecatlan, 12:10
Ueican, 12:111 (116)
Uei mollan, 8:10
Uei Quauhxicalco, 2:167 (181)
Ueuequauhtitlan, 3:31 (33)
Ueuetlan, 12:10
Uexotlan, 8:13–14; 9:24, 48
Uexotzinco, Huexotzinco, 4:25;
    6:114–15; 7:31; 8:9, 45, 65, 73, 77,
    88; 10:78, 151; 11:279; 12:39 (41)
Uitzcalco, 8:53; 9:64
Uitzilatl (spring), 2:131 (141); 8:2
Uitzilinquatec, Temple of, 2:174
    (188)
Uitzillan, 12:41, 84 (43–44, 86)
Uitzilopochco, 8:2; 9:13, 17, 24, 49;
    12:35 (37)
Uitzilopochtli, Temple of, 2:102, 112,
    124–25, 135–36, 161–62, 165 (109,
    121, 134–35, 146–47, 175–76,
    179); 4:77, 79; 8:61–62; 9:65;
    12:86 (88)
Uitznauac, 1:14 (33); 2:134, 136, 207
    (146, 148, 223); 3:7; 9:37;
    calpulco, 2:161 (175, 192); priest's
    house, 2:170 (183); pyramid, 2:170
    (183); Temple of, 2:169 (183);
    tribal temple, 2:178
Uitztepeualco, 2:169 (183)
Uitztlampa, 7:14
Uixachtecatl (mountain), 2:140
    (152); 4:143; 7:28; 11:259
Uixachtlan, 7:25, 27

126

White Cinteotl, Temple of, 2:170 (184)

Xalapa, 11:188
Xaloztoc, 11:260
Xaltenco, 11:143–44
Xaltepec, 8:2
Xaltocan, 7:9, 58; 8:7
Xicalanco, 9:17, 19; 12:13, 17
Xicocotitlan, 10:165, 167, 195
Xilotepec, 8:51–52
Xippacoia, Xippacoyan, 3:14; 10:168
Xiuhtecutli, Temple of, 1:12 (30); 2:148 (161)
Xiuhtzone, 10:168
Xiuitonco, 10:163
Xochcaatl (spring), 8:2
Xochicalco, 2:175, 177 189, 191); 12:103 (107)
Xochimilco, 4:143; 8:1, 7; 9:49, 80;

11:147, 152; 12:35, 91–92, 99, 100, 106 (37, 95–97, 103, 104, 110)
Xochipilla, 8:5
Xochiquauhyocan, 11:186
Xochitlan, 3:23, 29 (25, 31); 9:3
Xochtlan, 8:2
Xoconochco, 8:2; 9:31; 11:189
Xocotepetl, 10:184
Xocotitlan, 10:183; 12:95, 96 (99, 100)
Xocotlihiovican, 12:66 (68)
Xoloc (mountain, town), 12:73 (77)
Xoloco, Xolloco, 2:98 (103); 8:22; 9:64; 12:41, 83–84, 86, 117 (43, 85–86, 88, 121)
Xolteca, 10:65
Xomiltepec, 10:194
Xomolco, 12:109 (113)
Xoxocotla, 12:66 (68)
Xoxouiltitlan, 12:117 (121)

Yacacolco, 12:92, 99, 104–5, 109 (96, 103, 108–9, 113)
Yacatecutli, Temple of, 2:174, 175 (188, 189)
Yauhtenco, 12:93 (97)
Yiauhqueme (mountain), 2:43, 140, 179 (43–44, 152, 192)
Yoaltecatl (mountain), 2:43, 140 (43, 152)
Yolloxonecuillan. See Iolloxonecuillan
Yopicalco, 2:177 (191)
Yopico, Iopico, 2:2, 5, 44, 50, 55–56, 174, 199–200 (2, 5, 45, 51, 57–58, 188, 213); 8:85–86; 9:37, 69, 71; priest's house, 2:174–75 (188)
Yopitli, Temple of, 2:49, 56 (51, 58)
Yopitzinco, 10:187


Zapotlan, 2:195, 220 (208–9, 214)

# BIBLIOGRAPHY

# Bibliography

Acosta Saignes, Miguel. *Los pochteca: unbicación de los mercaderes en la estructura social tenochca.* Acta Anthropologica, Vol. I, 1945.

————. *Tlacaxipeualiztli, un complejo mesoamericano entre los caribes.* Caracas: Universidad Central, 1950.

Aguilar, Francisco de. *Relación breve de la conquista de Nueva España.* Mexico, D.F.: José Porrúa e Hijos, Sucs., 1954.

Alcocer, Ignacio. *Apuntes sobre la antigua Mexico–Tenochtitlan.* Tacubaya, D.F.: Instituto Panamericano de Geografía e Historia, 1935.

*Anales de Tlatelolco.* See Berlin and Barlow.

Ancona H., Ignacio, and Rafael Martín del Campo. *Malacología precortesiana.* Memoria del Congreso Científico Mexicano, Vol. VII, Mexico, 1953.

Anderson, Arthur J. O. "Pre–Hispanic Aztec Colorists." *El Palacio*, Vol. LV (1948), pp. 20–27.

————. "Refranes en un santoral en mexicano." *Estudios de cultura náhuatl*, Vol. VI (1966), pp. 55–61.

————. "Sahagún's Sahagún." *El Palacio*, Vol. LXIII (1956), pp. 195–201.

————, Frances Berdan, and James Lockhart. *Beyond the Codices.* Berkeley and Los Angeles: University of California Press, 1976.

Andrews, Richard J. *Introduction to Classical Nahuatl.* Austin and London: University of Texas Press, 1975.

Aubin, J. M. A. *Histoire de la nation mexicaine . . . réproduction du Codex de 1576.* Paris: Ernest Leroux, 1893.

Ayer, MS No. 1485. Newberry Library, Chicago.

Ballesteros Gaibrois, Manuel. *Vida y obra de Fray Bernardino de Sahagún.* León, Spain: Institución "Fray Bernardino de Sahagún," C.S.I.C., 1973.

————, ed. *Códices matritenses de la Historia general de las cosas de la Nueva España de Fr. Bernardino de Sahagún.* 2 vols. Colección Chimalistac Nos. 19–20. Madrid: Ediciones José Porrua Turanzas, 1964.

Bandini, Angelo Maria. *Bibliotheca Leopoldina Laurentiana, seu Catalogus Manuscriptorum qui nuper in Laurentiana translati sunt.* Florence: Typis Regiis, 1791–93.

Barlow, R. H. "Cinco siglos de las calles de Tlatelolco." *Tlatelolco a través de los tiempos*, Vol. IX (1947), pp. 27–34.

————. *The Extent of the Empire of the Culhua Mexica.* Berkeley and Los Angeles: University of California Press, 1949.

————. "Las ocho ermitas de Santiago Tlatelolco." *Tlatelolco a través de los tiempos*, Vol. IX (1947), pp. 62–67.

————. "Una pintura de la conquista en el templo de Santiago," *Tlatelolco a través de los tiempos*, Vol. VI (1945), pp. 54–60.

Baudot, Georges. "Apariciones diabólicas en un texto náhuatl de Fray Andrés de Olmos." *Estudios de cultura náhuatl*, Vol. X (1972), pp. 349–57.

————. "Fray Rodrigo de Sequera, avocat du diable pour une histoire interdie." *Cahiers du Monde Hispanique et Luso–Brésilien*, Caravelle 12 (1969), pp. 47–82.

————. "The Last Years of Fray Bernardino de Sahagún (1585–90). The Rescue of the Confiscated Work and the Seraphic Conflicts. New Unpublished Documents." In *Sixteenth–Century Mexico: The Work of Sahagún*, edited by Munro S. Edmonson, pp. 165–87. Albuquerque: University of New Mexico Press, 1974.

————. *Tratado de hechicerías y sortilegios de fray Andrés de Olmos.* Estudios Mesoamericanos, Series II, 7, Misión Arqueológica y Etnológica Francesa en Mexico, 1979.

————. *Utopie et histoire au Mexique: les premiers chroniqueurs de la civilisation mexicaine (1520–1569).* Toulouse: Editions Edouard Privat, 1978.

Bautista, Fr. Juan. *Huehuetlatolli, o pláticas de los viejos.* Mexico: 1600.

Beltrami, J.–C. *Le Mexique.* 2 vols. Paris: Delaunay, Librairie, 1830.

Berlin, Heinrich, and Robert H. Barlow. *Anales de Tlatelolco: Unos annales históricos de la nación mexicana y*

*Códice de Tlatelolco.* Fuentes para la Historia de Mexico, 2. Mexico, D.F.: Antigua Librería Robredo, 1948.

Biondelli, Bernardini. *Glossarium Azteco–Latinum et Latino–Aztecum.* Milan, Italy: Valentiner et Mues, 1869.

———, ed. *Evangeliarium, epistolarium et lectionarium aztecum sive mexicanum ex antiquo codice mexicano nuper reperto depromptum.* Milan, Italy: Typis Jos. Bernardoni Q.ᵐ Johannis, 1858.

Blake, Emmet Reid. *Birds of Mexico.* Chicago: University of Chicago Press, 1953.

*Boletín de la Real Academia de la Historia.* Vol. II (Madrid, 1883), p. 184.

———. Vol. III (Madrid, 1883), p. 209.

Brinton, Daniel G. *Rig–Veda Americanus. Sacred Songs of the Ancient Mexicans, with a Gloss in Nahuatl.* 1890. Reprint. New York: AMS Press, 1969.

Briquet, C. M. *Les Filigranes: Dictionnaire historique des marques du papier.* 4 vols. Geneva: Imprimerie W. Kündig & Fils., 1907.

Burland, Cottie A. *The Selden Rolls.* Monumenta Americana, edited by Gerdt Kutscher, vol. 2. Berlin: Verlag Gebr. Mann, 1955.

Bustamante, Carlos María de. *Historia general de las cosas de Nueva España, que en doce libros y dos volumenes escribió. El R. P. Fr Bernardino de Sahagún, de la observancia de San Francisco, y uno de los primeros predicadores del Santo Evangelio en aquellas regiones.* 3 vols. Mexico, D.F.: Imprenta del ciudadano Alejandro Valdéz, 1829-30.

———, ed. *La aparición de Ntra. Señora de Guadalupe de Mexico, comprobada con la refutación del argumento negativo que presenta D. Juan Bautista Muñoz, fundandose en el testimonio del P. Fr. Bernardino de Sahagún.* Mexico, D.F.: Ignacio Cumplido, 1840.

Calnek, Edward E. "Conjunto urbano y modelo residencial en Tenochtitlan." In *Ensayos sobre el desarrollo urbano de México,* by Edward E. Calnek; Woodrow Borah; Alejandra Moreno Toscano; Keith A. Davies; and Luis Unikel, pp. 11-65. Mexico, D.F.: Secretaría de Educación Pública, 1974.

———. "The Localization of the Sixteenth–Century Map Called the Maguey Plan." *American Antiquity,* Vol. XXXVIII (1973), pp. 190-95.

———. "Organización de los sistemas de abastecimiento urban de alimentos; el caso de Tenochtitlán." In *Las ciudades de América Latina y sus áreas de influencia a través de la historia.* Compiled by Jorge E. Hardoy and Richard P. Schaedel. Buenos Aires: Ediciones Sociedad Interamericana de Planificacion, 1975.

———. "Settlement Pattern and Chinampa Agriculture at Tenochtitlan." *American Antiquity,* Vol. XXXVII (1972), pp. 104-15.

Carochi, Horacio. *Arte de la lengua mexicana.* Mexico, D.F.: Imprenta del Museo Nacional, 1892.

Carrasco Pizana, Pedro. "El barrio y la regulación del matrimonio en un pueblo del Valle de México en el siglo XVI." *Revista Mexicana de Estudios Antropológicos,* Vol. XVII (1961), pp. 7-24.

———. *Los Otomíes.* Mexico, D.F.: Instituto de Historia, 1950.

———. "Sobre algunos términos de parentesco en el náhuatl clásico." *Estudios de cultura náhuatl,* Vol. VI (1966), pp. 149-66.

*Cartas de Indias. Publicadas por primera vez por el Ministerio de Fomento.* Madrid: Imprenta de Manuel G. Hernández, 1877.

Caso, Alfonso. *Los barrios antiguos de Tenochtitlan y Tlatelolco.* Mimeographed. Mexico, D.F.: Sociedad Mexicana de Antropología, 1954.

———. "Los barrios antiguos de Tenochtitlan y Tlatelolco." *Memorias de la Academia Mexicana de la Historia,* Vol. XV (1956), pp. 7-63.

———. "Instituciones indígenas precortesianas." *Memorias del Instituto Nacional Indigenista,* Vol. VI (1954), pp. 13-27.

———. "Land Tenure Among the Ancient Mexicans." *American Anthropologist,* Vol. XLV, No. 4 (Aug. 1963), pp. 863-78.

———. *La religion de los aztecas.* Mexico, D.F.: Imprenta Mundial, 1936.

Cervantes de Salazar, Francisco. *Crónica de Nueva España,* Vol. III. Papeles de Nueva España, 3rd Ser., Historia. Mexico, D.F.: Talleres Gráficos del Museo Nacional de Arqueología, Historia, y Etnografía, 1936.

Charney, Désiré. *Ancient Cities of the New World.* Translated by J. Gonino and H. S. Conant. New York: Harper, 1887.

Chavero, Alfredo. *Sahagún.* Mexico, D.F.: Biblioteca Aportación Histórica, 1948.

Chavez, Angelico, trans. and ed. *The Oroz Codex.* Washington, D.C.: Academy of American Franciscan History, 1972.

Chimalpahin Quauhtlehuanitzin (Domingo Francisco de San Antón Muñón). *Annales de Domingo Francisco de San Antón Muñón. . . .* Translated and edited by Rémi Siméon. Bibliothèque Linguistique Américaine, Vol. 12. Paris: Maisonneuve et C. Leclerc, 1889.

Civezza, Marcelino de. *Saggio di Bibliografia Geografica Storica Etnografica Sanfrancescana.* Prato, Italy, 1879.

Clark, James Cooper. *Codex Mendoza.* 3 vols. London: Waterlow and Sons, 1938.

Clavijero, Francisco Javier. *Historia antigua de México*. 4 vols. Edited by Mariano Cuevas. Mexico, D.F.: Editorial Porrúa, S.A., 1945.

Cline, Howard F. "Sahagún Materials and Studies." In *Handbook of the Middle American Indians*, edited by Robert Wauchope, Vol. 13, pp. 218–39. Austin: University of Texas Press, 1973.

*Codex Ríos (Il Manoscritto Messicano Vaticano 3738 detto il Codice* Ríos). Rome: Stabilimento Danesi, 1900.

*Códice Franciscano*. Mexico, D.F.: Editorial Chávez Hayhoe, 1941.

*Congrès International des Américanistes, Compte–Rendu de la Septième session, Berlin, 1888*. Berlin: Librairie W. H. Kühl, 1890.

Dávila Garibí, J. Ignacio. *Epítome de raíces nahuas*. Mexico, D.F.: Editorial Cultura, T.G.S.A., 1949.

Dibble, Charles E. *Códice Xólotl*. Mexico, D.F.: Universidades de Utah y de México, 1951.

————. *Historia de la nación Mexicana . . . Códice de 1576*. Madrid: Ediciones José Porrua Turanzas, 1963.

————. "The Nahuatlization of Christianity." In *Sixteenth-Century Mexico: The Work of Sahagún*, edited by Munro S. Edmonson, pp. 225–33. Albuquerque: University of New Mexico Press, 1974.

————. "Nahuatl Names for Body Parts." *Estudios de cultura náhuatl*, Vol. I (1959), pp. 27–30.

————, and Norma B. Mikkelsen. "La olografía de Fray Bernardino de Sahagún." *Estudios de cultura náhuatl*, Vol. IX (1971), pp. 232–36.

Dressler, Robert L. "The Pre–Columbian Cultivated Plants of Mexico." *Harvard University Botanical Museum Leaflets*, Vol. XVI, No. 6 (1953), pp. 115–72.

Durán, Diego. *Historia de las Indias de Nueva España y islas de Tierra Firme*. 2 vols. and atlas. 1867–80. Reprint. Mexico, D.F.: Editora Nacional, S.A., 1951.

Easby, Dudley T., Jr. "Ancient American Goldsmiths." *Natural History*, Vol. LXV, No. 8 (1956), pp. 401–9.

————. "Orfebrería y orfebres precolombinos." *Anales del Instituto de Arte Americano*, Vol. IX (Buenos Aires 1956), pp. 9–26.

————. "Sahagún Reviviscit in Gold Collections of the University Museum." *University of Pennsylvania, University Museum Bulletin*, Vol. XX, No. 3 (1956), pp. 3–15.

————. "Sahagún y los orfebres precolombinos de México." *Anales del Instituto Nacional de Antropología e Historia*, Vol. IX (1977), pp. 85–117.

Easby, Elizabeth Kennedy, and Dudley T. Easby, Jr. "Apuntes sobre la técnica de tallar jade en América." *Anales del Instituto de Arte Americano*, Vol. VI (1956), pp. 5–32.

Emmart, Emily Walcott. *The Badianus Manuscript (Codex Barberini, Latin 241), Vatican Library—An Aztec Herbal of 1552*. Baltimore: Johns Hopkins Press, 1940.

*Enciclopedia Universal Illustrada*. 70 vols. Madrid and Barcelona: Espasa Calpe, S.A., 1907(?)–30.

Espejo, Antonieta, and R. H. Barlow. "El plano más antiguo de Tlatelolco." *Tlatelolco a través de los tiempos*, Vol. I (1944), pp. 43–47.

Foshag, William F. *Mineralogical Studies in Guatemalan Jade*. Smithsonian Miscellaneous Collections, Vol. 135, No. 5. Washington, D.C.: Smithsonian Institution, 1957.

Foster, George. "Nagualism in Mexico and Guatemala." *Acta Americana*, Vol. 2, Nos. 1–2 (1944), pp. 85–103.

Friedmann, Herbert, Ludlow Griscom, and Robert T. Moore. *Distributional Check–List of the Birds of Mexico*. Pacific Coast Avifauna, Nos. 29, 33. Berkeley: Cooper Ornitholgical Club, 1950, 1957.

Galindo y Villa, Jesús. *Don Francisco del Paso y Troncoso. Su vida y sus obras*. Memorias y Revista de la Sociedad Científica "Antonio Alzate," Vol. 42 (1923), pp. 134–77; 541–51.

Gante, Pedro de. Letters to Charles V, 1532, and to Philip II, 1558. Archivo Histórico Nacional, Madrid. Docs. 113 and 158. In *Cartas de Indias*, p. xviii. Madrid: Imprenta de Manuel G. Hernández, 1877.

García Icazbalceta, Joaquín. *Bibliografía mexicana del siglo XVI*. Edited by Agustín Millars Carlo. Mexico, D.F.: Fondo de Cultura Económica, 1954.

————. *Fray Juan de Zumárraga*. 4 vols. Mexico, D.F.: Editorial Porrúa, S.A., 1947.

Garibay K., Angel María. *Historia de la literatura náhuatl*. 2 vols. Mexico, D.F.: Editorial Porrúa, S.A., 1953–54.

————. "Huehuetlatolli, Documento A." *Tlalocan*, Vol. I, Nos. 1–2 (1943), pp. 31–53; 81–107.

————. *Llave del náhuatl*. 1940. 2nd ed. Mexico, D.F.: Editorial Porrúa, S.A., 1961.

————. *La literatura de los aztecas*. Mexico, D.F.: Editorial Joaquín Mortiz, 1964.

————. "Paralipómenos de Sahagún." *Tlalocan*, Vol. I, No. 4 (1944), pp. 307–13; Vol. II, No. 2 (1946), pp. 167–74; Vol. II, No. 3 (1947), pp. 235–54.

————. *Panorama literario de los pueblos nahuas*. Mexico, D.F.: Editorial Porrúa, S.A., 1963.

————. *Poesía náhuatl*. 3 vols. Instituto de Investigaciones Históricas, Serie de Cultura Náhuatl, Fuentes 4–6. Mexico, D.F.: Universidad Nacional Autónoma de México, 1964–68.

————. "Relación breve de las fiestas de los dioses, Fray Bernardino de Sahagún." *Tlalocan*, Vol. II, No. 4 (1948), pp. 289–320.

———. *Veinte himnos sacros de los nahuas.* Fuentes Indígenas de la Cultura Náhuatl, Informantes de Sahagún, No. 2. Mexico, D.F.; Universidad Nacional Autónoma de Mexico, Instituto de Historia, Seminario de Cultura Náhuatl, 1958.

Gibson, Charles. *The Aztecs Under Spanish Rule: A History of the Indians of the Valley of Mexico, 1519–1810.* Stanford: Stanford Universiy Press, 1964.

——— and John B. Glass. "A Census of Middle American Prose Manuscripts in the Native Historical Tradition." In *Handbook of the Middle American Indians*, edited by Robert Wauchope, Vol. 15, pp. 322–400. Austin: University of Texas Press, 1975.

Glass, John B. *Sahagún: Reorganization of the Manuscrito de Tlatelolco, 1566–1569.* Pt. 1. Contributions to the Ethnohistory of Mexico, No. 7. Lincoln Center, Mass.: Conemex Associates, 1978.

Gómez de Orozco, Federico. "Huehuetlatolli." *Revista Mexicana de Estudios Antropológicos*, Vol. III, No. 2 Mexico, D.F., 1939), pp. 157–66.

Heikamp, Detlef, with contributions by Ferdinand Anders. *Mexico and the Medici.* Florence: Editrice Edam, 1972.

Hernández, Francisco. *Historia natural de Nueva España.* 2 vols. Mexico, D.F.: Universidad Nacional de México, 1959–67.

———. *Historia de las plantas de Nueva España.* 3 vols. Mexico, D.F.: Imprenta Universitaria, 1942–46.

Hewett, Edgar L. *Fray Bernardino de Sahagún and the Great Florentine Codex.* Archaeological Institute of America, Papers of the School of American Research. Santa Fe, New Mexico: School of American Research, 1944.

Hunter, Dard. *Papermaking: The History and Technique of an Ancient Craft.* New York: Alfred A. Knopf, 1967.

Ixtlilxochitl, Fernando de Alva. *Décima tercia relación de la venida de los españoles y principio de la ley evangélica.* Mexico, D.F.: Editorial Pedro Robredo, 1938.

———. *Historia Chichimeca.* Mexico, D.F.: Oficinia Tip. de la Secretaría de Fomento, 1892.

———. *Relaciones.* Mexico, D.F.: Oficina Tip. de la Secretaría de Fomento, 1891.

Jiménez Moreno, Wigberto. *Fray Bernardino de Sahagún y su obra.* Mexico, D.F.: Editorial Robredo, 1938.

Karttunen, Frances, and James Lockhart. *Nahuatl in the Middle Years.* Berkeley, Los Angeles, and London: University of California Press, 1976.

———. "Textos en náhuatl de siglo xviii," *Estudios de cultura náhuatl*, Vol. XIII (1978), pp. 153–75.

Key, Harold, and Mary Ritchie. *Vocabulario mejicano de la Sierra Zacapoaxtla.* Puebla, Mexico: Instituto Linguístico de Verano and Dirección General de Asuntos Indígenas, 1953.

Kirchhoff, Paul. "Los pueblos de la historia tolteca-chichimeca." *Revista Mexicana de Estudios Antropológicos*, Vol. IV (1940), pp. 77–104.

Kubler, George, and Charles Gibson. *The Tovar Calendar.* Memoirs of the Connecticut Academy of Arts and Sciences, Vol. XI. New Haven: Yale University Press, 1951.

Latham, Robert M. *Complete Book of the Wild Turkey.* Harrisburg, Pa.: Stackpole Co., 1956.

Leal, Luis. "El Libro XII de Sahagún." *Historia Mexicana*, Vol. V, No. 2 (Oct.–Dec. 1955), pp. 184–210.

Lehmann–Nitsche, Robert. "Tezcatlipoca und Quetzalcouatl." *Zeitschrift für Ethnologie*, Vol. LXX (1938), pp. 67–82.

Lehmann, Walter. "Der sogenannte Kalender Ixtlilxochitls. Ein Beitrag zur Kenntnis der achtzehn Jahresfeste der Mexikaner." *Anthropos*, Vol. III (Vienna, 1908), pp. 988–1004.

———. *Die Geschichte der Königreiche von Colhuacan und Mexico.* Stuttgart und Berlin: Verlag von W. Kohlhammer, 1938.

León–Portilla, Miguel. "Consejos de un padre Náhuatl a su hija." *América Indígena*, Vol. XXI, No. 4 (1961), pp. 339–53.

———. *La filosofía náhuatl estudiada en sus fuentes.* 3rd ed. Instituto de Investigaciones Históricas, Serie de Cultura Náhuatl, Monografía 10. Mexico, D.F.: Universidad Nacional Autónoma de México, 1966.

———. "Problematics of Sahagún: Certain Topics Needing Investigation." In *Sixteenth–Century Mexico: The Work of Sahagún*, edited by Munro S. Edmonson, pp. 235–55. Albuquerque: University of New Mexico Press, 1974.

———. *Ritos, sacerdotes y atavíos de los dioses.* Fuentes Indígenas de la Cultura Náhuatl, Textos de los Informantes de Sahagún, No. 1. Mexico, D.F.: Universidad Nacional Autónoma de México, Instituto de Historia, Seminario de Cúltura Náhuatl, 1958.

———. "Significado de la obra de Fray Bernardino de Sahagún." *Estudios de Historia Novohispana*, Vol. I (1966), pp. 13–28.

"Libro de entradas y profesiones de novicios, 1562–84." Bancroft Library, University of California, Berkeley. Mexican MSS 216.

Lockhart, James. "Y la Ana lloró." *Tlalocan*, Vol. VIII (1980), pp. 21–33.

López Austin, Alfredo. "Estudio acerca del método de investigación de Fray Bernardino de Sahagún." Unpub. licenciatura thesis, Facultad de Filosofía y Letras, Universidad Nacional Autónoma de México, 1969.

──────. "The Research Method of Fray Bernardino de Sahagún: The Questionnaires." In *Sixteenth-Century Mexico: The Work of Sahagún*, edited by Munro S. Edmonson, pp. 111–49. Albuquerque: University of New Mexico Press, 1974.

Lothrop, Samuel K. *Metals from the Cenote of Sacrifice, Chichen Itza, Yucatan.* Harvard University, Peabody Museum of American Archaeology and Ethnology Memoirs, Vol. 10, No. 2 (1952).

McAfee, Byron, and R. H. Barlow. "Anales de la conquista de Tlatelolco en 1473 y en 1521." *Tlatelolco a través los tiempos*, Vol. V (1945), pp. 32–45.

Martín del Campo, Rafael. "La anatomía entre los mexica." *Revista de la Sociedad Mexicana de Historia Natural*, Vol. XVII, Nos. 1–4 (1956), pp. 145–67.

──────. "Las cactáceas entre los mexica." *Cactáceas y suculentes mexicanas*, Vol. II, No. 2 (1957), pp. 27–38.

──────. "Ensayo de interpretación del Undécimo Libro de la Historia General de las Cosas de Nueva España." *Anales del Instituto de Biología*, Vol. IX, Nos. 3, 4 (1938), pp. 379–91; Vol. XI, No. 1 (1940), pp. 385–408; Vol. XII, No. 1 (1941), pp. 489–506.

Martínez, Maximino. *Las plantas medicinales de Mexico.* Mexico, D.F.: Ediciones Botas, 1933.

Matschat, Cecile Hulse. *Mexican Plants for American Gardens.* Boston and New York: Houghton Mifflin Company, 1935.

Mena, Ramón. *Filigranas o Marcas Transparentes en Papeles de Nueva España, del Siglo XVI.* Monografías Bibliográficas Mexicanas, No. 5. Mexico, D.F.: Imprenta de la Secretaría de Relaciones Exteriores, 1926.

Mendieta, Gerónimo de. *Historia eclesiástica indiana.* 4 vols. Edited by Joaquín García Icazbalceta. 1870. Reprint. Mexico, D.F.: Chávez Hayhoe, 1945.

Molina, Alonso de. *Vocabulario de la lengua mexicana.* Edited by Julio Platzmann. Leipzig: B. G. Teubner, 1880.

Monzón, Arturo. *El calpulli en la organización social de los tenochca.* Mexico, D.F.: Instituto de Historia, 1949.

Moreno, Roberto. "Guia de las obras en lenguas indígenas existentes en la Biblioteca Nacional." In *Boletin de la Biblioteca Nacional*, Tomo XVII, Nos. 1, 2, pp. 21–210. Mexico, D.F.: Universidad Nacional Autónoma de Mexico, 1966.

Motolinía, Toribio de Benavente. "Historia de los indios de Nueva España." In *Colección de Documentos para la Historia de México*, edited by Joaquín García Icazbalceta, Vol. I, pp. 1–249. Mexico, D.F.: Libreria de J. M. Andrade, 1858.

Muñoz Camargo, Diego. *Historia de Tlaxcala.* Mexico, D.F.: Ateneo Nac. de Ciencias, 1947.

Navarro, José Gabriel. *Los franciscanos en la conquista y colonización de América.* Madrid: Ediciones Cultura Hispánica, 1955.

Nicholson, H. B. "Sahagún's 'Primeros Memoriales,' Tepepolco, 1559–1561." In *Handbook of Middle American Indians*, edited by Robert Wauchope, Vol. 13. Austin: University of Texas Press, 1973.

Nicolau D'Olwer, Luis. *Fray Bernardino de Sahagún (1499–1590).* Historiadores de América, Vol. IX. Mexico, D.F.: Instituto Panamericano de Geografía e Historia, 1952.

──────. *Fray Toribio de Benavente (Motolinía). Relaciones de Nueva España.* Mexico, D.F.: Ediciones de la Universidad Nacional Autónoma, 1956.

──────, and Howard F. Cline. "Sahagún and His Works." In *Handbook of Middle American Indians*, edited by Robert Wauchope, Vol. 13, pp. 186–207. Austin: University of Texas Press, 1973.

Nuttall, Zelia. *The Book of the Life of the Ancient Mexicans.* Berkeley: University of California, 1903.

──────. "Francisco Cervantes de Salazar." *Anales del Museo Nacional de Arqueología, Historia y Etnología*, 4ª Epoca, Vol. 4 (1926), pp. 279–306.

Oliger, Livarius. *Breve compendio de los ritos idolátricos de Nueva España, Auctore Bernardino de Sahagún, O.F.M., Pio V Dicatum.* Rome: via Merulana, 124, 1942.

Olmos, Andrés de. *Grammaire de la langue nahuatl ou mexicaine.* Edited by Rémi Siméon. Paris: Imprimerie Nationale, 1875.

"Ordenanzas y cédulas de Indias." Biblioteca Nacional, Madrid. MS, Sig. No. 3045.

Orozco y Berra, Manuel. *Historia antigua y de la conquista de México.* 4 vols. Mexico, D.F.: Tipografía de Gonzalo A. Esteva, 1880.

Paredes, Ignacio de. *Compendio del arte de la lengua Mexicana.* Mexico, D.F.: Bibliotheca Mexicana, 1759.

Paso y Troncoso, Francisco del. *Descripción, Historia y Exposición del códice pictórico de los Antiguas Nauas que se conserva en la Cámara de Diputados de Paris.* Florence: Tipografia de Salvador Landi, 1898.

──────. "Estudios sobre el códice mexicano del P. Sahagún conservado en la Biblioteca Mediceo-Laurenziana de Florencia." *Anales del Museo Nacional de Arqueología, Historia y Etnología*, 4ª Epoca, Vol. 4 (1926), pp. 316–20.

Peñañel, Antonio, ed. *Cantares en idioma mexicano*. Mexico, D.F.: Oficina Tipográfica de la Secretaría de Fomento, 1904.

*Proceso criminal del Santo Oficio de la Inquisición y del fiscal en su nombre contra Don Carlos, indio principal de Tezcuco*. 1910. Reprint. Guadalajara, Jalisco: Edmundo Ariña Levy, Editor, 1968.

Puyol y Alonso, Julio. *El abadengo de Sahagún*. Madrid: Imp. de la Suc. de M. Minuesa de los Ríos, 1915.

Ramírez, José Fernando. "Códices mejicanos de Fr. Bernardino de Sahagún." *Boletin de la Real Academia de la Historia*, Vol. VI (Madrid, 1885), pp. 85–124.

Reccho, Nardo Antonio. *Rervm medicarvm novae Hispaniae thesavrus; sev plantarvm, animalivm, mineralivm mexicanorvm historia, ex Francisci Hernandez*. Rome: Ex Typographeio Vitalis Mascardi, 1651.

"Relacion y apuntamientos que dio el virey Don Antonio de Mendoça que lo fue del Reyno de nueua Espana a don Luis de vs^co su suçesor por mdo de su magestad." Biblioteca Nacional, Madrid. MS, Sig. No. 2816.

Ricard, Robert. *La conquista espiritual de México*. Mexico, D.F.: Editorial Jus, Editorial Polis, 1947.

Robelo, Cecilio A. *Diccionario de Aztequismos*. Cuernavaca: Imprenta del Autor, 1904.

———. *Diccionario de Mitología Náhuatl*. Mexico, D.F.: Ediciones Fuente Cultura, 1951.

Robertson, Donald. "Commentary." In *Investigaciones contemporáneas sobre historia de México. Memorias de la tercera reunion de historiadores Mexicanos. Oaxtepec, Morelos, 4–7, Noviembre de 1969*, pp. 91–95. Austin: University of Texas Press, 1971.

———. "Mexican Indian Art and the Atlantic Filter: Sixteenth and Seventeenth Centuries." In *First Images of America, The Impact of the New World on the Old*, edited by Fredi Chiappelli, pp. 483–94. Berkeley, Los Angeles, and London: University of California Press, 1976.

———. *Mexican Manuscript Painting of the Early Colonial Period*. New Haven: Yale University Press, 1959.

———. "The Sixteenth-Century Mexican Encyclopedia of Fray Bernardino de Sahagún." *Cuadernos de Historia Mundial*, Vol. IX, No. 3 (1966), pp. 617–28.

———. "The Treatment of Architecture in the Florentine Codex of Sahagún." In *Sixteenth Century Mexico: The Work of Sahagún*, edited by Munro S. Edmonson, pp. 151–64. Albuquerque: University of New Mexico Press, 1974.

Ruiz de Alarcón, Hernando, Pedro Sánchez de Aguilar, and Gonzalo de Balsalobre. *Tratado de las idolatrías, supersticiones, dioses, ritos, hechicerías y otras costumbres gentílicas de las razas aborígenes de México*. Mexico, D.F.: Ediciones Fuente Cultura, 1953.

Sahagún, Bernardino de. *Breve compendio de los ritos idolatricos de Nueva España*. Edited by Livarius Oliger. Rome: Via Merulana 124, 1942.

———. *The Florentine Codex: A General History of the Things of New Spain, Books 1–12*, translated by Arthur J. O. Anderson and Charles E. Dibble. Santa Fe and Salt Lake City: School of American Research and the University of Utah, 1950–81.

———. "Kalendario Mexicano, Latino y Castellano." Biblioteca Nacional, Mexico. MS No. 1628 *bis*, fols. 86–142.

———. *Histoire générale des choses de la Nouvelle-Espagne*. Translated and edited by D. Jourdanet and Rémi Siméon. Paris: G. Masson, 1880.

———. *Historia de la conquista de Mexico*. Edited by Carlos María de Bustamante. Mexico, D.F.: Imprenta de Galvan, 1829.

———. *Historia general de las cosas de Nueva España*. 4 vols. Edited by Angel María Garibay K. Mexico, D.F.: Editorial Porrúa, S.A., 1956.

———. *Historia general de las cosas de Nueva España*. Vols. V–VIII. Edited by Francisco del Paso y Troncoso. Madrid: Hauser y Manet, 1905–7.

———. *Historia general de las cosas de Nueva España*. Edited by Miguel Acosta Saignes. Mexico, D.F.: Editorial Nueva España, S.A., 1946.

———. *Historia general de las cosas de Nueva España*. 5 vols. Mexico, D.F.: Editorial Pedro Robredo, 1938.

———. *A History of Ancient Mexico*. Translated by Fanny Bandelier. Vol. I. Nashville, Tenn.: Fisk University Social Science Series, 1932.

———. "Primeros memoriales." In *Historia general de las cosas de Nueva Espana*, Vol. VI. Edited by Francisco del Paso y Troncoso. Madrid: Hauser y Manet, 1905–7.

Saldívar, Gabriel. *Historia de la Música en México*. Mexico, D.F.: Editorial "Cultura," 1934.

San Antonio, Juan de. *Bibliotheca universa franciscana*. 2 vols. Madrid: 1732–33.

Santamaría, Francisco J. *Diccionario general de americanismos*. 3 vols. Mexico, D.F.: Editorial Pedro Robredo, 1942.

———. *Diccionario de mejicanismos*. Mexico, D.F.: Editorial Porrúa, S.A., 1959.

Sauer, Jonathan D. "The Grain Amaranths: A Survey of Their History and Classification." *Annals of the Missouri Botanical Garden*, Vol. XXXVII (1950), pp. 561–632.

Saville, M. H. *The Goldsmith's Art in Ancient Mexico*. Museum of the American Indian, Indian Notes and Monographs, No. 7. New York: Hyde Foundation, 1920.

—————. *Turquoise Mosaic Art in Ancient Mexico.* Museum of the American Indian, Contributions, Vol. 6. New York: Hyde Foundation, 1922.

Schmidt, W. "Fray Bernardino de Sahagún O.Fr.M. 'Un breve compendio de los ritos ydolatricos que los yndios desta Nueva España usauan en el tiempo de su infidelidad.'" *Anthropos,* Vol. 1 (Salsburg, 1906), pp. 302–17.

Schultze Jena, Leonhard. *Alt–Aztekische Gesänge.* Stuttgart: W. Kohlhammer Verlag, 1957.

—————. *Gliederung des alt-aztekischen Volks in Familie, Stand und Beruf.* Stuttgart: W. Kohlhammer Verlag, 1952.

—————. *Wahrsagerei, Himmelskunde und Kalender der alten Azteken.* Stuttgart: W. Kohlhammer Verlag, 1950.

Seler, Eduard. *Codex Borgia, ein altmexikanische Bilderschrift der Bibliothek der Congregatio de Propaganda Fide.* 3 vols. Berlin: n.p., 1904.

—————. *Codex Vaticanus Nr. 7373 (Codex Vaticanus B).* Berlin: Druck von Gebr. Unger, 1902.

—————. *Collected Works.* 5 vols. Mimeographed. Edited by J. Eric S. Thompson and Francis B. Richards. Cambridge, Mass.: Carnegie Institution of Washington, 1939.

—————. *Einige Kapitel aus dem Geschichtswerk des Fray Bernardino de Sahagún aus dem Aztekischen übersetzt.* Edited by Caecilie Seler–Sachs, Walter Lehmann, and Walter Krickeberg. Stuttgart: Strecker und Schroeder, 1927.

—————. *Gesammelte Abhandlungen zur Amerikanischen* Sprach- und Altertumskunde. 5 vols. 1903–23. Reprint. Graz, Austria: Akademische Druck-u., Verlagsanstalt, 1960–61.

—————. *L'orfèvrerie des anciens mexicains et leur art de travailler la pierre et de faire des ornements en plumes.* Congrès International des Américanistes, Compte-Rendu de la Huitième session Tenue à Paris en 1890. Paris: Ernest Leroux, 1892.

—————. *Tonalamatl of the Aubin Collection.* London and Aylesbury: Hazell, Watson, and Viney, Ltd., 1901.

Serna, Jacinto de la, Pedro Ponce, and Pedro de Feria. *Tratado de las idolatrías, supersticiones, dioses, ritos, hechicerías y otras costumbres gentílicas de las razas aborígenes de México.* Mexico, D.F.: Ediciones Fuente de Cultura, 1953.

Siméon, Remí. *Dictionnaire de la langue nahuatl ou mexicaine.* Paris: Imprimerie Nationale, 1885.

Standley, Paul C. *Trees and Shrubs of Mexico.* Contributions from the United States Herbarium, Vol. 23, Pt. 3. Washington, D.C.: U.S. Government Printing Office, 1920–26.

Sullivan, Thelma D. *Compendio de la gramática nahuatl.* Mexico: Universidad Nacional Autónoma de México, Instituto de Investigaciones Históricas, 1976.

—————. "Nahuatl Proverbs, Conundrums and Metaphors Collected by Sahagún." *Estudios de cultura náhuatl,* Vol. IV (1963), pp. 93–177.

—————. "A Prayer to Tlaloc." *Estudios de cultura náhuatl,* Vol. V (1965), pp. 39–55.

—————. "Pregnancy, Childbirth, and the Deification of the Women who Died in Childbirth." *Estudios de cultura náhuatl,* Vol. VI (1966), pp. 63–96.

Tezozomoc, Alvarado Fernando. *Histoire du Mexicque.* 2 vols. Translated by H. Ternaux–Compans. Paris: P. Jannet, 1853.

Thompson, J. Eric S. *Mexico Before Cortez.* New York: Scribner's Sons, 1933.

Torquemada, Juan de. *Primera {segunda, tercera} parte de los veinte i un libros rituales i monarchia indiana.* 1723. Reprint in 3 vols. under the title *Monarquia Indiana.* Mexico, D.F.: Chávez Hayhoe, 1943.

Urbina, Manuel. *Plantas comestibles de los antiguos mexicanos.* Anales del Museo Nacional de México, 2ª Epoca (1904), pp. 503–91.

Velásquez, Primo Feliciano. *Códice Chimalpopoca.* Mexico, D.F.: Imprenta Universitaria, 1945.

Villa R., Bernardo. "Mamíferos Silvestres del Valle de México." *Anales del Instituto de Biología,* Vol. XXIII, Nos. 1, 2 (1952), pp. 269–492.

Vogelsang, Enrique G., and Rafael Martín del Campo. "Parasitología de los Nahoas." *Revista de Med. Vet. y Paras,* Vol. VI, Nos. 1–4 (1947).

Von Gall, August Freiherr. "Medizinische Bücher (ticiamatl) der alten Azteken aus der ersten Zeit der Conquista." *Quellen und Studien zur Geschichte der Naturwissen- schaften und der Medizin,* Vol. VII, Nos. 4–5 (Berlin, 1940), pp. 81–299.

Von Hagen, Victor Wolfgang. *The Aztec and Maya Paper Makers.* New York: J. J. Augustin, 1944.

Wasson, R. Gordon. "The Hallucinogenic Fungi of Mexico." *Harvard University Botanical Museum Leaflets,* Vol. XIX (1961), pp. 137–62.

Ximénez, Francisco. *Quatro Libros de la Náturaleza y Virtudes medicinales de las Plantas y Animales de la Nueva España.* Edited by N. León. Morelia, México: José R. Bravo, 1888.

Zavala, Silvio. *Francisco del Paso y Troncoso: su misión en Europa, 1892-1916.* Mexico, D.F.: Publicaciones del Museo Nacional, 1938.